D0876224

Vision
and Re-Vision
in Alexander
Pope

Wallace Jackson

Vision
and Re-Vision
in Alexander
Pope

Wayne State University Press
Detroit 1983

Copyright ©1983 by Wayne State University Press, Detroit,
Michigan 48202. All rights are reserved. No part of this book
may be reproduced without formal permission.

Library of Congress Cataloging in Publication Data

Jackson, Wallace, 1930-
      Vision and re-vision in Alexander Pope.

      Includes bibliographical references and index.
      1. Pope, Alexander, 1688-1744 — Criticism and
interpretation. I. Title.
PR3634.J3 1983   821'.5   82-20179
ISBN 0-8143-1729-4

To
M.K.J.

Contents

Acknowledgments

During the writing of this book I have managed to impose the manuscript upon a number of friends and colleagues at various stages of its progress. Oliver Ferguson and Grover Smith read an early version of the work, Clyde Ryals and Gerald Monsman a much later text. Deborah Wyrick's detailed observations and queries saved me from more than one infelicity. Robert Gleckner's support and advice were invaluable. The improving hand of Saundra Blais, the publisher's editor, is evident on almost every page. I leave to the end the expression of my gratitude to W. J. Bate and to Leigh DeNeef.

1 *Introduction*

My purpose in this study is to demonstrate the intellectual design of Pope's poetry through an encounter with thirteen texts written over the length of his career. The challenge I have set for myself is to reveal an enlarged and enlarging pattern to which these various works contribute, a pattern that indicates the unity of Pope's imagination. The reader will discover that I am less concerned with an allusive mode, and the various incorporations of a *tradition* to which that mode testifies, than I am with a coherent symbolism that arises from, to use Frye's phrase, an "inner logical discipline."[1]

I begin therefore with two specific assumptions. The first is very well established and needs no explanation. Pope rewrites his European predecessors even as, for example, he rewrites Homer in the act of translating him.[2] This action normally goes under the several heads of adaptation, imitation, influence, allusion, etc. The second assumption, nowhere explored as a sustained function of Pope's texts, is that he rewrites himself by continual acts of transposition, and that his poetic compels him to discover the burden of his own texts as they impose

11

themselves upon his consciousness and require re-articulation within a body of only seemingly discordant contexts. I want to work very far away from the propositions of recent Pope scholars who posit the resignation or collapse in the later poems of an "Augustan" mode[3] or argue the abandonment in such works of an "otherworldly vision."[4] I admit no such discontinuities, at least as they have been offered.

Further, I wish to show that Pope's central subject of order and disorder (the breaking away from and returning to divine design) necessitates sustained acts of mythopoesis that over and over again invoke metaphors of division, possession, obsession, and usurpation, which in turn are opposed by figures of unity, freedom, dedication, and authority. Even the philosophic center of Pope's vision, the *Essay on Man*, occurs within a psychological myth, itself a transposition of the garden from its objective to subjective status. Moreover, such works as the *Epistles to Several Persons* and *Horace, Imitated* are referable to this context and explicable within it. The *Epistle to Dr. Arbuthnot* sustains the self-evaluative acts of the *Essay on Man*, and the *Epistle to a Lady* bears comparable relation to the *Rape of the Lock*. Pope's poetry submits to a radical discontinuity of mode or genre, but responds to that discontinuity by recomposing its subjects within a steadily elaborated design.

His texts offer a coherent language of allegory that is not derived from standard seventeenth- or eighteenth-century critical theory, but is an invention consistent with epic practice (as Pope's "[Note]" to the *Temple of Fame* makes clear). Most neoclassical accounts of allegory are based on the principle of substitution, of this standing for that ("naive" allegory). For reasons that bear on the issue of poetic license (the credible vs. the incredible; the probable vs. the marvelous), Pope's texts do not work in this way. His is not a language of deferred or recondite meanings that we reach by proceeding, in Blackmore's terms, from a "*Literal* Sense" to "another *Mystical* or *Typical* Sense."[5] This method requires the reader to translate the text rather than to learn its language, and the translation must suffer in the manner usual to translations. I offer instead the suggestion that we read Pope in much the same way we read Blake. To fail to do so forces his poems, particularly the later ones, into narrowly conceived categories of satire or ethical formulas, and imposes upon us the problem of textual disjunctiveness rationalized in familiar ways.

I think I can illustrate my concern here by reference to the opening of the *Rape:*

> Say what strange Motive, Goddess! cou'd compel
> A well-bred *Lord* t'assault a gentle *Belle?*
> Oh say what stranger Cause, yet unexplor'd,
> Cou'd make a gentle *Belle* reject a *Lord?*

Neither motive nor cause is local or peculiar; motive is inherent in the form of rejection and assault, and the action of the poem recapitulates demonic possession, the appropriation by Belinda of an "Other," a fall engendered by sexual division, and a cycle of sexual warfare. The *Essay on Man* transposes this pattern (vision) by accommodating it to the internal relations among self-love, reason, and pride. Through the action of the subversive "other" (pride) upon reason, a new unit, pride and erring reason (selfhood), assimilates the divine datum (ruling passion) to its service.[6] The *Essay* re-imagines the *Rape* by further figuring the action of subversion, which is a possession and an obsession, a demonization of reason that results in the closure of the divine and an alienation from the order of nature now seen as emptied of its divine content.

Much the same sort of action is re-created in *Eloisa to Abelard,* wherein "rebel nature" forces another closure, another service to the "jealous God," another enslavement to a "darksom round." Generically, the *Rape, Eloisa,* and the *Essay on Man* have nothing in common. As myth they are interdependent parts of a unified vision, which is forged by extending the initial design into further and more elaborate contexts. In much the same way, Martha of *To a Lady* is a re-invention of Belinda, an articulation (with a difference) of the female within the same cycle of innocence, power, futility, and death. It is to break this cycle that Pope summons her. Equally, the conclusion of *To*

Burlington recapitulates that of *Windsor-Forest;* by inversion the close of the *Dunciad* re-invents the end of the *Essay on Criticism.*

If this study is at all successful, it should provide the basis for further inquiry into the forms of mythopoesis in eighteenth-century poetry, a subject that has been hardly explored at all. However sophisticated our current understanding of Pope, his position between Milton and Blake seems modelled on the principle of defective synapse. Pope is the bearer of few messages. I would hazard the guess that what has failed here are the ordinary and familiar terms of historicism, and that the cultural isolation of the Popeian poetic is one result of this failure. On the other hand, whatever Anglo-American structuralists may produce in the near future, by avoiding this poetic they now seem to be validating the bias of the old New Criticism. To some very large extent, the New Critical preference for a verse form *open* to the movements of the sensibility resident within it unhappily and tacitly sustained the Wartonian and Arnoldian verdicts on Pope's "didactic" and "prosaic" texts. Historically, the grounds of judgment shifted from rhetorical categories, but the result, where Pope was concerned, has remained largely the same. More recent criticism, Brower's and Wasserman's especially,[7] has responded by *opening* Pope's texts in the direction of allusion, and thus posited a greater play (ambiguity) than the New Criticism imagined to be possible. This, obviously, has been all to the good, but it also has had the peculiar effect of stranding both Dryden and Pope (once again) within the departing traditions of a "European" and "public" poetry. Worse yet, Pope's verse remains largely unmediated by a principle of composition, so that we still have no very satisfactory idea of the full bearing of Pope's texts upon each other. My purpose therefore has been to explore major poems by elaborating a coherence of symbolism within dissimilar modes or genres, an internally allusive pattern that permits Pope to recompose his poetic structures over a lifetime of writing. My intention is not to adhere strictly to Pope's order of composition, which, given his habits of revision and extension, would be impossible, but to illuminate an enlarged and complex context to which his works variously contribute. (Generic and tonal variety, so often praised in Pope's work, are unaccommodated to a logic of design, though both Paulson and Budick have briefly explored this subject in penetrating essay.[8])

Most generally, perhaps, Pope's "Augustan" mode is fabricated as a special status of sensibility and offered as exhibit A within one of history's more remarkable terminalisms. The usual label attached to his poetry is *satire*, which, if it means anything at all, commonly implies a cultural guardianship in the service of normative values. Thus from 1717 to the end of his life, Pope is largely incorporated within variations of Hogarthian or Reynoldsian modes, between "lively pictures of humanity in action" and the "Roman heroic."[9] If Pope offers a manageable knowledge, it is one supposedly invaded by reductionisms that make it so, and it is probably true that all Pope scholars write with the conviction that what is manageable is not therefore trivial. Yet the history of Pope criticism reveals a central concentration: Pope, it has been widely felt, will not surrender his sophistication, admit an archaism, acquiesce to the primitive, capitulate to dangerous knowledge. His "myth" (if he has one) is thus said to be predicated upon suppressions, his Apolline untempered, or unchallenged, by a Dionysiac. For Nietzsche, it has been said, "intuition and ecstasy are the only authentic modes of artistic creation."[10] This is the modernist moment, the authentication of the sublime. Such modes have more than a furtive existence in Shaftesbury and Young, but they are canonized by Collins and the Wartons, and all romanticists (it sometimes seems) have become genealogists of the sublime, historians of tragic ambivalence. Presumably, or so the friction runs, the old myths are no longer experienced in Pope, but have at best a contrapuntal, allusive textual vitality. He is thus remanded to the alien poetic kingdom of *wit*, an island empire divorced from the modernist mainland of the sublime.

I hope to show that this fiction will not do, that Pope's "language of allegory" bears remarkable similarities to Milton's and to Blake's. How could it be otherwise in a poet whose career is dominated by a consciousness of epic filtered through many modes: mock-epic, diminutive epic, anti-epic, translations of epic? I begin by considering a poet's consciousness of *place*, the contested territory, the spots of space and time threatened by closure. Mack speaks of the garden and the grotto as providing the "rallying point for [Pope's] personal values and a focus for his conception of himself—as master of a poet's 'kingdom.' "[11] "Kingdom" is exactly right, for it is the epic metaphor, invoking the serving figures of division, possession, usurpation, and closure, in turn opposed by the capable imaginings invested in unity, freedom, authority, and opening. These variables, arising from a consciousness of place, are accommodated to the formal element, to genre, and made to carry the burden of an unfolding design. Such constituent figures as "temple" (the temple of Fame and the "Temple of Infamy"), "glass" (Belinda's and satire's "impartial glass"), and "hecatomb" (Timon's and Zeal's) invoke a network of associations and function much like, to choose just one example, the recurrent fiction of predator and prey to sustain and enlarge the artistic pattern. Pope's vision is thus always a *re-vision*, a play among angles, a redistribution of what lies along the field of sight, as vision shifts and the field is variously reconstituted.

And this returns us to the question of textual ambiguity, or the "symbolic force"[12] of the allusive mode. Writing on the *Rape of the Lock*, Wasserman comments on the ways in which allusion synergistically qualifies the text, "incrementing and complicating its sense and tone."[13] And it surely does. But allusion, however various, rich, or complicating, does not provide a principle of constraint or formulation to which the text is subject. Allusion may evoke certain relations between a text and its predecessor text, as in the Miltonic allusions that inform the *Rape* or the *Essay on Man*. But allusion is too variable to submit to what Barthes calls the "constraint of recurrence."[14] In Pope's two Homeric translations, allusions "occur by the hundreds," says Mack, "in a verse whose vocabulary and context are potentially allusive at every moment."[15] The very richness of the mode and its constituent arbitrariness ("potentially allusive") are disqualifying. What we seek is a principle of stability, an operative fiction such as Paulson's "metamorphosis" or Budick's "displacement," which is at least offered as verifiably recurrent within a series (the canon).

Brower states that "For Pope, almost invariably, a mode of expression includes a mode of imitation, or allusion, a remark true even of the *Essay on Man,* probably the least obviously allusive of Pope's longer works."[16] He further reduces the mode of expression within the *Essay* to "modes of address," and it is for this reason that the "essence of Pope's 'drama' in the *Essay,* as in the later satirical epistles, lies in the play of tone." But "drama" presupposes an action, whereas Brower can find only a "tone" (and is thus right to put drama within quotation marks). What we are left with, then, is the sufficiency of rhetorical "play," and we are moved steadily toward Horace, on the one hand, and toward a "poetry of ideas" on the other. These movements fuse in Brower's conclusion that Pope writes "in Horace's manner a kind of systematic philosophic poem that is contrary to the genius of the style" and that by doing so Pope avoids "boredom." If Brower's inquiry handsomely adjusts Pope to Horace, it dispossesses the *Essay* of a functional relation to the canon, substituting in its stead a tonality, the "Horatian diatribe-epistle,"[17] whose "play" presumably compensates for the diminished allusiveness of the poem.

This sort of exercise keeps us busily on the lookout for contexts that qualify the text, but deflects us from the canon as a system of functions founded on recurrence. Once we begin to identify recurrences as units of meaning, in the way, for example, that Sitter identifies "temple" as a "single allegorical principle" linking the temple of Fame to the "Temple of Infamy,"[18] we are positioned to pursue their organizing purposes within a common allegorical vision. When therefore we meet again with "temple" in the *Essay on Man* ("In the same temple, the resounding wood, / All vocal beings hymn'd their equal God" [III, 155-56]) we might begin to suspect that the text is revitalizing an allegorical vision consonant with the earlier and later poems. Some one hundred lines later, "altar," re-emergent from the dedicatory contexts of the *Rape* and *Eloisa* ("Altars grew marble then, and reek'd with gore" [III, 265]), suggests that a complex sign system, based on an analogy of functions, is involutedly designating a common context. Such correspondences imply a poetic consciousness folding into and expanding from a central idea, moving outward from a motivated center, much like Pope's image of expanding and concentric circles. Given this activity, we should be prepared for a poetry that displaces and reconstitutes its own myths, thereby signifying its principle of growth and vitality.

Throughout his career, Pope appears particularly alert not only to various manifestations of error and folly (which we well know), but especially to the forms of human aggression. In *Windsor-Forest* his notations on this subject arise from a reflective engagement with history and the pervasiveness of its ruling principle, "blood." In the *Temple of Fame* personal ambition is objectified in a vision which is itself a dream of desire, finally repudiated as the full significance of "rising" is revealed in the poem's meditation. Belinda's aggression and Eloisa's "rebel nature" neatly contextualize the militant ego attempting to fulfill its own dreams of desire. And the *Essay on Man* defines the self as the field on which warring impulses contend for mastery. At its most intense, Pope's poetry confronts the ego brimming over with the ambition to flood the possibilities that lie at the periphery of perception, to become its own image of itself, to fulfill itself in various acts of transgression that constitute a raid on the possible. It is for such reasons that Pope enters his own dramas of internal subversion and betrayal, alert to those confusions of identity and purpose that baffle the aspiring ego. Not uncommonly, in Pope's poetry such concentrations as I have suggested above are refracted through an engagement with the word, with *blood* in *Windsor-Forest*, with *rising* in the *Temple of Fame*. These poems enact, respectively, a purgation of the compulsions inherent in *blood* and an opening of *rising* to its self-reflexive bearing upon the status of Pope himself.

His dramas are those of man fulfilling or subverting the divine design, and thus they commonly focus on the authority that may (or may not) be invested in such recurrent terms as *knowledge* or *power*. Wherein lie the sanctions that legitimize desire or reflect its purposes as the self moves outward to realize its informing data within the larger contexts of society and nature? How, then, does Pope's imagination continue to accommodate the urgencies that inspire his exploration of related subjects, and in so doing to deploy an immense cast of characters allusively and complexly related to each other? How, finally, does one speak critically of the knowledge of text as intertext, of text and subtext? Such questions as these guide my procedure here, an effort initiated by the unitary principle underlying my methodology and predicated on the coherence of Pope's art. I seek, therefore, one universe of discourse within the multiple discourse of thirteen texts, a field on which is disposed the imaginative figure that is uniquely Pope's. My purpose is to disclose the hidden paths leading from poem to poem, to break down those disjunctions that have historically mocked a holistic criticism of Pope and have too often left us contemplating the fragments of an "ethical system," puzzling over the purposes of a projected and abandoned epic, or merely meditating the inconsistencies of a "poetic manner"[19] seeking an imaginative center.

Johnson's appraisal of Pope is perhaps the finest we have yet had, but it is founded on an implicit discrepancy. Pope's mind was "in its widest searches still longing to go forward, in its highest flights still wishing to be higher; always imagining something greater than it knows, always endeavouring more than it can do." Yet, "he excelled every other writer in *poetical prudence*; he wrote in such a manner as might expose him to few hazards."[20] The crucial relation is that between "powers" and "good sense," [21] between the risks his poetry will not take and the energies that animate it. To my knowledge this issue has never been directly addressed, nor can it be until Pope's assimilative intelligence is granted the same sort of imaginative purposiveness we readily concede to Milton's or to Blake's. And this means reversing the critical presumptions that grant priority to the *tradition* rather than to the imagination that deploys the tradition, thereby subjecting the literary past to the design the imagination obliges it to serve. This is the premise animating my method here, an adventuring among texts to discover the synoptic design with which each is imbued.

2 The Word and the Desiring Self

Windsor-Forest and The Temple of Fame

In *Windsor-Forest* Pope moves from his apprenticeship in pastoral to a specifically English setting in which the attempt to reconstitute Dryden's myth of England is the evident purpose of the poem. The ambivalences of his vision here define the inception of his major and most characteristic poetry. To assert the imperial power of the realm much as Dryden might have conceived it, to envision England passing beyond the precincts of her island kingdom, are aspirations deeply threatened by the elements of passion marshalled by Pope against the hopeful claims of empire. The substitutive acts of the poem—the hunt that takes the place of war, the good passions that displace the bad—are conclusions the poem's argument both resists and forwards, thus isolating what will become a persistent engagement with the role and disposition of the passions. The history that the poem explores is relevant to this topic, a purgation through time of the passions associated with Norman tyrants, and thus a working out of the barbaric past, metaphorically purified by the flow of Father Thames and the convocation of tributary English rivers.

21

This is the burden of *Windsor-Forest*. It marks the beginning
of Pope's engagement with man as a historical being and initiates the purification of the special place as a principal effort of
his imagination. To make England "look green" (8) again is to
re-create the Edenic myth, to re-establish Pan, Pomona, and
Flora now that "a Stuart reigns" (42). *Windsor-Forest* richly commemorates past griefs and the blood-letting that such griefs
memorialize. Nimrod is the type of the "haughty Norman" (63)
who "first the bloody Chace began" (61). William I and his sons
bear testimony in their deaths to the truth that blood is exacted
as the price of blood-letting. As Rufus "Bleeds in the Forest"
(84), so too does France "Bleed for ever under *Britain's* Spear"
(310). The pheasant "Flutters in Blood" (114). Internecine warfare and the death of kings have made Albion bleed (322), the
"silent *Darent* [is] stain'd with *Danish* Blood" (348), and martial
adventuring abroad has exacted "*British* Blood" (367). If the
archetypal act is itself the bloody chase, the purpose of the poem
is to exile to "deepest Hell" (413) the predatory passions that
have brought about the repeated ceremony of blood and now
will "thirst for Blood in vain" (422).

One of the adventures of this poem is to address the
primitivism that fulfills itself in blood and informs both human
nature and human history, and it is in this sense that *Windsor-
Forest* initiates for Pope the warfare against the darker powers of
human energy. And these powers in turn suggest a curious affiliation between predatoriness and sexual aggression. Pan's attempted rape of Lodona links strangely with France bleeding
under Britain's spear, and with those English swains whose
fields under the Norman tyranny had been "ravish'd from" (65)
them. Tyranny and martial assault contain in latent form the
terms of sexual abuse or humiliation, the darker passions not
merely predatory but rapacious. Thus Pope seems to question
the propriety of the male ideal as warrior-predator. In one way
the poem reveals its awareness of this subject through a seemingly conventional reference to sexual aggression. The las-
civious Jove contemplating the bright female beauties on
Windsor's banks is "subdu'd by mortal Passion still" (233). If

the seduction of Jove is a moral defeat of sorts (he is "subdu'd"), it is one that testifies to the vitality of "mortal Passion" and inevitably links the male principle of desire to sexual aggression. How this recognition may qualify our reception of Pan's pursuit of Lodona remains something of an open question, if only because the question of male propriety remains momentarily at least unresolved. In much the same way, for example, those blooded youths (93) who exercise the skills of the chase practice a variation of the martial arts, of subversion and blood-letting, that culminates, by analogy, in the capture of some "thought-less Town" (107), and, more immediately, in the death of the pheasant who "Flutters in Blood."

Pope's linguistic formula insists not merely upon the vulnerability of the town, but upon that vacancy which justifies its fate. Albion's armies, made up of "eager Sons" (106) and hunters who "rush eager to the Sylvan War" (148), define the chase and the war as proximate acts compelling the same emotions from the same youths. Pan's pursuit of Lodona inspires her flight: "her Flight," says Pope, "increas'd his Fire" (184). The relation between "eager" and "Fire" is arbitrated only by "mortal Passion" and suggests that martial and sexual aggression have the same source and contribute equally to the formation of the male ideal. Nimrod, Pope told us, was a "mighty Hunter, and his Prey was Man" (62). That Nimrod was himself a type of tyrant further enforces the relation between hunter and despot, between predator and warrior. Pan's pursuit of Lodona bespeaks an archetypal assault in its own way parallel to Nimrod's predatoriness. To hunt man or nymph is a compulsion of the male principle consistent with mortal passion, and the verification of this premise exists as a fact both of history and of myth. Within the forest that is variously England or Nature, Nimrod, Rufus, Pan, and Jove stalk their prey.

Whether or not we conventionally agree that each of the preceding figures is wrong, we nevertheless find the issue inevitably refers to questions of male decorum that the poem is hesitant to address directly. When it does so, it creates the happy man (235) approved by the Stuart court, though the happy man is curiously without a specific context or particular action. He is merely someone whom the "bright Court approves / His Sov'reign favours, and his Country loves" (235-36). One may assume that the series—"approves," "favours," and "loves"— rises intensively, but once again it would be difficult to measure the value of these terms in relation to mortal passion. If the poem requires, as seems obvious, a certain sort of adventuring in which to invest the male ideal, Pope cannot find this in the man approved by courts merely for actions that remain unspecified. Nor can Pope locate that spirit in the retirement motif, which follows directly upon the lines cited above. "Successive Study, Exercise and Ease" (240), however admirable they may be, function only to set off by contrast the more vigorous life of the chase or war. It may be for this reason that we can here find Pope himself in the poem through the reference to "Ye sacred Nine! that all my Soul possess, / Whose Raptures fire me, and whose Visions bless" (259-60). The significant term is apparently "fire," and one need only remark upon the verb's earlier application to Pan to perceive not a continuity of context, but a fervor that incorporates Pan and poet.

A somewhat more modernistic critic might here comment upon the anxiety that penetrates Pope's conception of his own role and the vigorous envisioning of what England's poets have been. For example, Surrey was the Granville "of a former Age: / Matchless his Pen, victorious was his Lance" (292-93). One gets the impression that pen and lance are interchangeable instruments, each equally adequate for dealing with fools and foes. As a defense of Pope's own vocation the reference comes in exactly where one might expect, given the argument I am following, at the very beginning of the second part when the poem was taken up again in 1713. In any event, pen and lance define a heroic consciousness, which inevitably draws into itself the fair objects of Surrey's and Granville's desire, the ladies Geraldine and Myra. Here again Pope is appealing to—and re-creating—a masculine ideal of warrior-poet-lover to which presumably his own "fire" is not irrelevant. Such fire then leads him to sing of "what Heroes *Windsor* bore" (299), the poet's own credentials for singing of heroes again presumably patent in the high heroic role that poets have fulfilled. And this leads in turn to the timeless poetic icon of "vanquish'd France . . . / bleed[ing] for ever under *Britain's* Spear." One may have good reason now to distrust that spear, for we know that it is cognate at least with pen and suggests an instrument borrowed from another context.

My main point, however, is that it is very difficult to get rid of the aggressive element, since Pope has tied it so firmly to the male role. To hunt man with Nimrod, or nymph with Pan, or pheasant with swain, or France with England provides a variety of exercises that are all highly interchangeable and compatible. When we look back upon the episode of Pan and Lodona we are reminded of the relation between "fierce Eagle" and "trembling Doves" (187-88). Pan pursues Lodona as eagle pursues doves, Pan's fire equivalent to eagle's ferocity, doves' trembling analogous to the "fainting, sinking, pale" nymph (191). Such a strong suggestion that predatoriness is a fact of nature, and thus a law by which human and animal live, seems to establish the metaphysics of assault as the basis of natural law. If Pope thereby validates the despot's right to hunt his kind, Pan's right to pursue Lodona, England's right to impale France, then we may well question the basis for the many seemingly elegiac moments in the poem. The poet's lament for the dying pheasant ("Ah! what avail his glossie, varying Dyes" [115]) may seem a pointless sentimentality or simply a regret that things are as they are. Eden, after all, did not include the hunt. Yet in the fallen world the sensible evidence of human vitality is present in the chase or war or in the glorious representation of either.

Clearly, however, the poem invites us to divide our sympathies, and the elegiac mode reaches deeply into *Windsor-Forest*. Diana weeps for Lodona (209-10). The deaths of "old Warriors" (301) have provoked the bereavement of "weeping Vaults" (302). "Marble weeps" (313) over the "Martyr-king," Henry VI, and regicide has caused Albion itself to shed tears (321) over old wounds and bleeding new ones (322). The torn and violated body of Albion gathers the poem's various transgressions and focuses them: "She saw her Sons with purple

Deaths expire, / Her sacred Domes involv'd in rolling Fire, / A dreadful series of Intestine Wars, / Inglorious Triumphs and dishonest Scars'' (323-26). If the principal acts of history are such as to evoke the commemorative tear, it is surely worth reminding ourselves that such acts are *natural* in the simple sense that mortal passions compel various adventurings, even as their consequences force the tribute of a tear. The absurd cycle of death and lamentation, of blood-letting and elegiac memorializing, is brought to a conclusion by ''great ANNA'' (327). Except as a function of Pope's rhetoric, and excluding also the precise historical reference he intends, the fiat is too miraculous to accept. However much the poem owes to the Peace of Utrecht, it owes far more to its own presiding problems and to the role of blood that has dominated the perceptions of the poet.

Wasserman suggests that ''commerce, which had not yet lost its large human significance . . . is the perfect symbol of peaceful war, the continuous energy of *concordia discors,* the well-accorded strife.''[1] And this is of course true. But it seems more important to remark that the passions and their control remain at the heart of *Windsor-Forest,* and that the central proposition of the poem is a variation of the theme of *An Essay on Man,* that self-love is social. In *Windsor-Forest* Pope's subject lends itself to the aphoristic reduction that passion has imperial ends to serve, and that man is saved from himself by assimilation into the larger stream of national dedication. So in this way are we returned to the permissible terms of blood-letting. One strategy recommends that ''Arms [be] employ'd on Birds and Beasts alone'' (374), thereby staunching the flow of ''*British* Blood'' that foreign wars have exacted. Another advocates commercial enterprise as a substitute for war, and Father Thames's prophecy of English commercial glory focuses the resolution: ''For me the Balm shall bleed, and Amber flow'' (393). The ''red[dening]'' coral and the ''glow[ing]'' ruby (394) extend the metaphoric sacrifice and tribute that nature pays to empire. In other words, a certain amount of bleeding is necessary to peace and empire, the regeneration of which requires blooded youths but not the blood of youth. The mortal passions of poet, hunter, and patriot-voyager do not negate the predatory impulse but raise that impulse into a symbolic ceremony of blood in which each participates. The poet who commemorates, the hunter whose vigor is confirmed in the chase, the patriot-voyager who exacts the treasures of a yielding nature enact a heroism purified of the death of kind.

The artifice of Pope's resolution sublimates blood-letting into peaceful bleeding, preserving thereby the dynamic of strife but transmuting its death-giving qualities into life-giving ones. The resolution affords us a sense of the displacements or substitutions whereby the despot is displaced by the good monarch, Anne, and the foraging and predatory Pan by the greater god, Father Thames. And it brings us also to the brink of the sacramental vision within the poem that, as it pacifies blood-letting, pacifies equally the sexual assault consonant with it. We need something of an analog here with an earlier work, with the pattern of resolution *Lycidas* provides. The "rev'rend" (330) figure of Father Thames emerging from his "Oozy Bed" (329) suggests affiliation with Lycidean "oozy locks" (*Lycidas*, 175), even as Pope's pastoral pose ("Enough for me, that to the listning Swains / First in these Fields I sung the Sylvan Strains" [*Windsor-Forest*, 433-34]) agrees with the Miltonic resolution ("Thus sung the uncouth Swain to th' Oaks and rills" [*Lycidas*, 186]). If Pope's poem presses allusively back upon *Lycidas*, it does so to seek its own resolutions, not only within an enlarged conception of historical progress, but within the divine idea, for that has been largely at question throughout the poem. The envisioned figure of "Peace descending" (429) is the promise of beneficient futurity, a guardianship mutedly trinitarian ("Dove-like Wing" [430]) and providentially covenantal. If Milton's Christian humanism orchestrates Lycidas's fate within the pattern of death and resurrection, Pope's poem rehearses the ceremony of blood that so far has bound man to man within the disharmony sponsored by warring and predatory passions.

This has been the pattern of truth that history, myth, and nature present. To break this pattern Pope offers the promise not of the Redeemer's blood but of a blood-letting that itself has been redeemed. And if Lycidas hears the "unexpressive nuptial song" (176), Pope sings of the new sacrament that binds Anne to Thames, the monarch to the god. The alliance establishes the new holy place that is England, the dangerous passions cast out: "Exil'd by Thee [Peace] from Earth to deepest Hell" (*Windsor-Forest*, 413). What have been exiled are discord, terror, pride, the entire panoply of rebellious emotions that have lived on blood, that have evoked the elegiac lament of Albion, and that have been now finally banished. And this is so not because such passions are unnatural, but because their function has been negated by those sublimations the poem has created and encouraged. The Satanic host has not been defeated finally but merely neutralized by the permissible blood-letting advocated in the poem's conclusion. As a strategy it may leave something to be desired, and it suggests one of the ways Pope imports the context of *Paradise Lost* to serve his purposes. If seems fair, however, to remark that such passions have only gone underground to emerge later. When Brower observes that Pope was "not to see Nature or England quite like this again,"[2] we may well understand why not.

The pervasiveness of *blood* in *Windsor-Forest* imbues the word with a quasi-Shakespearian intensity, for "blood" as sexual emotion and predatory impulse has been the very driving force of vitality in action, and it is this motive power that is addressed as a function of history, myth, and nature. Within the boundaries of Pope's poem, "blood" is a contagion of the soul, operative from generation to generation, a compulsion of the male ideal, a baseness within human nature that is cured here by the emergent English deity who now enters the poem (and re-enters English history) at the precise moment that "great ANNA" pronounces her Peace of Utrecht. The poet's vision commemorates a displacement of suffering and it is nature that now suffers the harvest reaped by the passions in action and sanctified by the god. Reason cannot oppose the scale of desire which ranges in the poem from lust to slaughter. Pope sees the bestiality underlying human passion, but it is this passion he would raise and so reconstitute its very essence, symbolically centered in "blood." In the poem's most curious sublimation, blood is made to substitute for blood and one sort of bleeding is made to displace another. The imperial adventure (the myth of kingdom) atones for the savagery of the past, and England is redeemed by actions that transmogrify the Christian myth of sin and redemption within a new vision of universal harmony: "The Time shall come, when free as Seas or Wind / Unbounded Thames shall flow for all Mankind" (397-98). The god acts for "all Mankind" and redemption is thus predicated on a freedom from the barbarous past bound by its own cycle of transgression and lamentation and on a freedom in which the reign of Peace will grow "Till the freed *Indians* in their native Groves / Reap their own Fruits, and woo their Sable Loves" (409-10). The resolution depends upon the odd and incongruous conjunction of a myth of empire and innocence. It is no wonder that Pope could not sustain it.

As constituent elements of Pope's psychological myth, the dangerous passions have been rendered purposeless and their departure made contingent upon Pope's intentions here: to make England look green again, to build once more the Edenic garden. This is one way, as I have been suggesting, that Milton's epic bears upon Pope's resolutions. At the close of the work, however, we are left arbitrating the relation between a fiction and a myth, perhaps one of the reasons why the apocalyptic declaration is given by the god, a judgment consonant with his emergence as the presiding deity of England's commercial glory. The prophecy is a vision of the grace attendant upon England's fidelity to Anne's fiat, and is therefore conditional. Father Thames is the god within the kingdom, deriving and consolidating his grandeur from the separate and distinct tributary streams that swell his power, and thus analogous to the master passion of the *Essay on Man*. As the latter gathers the lesser passions under its governance, the Thames assimilates all other and smaller streams, and as the ruling passion is the sensible evidence of God within man, the Thames is the god within England.

Under the aegis of a Stuart restoration the primeval energies of England emerge as masculine and aggressive. The object

of such passions is strenuous commercial competition among
nations, and in their service nature willingly yields her bounties.
If we circle over our own premises it seems apparent that
Thames's declaration establishes the terms of a pacific compli-
ance that further and ironically illuminates a past predatoriness.
"For me," says Thames, "the Balm shall bleed, and Amber
flow," and it is clear that the god's action upon the body of
nature does not impose despoliation but engenders voluntary
tribute. The role of passion in this world is secured and validated by the kind of heroic adventuring that is itself consonant
with romance. For, as Thames continues, "The Pearly Shell its
lucid Globe infold, / and *Phoebus* warm the ripening Ore to
Gold" (395-96). The maturing bodies of shell and ore imply
more directly than we require an offering latently sexual. In such
terms the beau ideal of the poem is defined and the predatory
passions are dispelled in the amorous adventuring of patriot-
voyagers.

Such loving receptivity of the bounties of nature suggests
a new version of the old Adamic ideal: the cultivation of England's imperial garden is a task worthy of full-blooded men acting under the aegis of the nation's tutelary deity. How men
might serve the god in this fallen world seems the pertinent
question, to which Pope has provided a lengthy answer. We
may take both question and answer as defining constituent elements of the greater myth of fall and redemption. If the dangerous passions are securely locked behind bars, if the old Satan
has been confined more carefully than ever Milton could contain
him, then what remains is an Adam protected against those
temptations that arise from within. On the other hand, the
poem admits the persistence of "War or Blood," but only in the
"Sylvan Chace" (372). The prescription is rather too hopeful (as
Pope came quickly to realize), and it may lead us to query the
poet's elegiac cry over the fate of the varicolored pheasant. But
his is a concession consistent with Anne as patron of the hunt
and therefore with Diana as the type of the English queen.

Once we cast the poem into these terms, we can further
recognize certain affiliations between *Windsor-Forest* and the

Rape of the Lock. Both poems are remarkably interested in predator and prey and in the conditions that create or necessitate this
relation, and it may seem that the movement from one poem to
another is to a large extent a substitution of contexts. The forest's primeval reality is opposed by Hampton Court's urbane
sophistications, but the structures of human action motivated by
the predatory (including sexual) passions remain constant. The
issue of motive and desire opens into the subject of familial relations that lies close to the center of *An Essay on Man,* and bears
on the presiding domesticity governing the interaction between
self-love and reason. More darkly, the subject opens into the
courtship of the goddess Dulness which the *Dunciad* details. But
also at issue is the stability of the self and the terms that make
the myth available for social criticism and for the continued writing of poetry.

Budick notes that the ''vision of perfectibility presented in
Windsor-Forest is, in fact, a reversal of the terms of regeneration
envisioned in *Paradise Lost*: now man is encouraged to cultivate
and exploit his materialistic nature rather than to alter it; the
trajectory of man's expulsion from Eden becomes the route to a
demi-paradise of controlled commercialism.''[3] All of this would
be more convincing and appropriate if Pope's vision here was
not qualified by the blood-letting that links alternately to death
and to energy. This dual focus in *Windsor-Forest* tacitly proposes
the price of empire, that ceremony of blood to which I referred
above. If, indeed, empire is the ideal of *Windsor-Forest,* it should
be clear that the poem has proceeded with substantial irony at
the expense of the ideal. In one sense the dangerous passions
are expelled, cast out; in another they are cast outward, and
man's blood-lust is to be controlled in the disciplined actions of
hunt and trade. Yet the bleeding balm reminds us emphatically
that in the fallen world passions may be sublimated but not
excluded. The ritual function of the poet is both to discover and
to memorialize such displacements.

Yet the legacy of *Windsor-Forest* is for the poet the imaginative act that uncovers ambivalence itself and encounters it as a
function of language, the very substance of the poetic perfor-

mance. The word *blood*, here redeemed by redefinition, remains nevertheless the word within which the simulacrum of meaning challenges the redemptory poet. What is cancelled here in the poem's reconciling myth is elsewhere in the canon invasive, for *Windsor-Forest* initiates Pope's engagement with ambivalence. The implications of this engagement echo throughout the early poems and permit us to define *Windsor-Forest* and, as I will argue in the next section, the *Temple of Fame* as dialectical efforts of one imagination. If the principal intention of *Windsor-Forest* is to defeat the accretions of time by sublimation of the more destructive passions, the effort of the *Temple of Fame* is to raise up a visionary structure of human perfection in which the independence of the imagination, free from those compulsions that plague action, is celebrated and enshrined. The dialectic that is sustained by these poems is suggested by the fact that *Windsor-Forest* looks to the future and the *Temple of Fame* looks to the past. The *Temple of Fame* defines an uncompromised act of the imagination accomplished by the masters of the word, of those who have subdued the word and its import to their purposes, and for whom the effort of mastery and control has not issued in that act of self-violation that Pope now turns to address. Spirit is made counterpoint to matter, art to commerce, in a manner that anticipates the dialectic between grace and nature in *Eloisa to Abelard*. And the recurrent imagery of both poems forces upon Pope a reconsideration of the role of the poet in the world.

In *Windsor-Forest* "fire" is a lust (Pan's) and a rapture (poet's) and a national disaster (Albion's). In the *Temple of Fame* "fire" is the energy animating the epic vision (Homer's and Virgil's) and the destructive principle inherent in capricious judgment. The issue of Fame's black trumpet is a roaring fire ("long flaky Flames expire, / With Sparks, that seem'd to set the World on fire" [414-15]). Rumour's mansion includes "various News" (448) of "Fires and Plagues" (453), resulting in "Tow'rs and Temples [that] sink in Floods of Fire" (478). Moreover, to this mansion "arise / All various Sounds from Earth, and Seas, and Skies" (432-33), "As Flames by Nature to the

Skies ascend'' (428). Fire is a rising and a falling (''sink in Floods of Fire''). Yet the reward for being fired (enraptured) is to be raised up. Homer's *Iliad*, figured on the pillar, ''prov'd the Master's Fire'' (193). On Virgil's ''Golden Column'' (196) ''Troy flam'd in burning Gold'' (208). Pindar's baroque column is emboldened by ''fiery Steeds'' (219), though ''Pindar's fire'' is ''temper'd'' by Horace (223). Above these ''massie Columns [that] in a Circle rise'' (244) is *Fame's* Imperial Seat'' (248), ''And all on fire appear'd the glowing Throne'' (255).

In the *Temple of Fame* fire is a rising validated by the art that it makes possible, or fire is an uprising feeding on that which it consumes. Thus the fire connoting art and vitality and glory within the temple metaphorically signifies just the opposite outside the temple: the civilization that flames in the burning gold of Virgil's designed artifact merely burns in the accidental fires set by Rumour (''So from a Spark, that kindled first by Chance'' [475]. When in the *Essay on Criticism* Pope wishes to praise ''each *ancient* Altar'' (181), he remarks that it is ''Above the reach of Sacrilegious Hands, / Secure from *Flames*'' (182-83). Yet as he hopes to emulate the masters of the word, he says, ''Oh may some Spark of *your* Coelestial Fire / The last, the meanest of your Sons inspire, / (That on weak Wings, from far, pursues your Flights)'' (195-97).

The fire that flames up enviously and sacrilegiously (like a lust rather than a rapture) is an uprising that corrupts and destroys. The fire that is imparted from a leader to a follower (as in a legacy) ennobles and inspires emulation. An image that provokes such oppositions suggests a fundamental division in the author's mind that is itself reflected in Fame divided so as to encompass her opposite, Rumour. The division indicates a ground of conflict incorporating the speaker. He wants to rise but fears his ambition is unfounded: ''Or if no Basis bear my rising Name'' (519). Thus, if there is no clear support for his rising, it is merely an act of pride and impiety. On the other hand, if the only basis for rising be ''the fall'n Ruins of Another's Fame'' (520), then it is the same basis signified by those ''Tow'rs and Temples [that] sink in Floods of Fire.'' Further, an ill-founded attempt may provoke the black trumpet whose "Sulphureous Flames" (339) will scorch his name, making him the victim of "Loud Laughs . . . and bitter Scoffs" (403).

In a poem so concentrated on the act of rising, we may expect a very fair attention to the verb itself:

rising Flowers (2)	in a Circle rise (244)
Phantoms in wild Order rose (9)	her tow'ring Front she rais'd (261)
Mountains rise (14)	Wings raise her Arms (267)
Temples rise (18)	they raise the Voice (273)
Rise white in Air (54)	bade the Muses raise (306)
Cities rais'd (71)	they ev'ry moment rise (312)
Sculpture rising (78)	Rise! Muses, rise! (370)
Like Exhalations rise (91)	their proper Place, arise (432)
round them rise (103)	Hosts rais'd by Fear (461)
huge Colosses rose (121)	thy rash Ambition raise (499)
Rais'd on a thousand Pillars (139)	bear my rising Name (519)

To rise is thus commensurate with *to bleed* in *Windsor-Forest*; a similar ambivalence inhabits each verb and dictates the burden of the respective tests.

Traversi, speaking of *The Winter's Tale*, notes Shakespeare's "effort to bring the *impasse* suggested by his exploration of the part played by 'blood' in human experience—a part at once destructive and potentially maturing—into relation with feelings which imply the understanding of a positive spiritual conception."[4] In the context of *Windsor-Forest*, *blood* undergoes a similar transformation, becoming the product of the unspoiled natural world in which the national deity holds a property; for, among other topics, it is the rational basis of property that the poem brings under scrutiny. If blood-letting denotes one kind of appropriation (of man by man, of nation by nation) that is cancelled in the poem's reconciling myth, the bleeding balm specifies another property consistent with the purification of the passions (the "positive spiritual conception") promoted at the poem's close. Similarly, yet differently, Pope's action upon *rising* denotes another opening of the word, though in this case the word is opened so as to incorporate its lapsarian causality. In Pope's texts the two words are passing each other in opposite directions, *blood* bearing its share of the naive optimism invested in the myth of empire, *rising* sponsoring a dubiety that enters the poem to complicate the narrator-poet's relation to his own vision.

In both poems, Pope also creates a disjunction within the temporal context (time past and time present) by the way he uses each significant verb. In the *Temple of Fame* the narrator is encompassed by the myth of the Fall, the precise context to which his aspirations have led him. In *Windsor-Forest* he is able to leap beyond fallen nature toward the promise explicit in the vision of *Britannia Redivivus*. In this way the two poems bear something of a Janus-like relation to each other, not dissimilar from the relation between the *Essay on Man* and the *Dunciad*. This sort of juxtaposition seems to serve an odd requirement of Pope's imagination; another variation is again evident in the similar-dissimilar circumstances of the *Rape of the Lock* and *Eloisa to Abelard*. More about this later.

In the *Temple* the renunciatory activity of the speaker focuses the problem, specifies *rising* as a goal to be qualified by the moral legitimacy with which the word may or may not be invested ("Or if no Basis. . . ."). Moreover, the close of *Windsor-Forest* and the opening of the *Rape* re-examine *rising* within contexts that alternately enclose the word within opposite significations, suggesting further a coalescence of contexts in which the word is arbitrated and known. Father Thames salutes "Sacred *Peace*! hail long-expected Days, / That *Thames's* Glory to the Stars shall raise!" (355-56). And again: "Behold! Augusta's glitt'ring Spires increase, / And Temples rise . . . " (377-78). In the *Rape* Belinda adorns herself: "Now awful Beauty puts on all its Arms; / The Fair each moment rises in her Charms" (I, 139-40). And this rising is compared to the sun's: "Not with more Glories in th' Etherial Plain, / The Sun first rises o'er the purpled Main" (II, 1-2). Any further study of this action in the *Rape* would run into those suns that "sett" (V, 147) and the lock that rises, so that the ending of the poem concedes equally to its rhetorical principle (the sublime) and its elegiac one (the end Belinda is advised to recognize).

In the *Temple of Fame* the meaning of *rising* is suspended between positive and negative, between renewal, rebirth, re-creation (Troy flames again but in burning gold), on one hand, consistent with the terms of adoration, praise, wonder, etc., and, on the other hand, an *uprising* that is presumptuous, rash, egotistical, and sacrilegious. Rumour's "Hosts rais'd by Fear" (461) correlate with Fear's "Devils" in the *Essay on Man* (III, 256), evoked under the agency of Superstition, the goddess correspondent to Rumour. Yet the issue of rising is further complicated, since the hosts raised by Fear are "Phantoms of a Day" (*Temple*, 461) and thereby correspond to that "Train of Phantoms" (9) with which the poem begins. Equally, the phantoms of a day are phantoms of a morning dream and correlate with those of Belinda's morning dream in the *Rape*. If Belinda's morning dream is composed of a promise and a warning (a promise of rising and a warning of falling), Pope's dream in the *Temple* is made up as well of alternate visions of fame and infamy. Is Belinda's rising, then, the transposed form of a comparable rising rejected by the poet in the *Temple*? If so, a rising is sponsored by the alternative agencies of god and demon, and the self is advised to meditate its own impulses within the context that language itself provides. The recognition of ambivalence is the pre-condition of knowledge, the basis of that self-reflexive act on which the proper study of mankind is initiated.

The bearing of these remarks on *Eloisa* and the *Essay on Man* will be clear before long. For the moment it is enough to notice that the relation between Fame and Rumour, a rising and an uprising, dramatizes the Freudian principle of condensation, the idea that "latent elements sharing some common characteristic are in the manifest dream put together, blended into a single whole."[5] Empson states that "a Freudian opposite at least marks dissatisfaction; the notion of what you want involves the idea that you have not got it. . . . In more serious cases, causing wider emotional reverberation, such as are likely to be reflected in language, in poetry, or in dreams, it marks a centre of conflict; the notion of what you want involves the notion that you must not take it.''[6] Or, in this case, that you must not risk taking it. In the *Temple of Fame,* Pope says that if the purchase of fame requires ''soothing Folly, or exalting [raising] Vice'' (516), he will not pay the price, whereas a price he will not pay has already been identified. He will neither fall willing victim to Rumour nor submit to the vagaries of Fame's judgment in the world. The ambivalences reflected in both *fire* and *rising* are sustained in the instruments of judgment (the double trumpets) and are further reflected in the progeny issuing from Rumour's mansion, the ''Inseparable . . . Truth and Lye'' (494) who fuse together in passing through the ''narrow Vent'' (492).

The speaker who arbitrates the meanings of *rise* and *fire* arbitrates as well the relation between Fame and Rumour. In itself the action suggests another form of displacement: the transposition of the Edenic context into the terms of a dream vision, wherein temptation and rejection define the poet's self-reflexive engagement with his desire to rise and the ''rash Ambition'' the desire conceals. Also, the relation between Fame and Rumour defines the distinction between the goddess and her malign simulacrum, between Fame in her temple and Rumour in the prolific whoredom of her mansion. To read the poem in this way is to recognize Pope's treatment of the life of man polarized between the ideal and reality, between the fuller life of the imagination and the minimal life of man limited by the illusions of the present moment, and thus included among those ''Confus'd, unnumber'd Multitudes . . . / Who pass, repass, advance, and glide away'' (459-60). Yet the very ambivalence with which the *Temple* contends is re-emergent in *Eloisa,* in which *love* is subject to the contrary demands of the ''jealous God'' (81) and Christ. That dispute defines the distinction between possession and freedom, between an enforced servitude and devotion. And in the *Essay on Man* a comparable ambivalence governs the internal argumentation in which the

self contends with its "other," the "I" speaks to its "you," and
self-love opposes the usurpations of the selfhood.

If the burden of *Windsor-Forest* is to confront the ambivalence within *blood-letting,* and by substitution to displace one significance of the word by another (a displacement that permits
the poet to find the act restorative of empire and commensurate
with the beau ideal of the poem), the corresponding burden of
the *Temple of Fame* is to discover and maintain an ambivalence
that cannot be cancelled within a reconciling myth. The word
cannot be purged of its ulterior significance. This is so because it
is the very act of choosing that is at the perilous center of the
poem. To rise involves the corollary proposition, to fall, even as
to master the fire is shadowed by the possibility of being consigned to it, and to court fame is to risk infamy. It is a question
therefore of what can be chosen, of the enabling knowledge that
permits the poet to escape the disabling and limiting desire of
"rash Ambition." Whatever may be true of the "symbolic eternity"[7] represented by Fame's "hallow'd Quire" (178), in that
temporality in which man has his being Fame and Rumour are
coexistent contraries, inevitably as "strict Companions" (495) as
"Truth and Lye."

Barthes observes of the Racinian being that his "disease is
to be disloyal to himself and too loyal to the Other."[8] This is
precisely Belinda's predicament, and it is exactly what Pope
would avoid for himself in the *Temple.* These poems pose a question of knowledge, of the problematic that incorporates the
Edenic context and summons before the reader the very basis on
which choice rests, the knowledge, or lack of it, that conditions
and determines choice. The dreaming self that images simultaneously its desire and fear creates the Freudian "dream-work
. . . [that] strives to condense two different thoughts by select-
ing after the manner of wit, an ambiguous word which can suggest both thoughts."[9] The dream itself is a specific vehicle of
ambivalence, a fact which more than any other necessitates
Pope's form here and results in the partial Chaucerian imitation
that is the *Temple of Fame.* The self-reflexive action of the poet is
therefore focused on *detachment,* the detachment of the self (as

in *Windsor-Forest*) from its now recognizably "guilty" (521) pre-
tensions, its refusal to recapitulate the Edenic sin, to aspire
falsely (rise), to be judged, and to fall again. And this knowledge that is the poet's is the knowledge of an inherent *otherness*
implicit within the temptation. At issue therefore are the stability of the self and the choices that threaten it. The manifest
dream-work holds the conflict and focuses it; the latent significance is revealed through an interpretive encounter with ambivalence itself.

In *Paradise Lost,* what separates Eve's dream of rising and
falling (V, 86-92) from the poet's is this knowledge, the special
alertness to deception that orients Pope's early work and, as I
will demonstrate later in this chapter, is at the heart of both the
Rape and *Eloisa.* It is for this reason that *to know* is the principal
verb in Pope's lexicon, the mandatory and essential premise on
which belief and behavior are predicated: "What can we reason,
but from what we know?" (*Essay on Man*, I, 18). And what Pope
knows is that the sublime and its gothic cognate coexist. A rise
involves a fall; the inversion of a ruling passion is an idée
fixe. It is what Belinda and Eloisa do not know that occasions the
two major works of Pope's early career; not knowing is what
both women share. Conversely, the poet is the one who does
know, who has been granted the vision and is alert to the
ambivalences of meaning it contains, the temptations and
deceptions inhabiting it. The poet who purges Windsor Forest
of its ancient guilt here purifies himself of the far more ancient
desire to be promoted in the scheme of things. The same theme
re-emerges in the *Essay on Man,* and even more subtly and self-
evaluatingly in the *Horace, Imitated.* The *Temple of Fame* and
Windsor-Forest give Pope his subject *and* his authority, give him
that angle of vision, that place to stand of which Mack speaks,
and in the figure of Rumour he enlists the first shadowy goddess who will lead finally to Dulness herself.

The Rape of the Lock *and* Eloisa to Abelard

The *Rape of the Lock* and *Eloisa to Abelard* present the leading

characters in similar circumstances, though initially their situa-
tions appear radically different. Belinda is the belle of highly
polished London society; Eloisa is a twelfth-century French
woman relegated to a convent after the castration of her lover.
Yet both poems deal with erotic love, with this emotion as it is
awakened in young men by the beautiful Belinda and experienced by Eloisa incarcerated within the Paraclete. And if Belinda
is a "Goddess" of love victimizing others by her seemingly
unattainable beauty, Eloisa is herself victimized by the "jealous
God" (81) of love who torments her isolation. In each poem a
conversion of sorts is advocated if not experienced. The conclusion of the *Rape* accommodates Belinda to the tradition of *ars
moriendi,* to an elegiac motif that requires Belinda to view herself
sub specie aeternitatis. In *Eloisa to Abelard,* Eloisa dies to Abelard
while awakening to Christ.

Both poems invoke the elegiac mode as a perspective
through which to view a rising (Belinda's) and the fires of desire
(Eloisa's), and thereby they come round in their different ways
to ideas suggested in the preceding works. If the purpose of the
Rape and *Eloisa* is to purge both women of the obsessions that
define them, the route leads through the elegiac consciousness,
even as *Windsor-Forest* pays elegiac tribute to those victims of
mortal passion, another principle of nature exacting another
kind of death. The elegiac mode thus sustains the ambivalences
within nature and within time. Moreover, those erosions to
which Fame's temple testifies suggest a consciousness of mutability and loss that deeply informs Pope's texts, and such an
awareness may in itself indicate the impulses leading to those
stabilities that are vigorously asserted by the *Essay on Man.* If I
am right in isolating the elegiac consciousness in Pope, we may
on this basis also learn something new about his imagination.
Troy's ruin is the very stuff of the *Iliad,* but it is equally the fire
on which the imagination feeds, and the conversion of an
energy that destroys into an energy that preserves seems a paradox of mortal passion.

Both the *Rape* and the *Eloisa* also maintain the theme of the
special place. In the former, Hampton Court is the place where

predatory man and predatory woman enact their ritual of coquetry and desire, a displacement of the Edenic setting consonant with the fallen and contemporary world. The predatory theme links the *Rape* to *Windsor-Forest*, joins Baron and Belinda to Pan and Lodona. In each case the female huntress becomes subsequently the hunted, and the Baron's totemic rape of Belinda parallels Pan's attempted rape of Lodona. In *Eloisa to Abelard*, the Paraclete is another form of the special place, made dismal by the *genius loci* of "Black Melancholy" (165) acting under the aegis of the jealous god of love. The *Rape* also offers its version of *genii loci*, Ariel and the guardian sylphs, who promise to take Belinda under their protection and guarantee her chastity and "honour." Yet the sylphic idea of the good society is of one inhabited by sexually abstaining coquettes, who, though they flirt, do not fall.[10] Another witty variation of the special place in the *Rape* is the mons veneris. By assuring the integrity of this place, Belinda shall remain "fair and chaste" (67).

The temptation to chastity, however (if that is exactly what it is), is not without certain Amazonic overtones, for the nymph who "Rejects Mankind, is by some *Sylph* embrac'd" (68). That the sylphs were "once inclos'd in Woman's beauteous Mold" (48), and now "Assume what Sexes and what Shapes they please" (70), suggests a wantonly capricious sexuality underscoring their mock-diabolism and their plan to subvert the natural interactions between men and women. The role of the sylphs is to guarantee that self-love is not social. The predatory passions return transmogrified into the passions of sexual gaming, and what first appears as the high comedy of sylphic intervention is revealed to be a low affair of scheming retribution, of sylphs who might almost be said to "haunt the places where their Honor dy'd" (*Epistle to a Lady,* 242).

In the *Rape of the Lock*, "*Honour* is the Word with men below" (I, 78). Yet what kind of word is *honor,* for which power and knowledge contend? The *Rape* explores the opposition between power and knowledge and attempts, through the mediation of honor, to unify and harmonize the two. Ariel's discourse to Belinda concentrates on the necessity to know.

"Know then" (I, 41), he says to her, and "Know farther yet" (I, 67). And though honor may be the word with men below, "the wise Celestials know" (I, 77) something else, know that it is their sylph who "guards the Purity of melting Maids" (I, 71). The "World" may "imagine" that women stray (I, 91), feminine inconstancy "erring Mortals Levity may call" (I, 103), but only the sylphs *know*. The word *know* is the authority principle of Ariel's discourse, wherein *honor* is reductively the illusion of virtue. Knowledge is the revealed truth of female honor, the vision of right naming that Belinda is granted. And the right name for honor (or so Ariel would have her believe) is grace, the sylphic intervention that protects the prey from predatory man.

On the other hand, power is the agency of totemic murders and totemic rape. Belinda rising in her charms (I, 140) recapitulates the rising rejected by the poet in the *Temple of Fame*, while parodying Fame's rising. Belinda's assumption of power affiliates by analogy with the sun's rising (II, 2), a glory that indicates the obsessional effect of her beauty, which "fix'd" every eye "on her alone" (II, 6). Her rising is accommodated to a firing, which suggests the continued play upon these related terms, now translated into the context of the comic vision and adapted to the fairy way of writing: "For when the Fair in all their Pride expire, / To their first Elements their Souls retire: / The Sprights of fiery Termagants in Flame / Mount up and take a Salamander's Name" (I, 57-60). Like that sun with which she is compared, Belinda *burns:* "to encounter two adventrous Knights" (III, 26), and, the lock lost, "with more than mortal Ire" (IV, 93). The Baron asks to "burn in *Cupid's* Flames,—but burn alive" (V, 102). Such heats imply a parodic accommodation of *Windsor-Forest's* warfare and a metamorphosis of the poet's sense of his own situation in the *Temple of Fame*. The historical progression that charts a line from *Windsor-Forest's* antique conflicts through the historical consciousness of the aspiring poet in the *Temple of Fame* leads now into the historical present, a present in which rising and firing continue to symbolize desires that constitute human nature. By continuing to re-examine the same and related terms, Pope is able to play over the extended surface of human life and to explore those substantive realities that emerge and re-emerge.

What distinguishes the Baron from Pan are "three Garters, half a Pair of Gloves" (*Rape*, II, 39). Pope's technique of forcing us to think of one context in relation to another functions as a strategy for exposing the same motivational cluster. Pan who burns with lust, poet who burns with poetic fervor, and Belinda who burns with martial zeal are gathered within the complex relation sustained by *fire*. Pope's texts thus dissolve meanings to reconstitute them within widely dissimilar contexts that are, upon examination, not very different at all.

In the context of the *Rape*, power is the causative agency of obsession, and an obsession is a contraction of vision, comparable in its way to the contraction of Belinda's image to the "Glass" in her hand. The play, at the moment, is between goddess and victims, between power and powerlessness, and the predatory theme resonates within a relation that has not yet reversed its terms. But the Baron has his own powers, "chiefly *Love*" (II, 36-37), and these "Pow'rs gave Ear" (45). The ironic moment encapsulates Belinda within the power of knowledge and the knowledge of power, engendering in turn the rebellious invocation of one kind of power to oppose another power. Within this context, Belinda's altar and the Baron's are places denoting a ritual eroticism, sanctifications of those "murders" Belinda will commit with her eyes, of that "rape" that sustains the principle of male aggression. Between these corruptions that define a rising and a rebellion there is no distance at all; rather, there is a concordance founded on and justified by the prevailing predatory acts that define Hampton Court.

Such a concordance keeps us focused on the poem as an invocation of the will to power, which here sponsors a violent reciprocity, but the relation between rising and falling is enacted within a culture that has been diminished and is only comically present in the poem. This alone is what keeps it from tragedy, for there are and can be only mock murders, pseudo-rapes. Girard remarks that the "mechanism of reciprocal violence can be described as a vicious circle. Once a community enters the circle, it is unable to extricate itself," and it follows that when "a community succeeds in convincing itself that one alone of its number is responsible for the violent mimesis besetting it; when it is able to view this member as the single 'polluted' enemy who is contaminating the rest; and when the citizens are truly unanimous in this conviction—then the belief becomes a reality, for there will no longer exist elsewhere in the community a form of violence to be followed or opposed, which is to say, imitated and propagated."[11] But there is no such consensus within the community of Hampton. Clarissa is there to speak the truth about Belinda, but Thalestris is there to incite division, which in itself turns on the issues of power and knowledge. Thalestris's notion is one of cosmetic suffering serving the ends of power, but it incorporates a conception of honor that forces redefinition. Her vision is of Belinda impaired in her power: "Already see you a degraded Toast, / And all your Honour in a Whisper lost!" (IV, 109-10).

The self debased through its loss of reputation incorporates the "incessant Rumours" and "gath'ring Scandals" of the *Temple of Fame* (336-37), and honor, which is reputation, is equally the very substance of power.[12] The alliance defines another ambivalence on which the divisiveness between the sexes is predicated, and the totemic power of the word *honor* rivals the totemic significance of Belinda's rape. In such a context, coffee-pots are not coffee-pots, china is not china, rape is not rape. Neither the word nor the object is exactly what it seems to be, for each is based on a symbol-making consciousness that continues to fabricate identity on successive refinements of *power* and *knowledge* until the very divisiveness inhabiting each word is extended into the society which now wars on itself. Thalestris's *honor* is consistent with the Baron's, and her outrage and his exuberance make explicit the shared meaning of the word. Following the rape he says: "So long my honour, Name, and Praise shall live!" (III, 170). So that honor, which is a kind of fame, is opposed by dishonor, which is a kind of infamy ("'Twill then be Infamy to seem your friend!" [IV, 112]), and fame and infamy are reconstituted as the polarities of reputation. This is the basis of Thalestris's appeal to Belinda, an appeal to power in terms of the only knowledge (reputation) that serves it and on which self-identity is founded.

Conversely, Clarissa proposes a conception of ends commensurate with human frailty, with the inevitable decay and diminution of power. Clarissa's emphasis is on knowledge, on knowing the human condition, and on the right ends to which power is disposed: Since "she who scorns a Man, must die a Maid; / What then remains, but well our Pow'r to use" (V, 28-29). The strategy of both Thalestris and Clarissa is to ask intentionally rhetorical questions of Belinda; the implied answers suggest the dichotomy between power and knowledge, and the further significance of honor with which either power or knowledge is invested. To Thalestris, honor is reputation; to Clarissa, it is newly defined as "Merit" (V, 34). These terms largely divide the issue, as knowledge gathers to itself the elegiac component (implicit in setting suns) and imposes the perspective under its aegis. The respective advocacies of Thalestris and Clarissa tend to allegorize these principals as psychomachian elements, not unlike other equivalent oppositions in Pope's later works. Part of the poem's effort therefore is to free honor from the falsely synonymous reputation, and thereby to call the thing by its right name.

Yet power, we are given to understand, may serve the ends of knowledge, an accommodation that illuminates Clarissa's agency in the rape itself. *Power*, like *blood* in *Windsor-Forest*, or *rising* in the *Temple of Fame*, is the agency of a deceptive self-consciousness on which, as I suggested before, self-knowledge is predicated. Thus power is to be drawn from its various subversive affiliations: from Ariel, who "found his Pow'r expir'd . . . , and with a Sigh retir'd" (III, 145); from Spleen, whose "Pow'r" Belinda "disdains" (IV, 65); and from the militant warrior queens of the ombre deck (III, 40, 77) whose power sustains and perpetuates the prevailing predatory antagonisms. The reunion of power and knowledge, and thus the redefinition of honor, signifies the real relation of the poem to the Miltonic context. The self-sufficiency of power is the illusion knowledge destroys, whereas the legitimate efficacy of female power is the reality knowledge guarantees. The reintegration of power and knowledge signifies one of Pope's more successful marriages; the goddess in the glass is advised to read her fate in the brilliance she rivals, in those suns that "sett." This is the knowledge of power on which the poet's, and Clarissa's, advocacy rests.

Belinda is a woman who would destroy herself by rising too high; in the *Temple of Fame* Pope is the young petitioner and candidate for fame who resists the temptation to rise. Of the relation between the two poems I wish to suggest only that the *Rape* provided Pope with the opportunity to dramatize a rising coincidental to the one he rejects for himself, while at the same time it mediates the tension between power and knowledge. Such a mediation bears on what de Man calls "the psychological dangers and satisfactions open to the transcendental self that is constituted both by and in the work of art."[13] The aggressive elements constituted by predator and prey in *Windsor-Forest*, by the rash ambition of rising in the *Temple of Fame*, are re-addressed within the *Rape*, and the militant ego is rebuked, purified in such a way (or so the close of the *Rape* prophesies) that the very consciousness of self is altered in the alteration of the self's objects. In *Eloisa to Abelard* a similar effort of deflection is evident in the movement of the ego from contraction to expansion, from "darksom round" to "roseate bow'rs," which describes another surrender of the object on which identity had been based. If Belinda is the tyrant, Eloisa is the rebel, and there is a strong affinity between the two, though Pope is coming at related problems from two different perspectives.

The self-seeking imagination constructs its fables of identity, contextualizes itself in ways that the *Rape* exposes and corrects. Belinda is at one moment in the poem a character out of the *Temple of Fame*, one whom "Thirst of Fame invites" (III, 25); the lock lost, she envisions herself within a gothic pastoralism: "Oh had I rather un-admir'd remain'd / In some lone Isle, or distant *Northern* land" (IV, 153-54). Her special vulnerability is to the falsely contextual, exactly the issue of all the early poems and the principal topic of the *Essay on Man*. Eden is not merely lost; it is displaced: onto Windsor Forest, onto Fame's temple, and onto Hampton's graces. And each of these displacements is a loss but also a survival. Thus also at issue are the terms of that survival. As Eden closes to man it opens again, transposed into the form of Hampton, yet now less than it was, its fallen form signified by the dedicatory altars that promote the reality of malign divinities. This corruption is itself the sensible evidence of *fall*, and the immediate and specific manifestations of falling are explicit in those fictions of identity of which Belinda is composed.[14] As the garden closes it opens again as the direct result of *rising*, the self-enchantments that are the consequence of "mean Self-love" (*Essay on Man*, II, 291). Eve is now Belinda, the sylphs are Satanic subverters, and Adam's new relation to woman is that of the Baron's to Belinda. The garden that sanctified connubial bliss has been transformed into the forest of stratagems and violent practice. Baron hunts Belinda as Pan hunts Lodona; the primordial episode is superimposed upon the contemporary event, and the timelessness of the montage suggests the reversibility of history and process. Pope's most structurally cogent allusions are to a special place that has closed before and now threatens to close again. The latent possibility is of yet another fall, a progressively downward spiraling of that special place until it merges with chaos and is no more. This is the reality of the *Dunciad's* end. In the *Rape* the same awareness sponsors the visit to the Cave of Spleen. Here the "Dismal Dome" (IV, 18) of Spleen's cave correlates with the "sacred Dome" of Dulness (*Dunciad*, I, 265). In the "Temple's last recess inclos'd" (III, 1), Cibber

> hears loud Oracles, and talks with Gods:
> hence the Fool's Paradise, the Statesman's Scheme,
> The air-built Castle, and the golden Dream,
> The Maid's romantic wish, the Chemist's flame,
> And Poet's vision of eternal Fame.
>
> (III, 8-12)

In Spleen's cave

> A constant *Vapour* o'er the Palace flies;
> Strange Phantoms rising as the Mists arise;
> Dreadful, as Hermit's Dreams in haunted Shades,
> Or bright as Visions of expiring Maids.
> Now glaring Fiends, and Snakes on rolling Spires,
> Pale Spectres, gaping Tombs, and Purple Fires:
> Now lakes of Liquid Gold, *Elysian* Scenes,
> And Crystal Domes, and Angels in Machines.
>
> (IV, 39-46)

Weiskel comments that the sublime is "apocalyptic in the strict sense that it reveals final things, and [that] the defeat of the sensible imagination accomplishes subjectively the end of the natural order."[15] This seems to me quite the point of such visionary experience, in that by transcending nature it negates nature and the entire context of signs and significations that nature embodies, signs which are themselves, as the *Essay on Man* makes clear, referents to cosmic design. And, again quoting Weiskel, "if the sensible world is too strongly negated, the usurpation loses its 'strength,' and the sublime is reified into a permanent attitude of alienation from nature." The egotistical sublime correlates with the apocalyptic visions of Spleen's cave (another illusory *rising*); each defines a different manifestation of alienation consonant with one or another kind of sublime experience, but with presumably one difference. The egotistical sublime is a stage in the process of alienation, leading progressively to exaltation of the unconscious as the ultimate repository of value. At this moment both history and nature are negated, and the chaos that *rises* is itself the dissolution of all "Relation" (*Dunciad*, IV, 479), the return of all things to their fundamentally unorganized state of pure matter.

Thus the strife Belinda engenders through the "Murders" (V, 145) of her eye and the battle between the sexes should remind us, given what has preceded it, of the mindless, warring strife of chaos and the alienation from nature that is the goal of the egotistical sublime. Thalestris signifies the total freedom of the female principle, which, now emancipated from all *relation* to the male, turns aggressively upon it. Almost one hundred years later Blake will identify this state as the separate female will. Regardless of what we call it, Thalestris represents the ancient desire of the female to rise above the male. Followed to its inevitable conclusion, the result is closure, the contraction of nature into a "darksom round," the maintenance of sexual interaction on the principle of predator and prey. Belinda, who has been the remote and mysterious beauty, is enlisted after the rape under the Amazon queen, Thalestris, and this action begins presumably another cycle of separation and warfare that the poem does not pursue. Yet the *Rape* moves through several clearly demarcated stages: from the creation of the goddess of love to the rebellion of the lover and the rape of his mistress, to the separation of the sexes into hostile opposites. Underlying all of this is the myth of fall, the alienation from nature that the egotistical sublime promotes, and the threat of chaos rises in the *Dunciad*-like apocalypse of Spleen's cave. Pope brings his poem to the moment of epiphany, which, by way of elegy, informs the moral: "*This Lock*, the Muse shall consecrate to Fame, / And mid'st the Stars inscribe *Belinda's* Name!" (V, 149-50). The lost lock has become part of the natural sublime, "mounted to the Lunar Sphere" (113). But there "Heroes' Wits are kept in pondrous Vases, / And Beaus' in *Snuff-boxes* and *Tweezer-Cases*" (115-16) along with such other stuff as "Lovers' Hearts," "Courtier's Promises," and the "Smiles of Harlots" (118-20). That the epiphany is enfolded in fictions of feeling strikes at the heart of transcendence, another and last attack upon the authority of the sublime and those who profess to read human fate in the heavens. Yet the poem reserves such a privilege for the poet: "But trust the Muse—she saw it upward rise, / Tho' marked by none but quick Poetic Eyes" (123-24).

The ascendant lock is another rising, another predication of the word on another fiction inhabiting it. Simultaneously, its sublime is legitimized within the province of poetic license; it becomes then a function of the poem's rhetoric, a mock-rhetoric consistent with mock-epic, and that Pope delivers this authority to the poet suggests the ways in which the rhetorical sublime can play against the egotistical sublime. Belinda is offered a fiction to replace other fictions, a rising to substitute for other risings. The localization of the lock in a context of emotional deformations qualifies the apotheosis: "Then cease, bright Nymph! to mourn thy ravish'd Hair / Which adds new Glory to the shining Sphere!" (141-42). If the lock merges with the natural sublime ("shining Sphere!") still those "fair Suns shall sett, as sett they must, / And all those Tresses shall be laid in Dust" (147-48). Pope's vision cuts two ways, as it has throughout the body of the poem. It both celebrates and diminishes, and realizes its own ironic conclusion: "Not all the Tresses that fair Head can boast / Shall draw such Envy as the Lock you lost" (143-44). The oddly discordant conclusion in which loss is the object of envy leagues, however, with another discordance: the paths of glory lead but to the grave. It is the purpose of the poem to drive these two discordances into harmony. That those "fair Suns shall sett" draws the poem back into the natural cycle of rise and fall, vitality and death. The sun is itself subject to a law greater than its own, and its authority must therefore reckon with a context that inevitably includes the elegiac moment. This awareness is sufficient to bring into the poem yet another occasion of falling, but one accommodated to the law of nature designed by the divine mind. This *fall* is not occasioned by an act of impiety; on the contrary, the recognition of its necessity is the surest sign of a mind obedient to the proper forms of self-love. Belinda is thus "rival" to the sun in ways she had not expected, and a further ironic strategy is to surprise pride by drawing out and fulfilling the implications of its assumptions. Pride, like the Satanic subverter it resembles, is caught within the fate of the sublime wherein it seeks to locate its own authority. On the other hand, the sun is the visible god of this world. Belinda's creative power has been transformed into a destructive power ("Murders"), the corruption of the God within her. This action in turn affiliates with the perversion of the creative power in man, the ruling passion, which, under the aegis of pride and erring reason, becomes subversive and tyrannical, resulting in a denial of the power of the Godhead vested in man through that passion.

But because our lives are governed by solar rhythms, Pope is calling attention to the natural cycle of birth and death to which the sun itself is subject. In other words, Belinda contains a reflection of the Godhead, but is not God; the natural is informed by the divine and not the other way round. Belinda's error is to believe that the natural can assume the divine; Eloisa's mistake is to imagine that the natural precludes the divine. In the relation between nature and the divine Belinda represents one type of error and Eloisa another of comparable though differing kind. Both misapprehend the reality of the special place, nature itself, and in the poems Pope studies the ways in which Hampton and the Paraclete are, or should be, continuous with Eden. This is much the same problem we witnessed earlier in the *Temple of Fame,* the difference being, however, that Rumour's mansion is merely the parodic or fallen form of Fame's temple, so that the world and the idea can never be reconciled. And in *Windsor-Forest* the forest is itself the displaced form of Eden, now purged of its dark and bloody history and ready to enter into a new cycle of commercial glory and expansionism. Both *Windsor-Forest* and the *Rape of the Lock* bring us to the edge of new historical cycles, though that to which we are conducted in the *Rape* is poised diametrically against that to which *Windsor-Forest* leads.

In itself this is a complex matter bearing upon Pope's own uncertainties about where history is leading, and the only way to deal with this problem in his poetry is to refer it to the dialectic sustained by the *Essay on Man* and the *Dunciad.* The *Essay* might bear the subtitle, Civilization Secured; the *Dunciad* is a vision of Civilization Lost, and both poems derive from Pope's early works and the ambivalences informing them. These dualities are made more apparent if for the moment we reflect on the drama of oppositions. Thalestris is opposed by Clarissa, Rumour by Fame, the weak queen Diana by the Stuart monarch, and Eloisa by the sainted "sister" she aspires to become. Such

conflicts are prelude to the larger antithesis of the *Essay*, the conflict between self-love and selfhood, the internal agencies of the
psyche that now contend for mastery and dominion over the
special place, man's middle kingdom.

When we look at Pope's poetry from this point of view we
see it unfolding from an imaginative center that necessitates the
creation of two irreconcilable acts. That the patriarchal God of
the *Essay* confronts the matriarchal goddess of the *Dunciad* suggests an encounter between potent mythological powers who
now contend for control over history. Mythologically, Dulness
affiliates with the Whore of Babylon; commonly she is identified
with chaos, ''and her whoredom represents the possessive love
of the jealous Selfhood . . . , the ultimate fallen form of nature.''[16] On the other hand, God endows man with the power
that conciliates knowledge; neither polarity is abrogated in the
engagement with the self that is at the center of creativity. The
choice is between becoming ''fix'd'' in one's own self-image,
the illusion sponsored by power, or free within the self-reflexive
reading of the datum (self-knowledge). In Pope a misreading is
always a contraction and a contraction is always a loss of knowledge, the ''giddy Circle'' (I, 93) in which Ariel and his creatures
have their being.

For the moment it is enough to recognize that the issue in
question is history, its direction and progress. No power of reconciling the *Essay*'s God with the disnatured goddess of the
Dunciad is available to Pope or to his culture. When the subject is
taken up again by the only writer following Pope capable of
applying himself to it, the problem will elicit the extraordinary
solution wherein both God and goddess are revealed as compatible realities, equally enchaining the mind to a delusory and
tyrannical nature. But before this occurs English poetry will pass
through a stage in which the passions are both demonized and
deified, and the unconscious is cultivated as the source of creative energy. The fact alone is enough to suggest the historical
pertinence of Pope's dialectic.

Eloisa to Abelard embodies another form of the dialectic, and
Eloisa's consciousness is the field for the conflict between nature

and grace. In this context the garden rises again, but as the transformed ''darksom round'' (17) of the Paraclete, the fallen form of nature in which Eloisa's eroticism provides the basis for the compulsive repetitions that bind her freedom and engender the anxious spirit of place, ''Black Melancholy.'' The gothic landscape of the Paraclete corresponds to the demonization of Eloisa's sexuality, and her alienation, felt as a disjunction from the deepest springs of her being, correlates with the Paraclete as a place of formidable psychic and emotional dislocation. Pope's choice of a twelfth-century romantic tragedy suggests the effort to analyze, apart from the contemporary context, the effect of eroticism on a woman of strong sensibility when the object of that eroticism is withdrawn and the mind seeks another object in which to invest itself. The problem is complicated by the displacement of one context (nature) onto another (grace), but the displacement permits Pope to continue to explore the relation between natural and divine. The erotic element serves to challenge the relation between the two realms, to bring their presumed incompatibility into sharpest focus, the reason why, as the Twickenham editor points out (without explaining), Pope adds ''a religious conflict to the usual Ovidian ones.''[17]

It seems apparent that for Pope, as well certainly as for other eighteenth-century writers, the gothic is cognate with the sublime—the former a penseroso state—and each engenders alienation.[18] Yet alienation in *Eloisa to Abelard* is not, as in the *Rape*, a function of power misapplied or misapprehended, but rather of powerlessness. Eloisa's passion is denied its object: the castrated figure of her lover is lost to her; and the effect of this denial is to enclose her within the darkness of nature, its night unilluminated by the vital principle with which, however ironically, Belinda is associated in the *Rape*. It is partly the relation between Belinda's light and Eloisa's darkness that drives these two poems into proximity, but Belinda's light moves toward its negation through the poem's second fall, whereas Eloisa's darkness is latterly irradiated by the illuminations of grace. So the poems tend to cross each other, the *Rape* moving from light to darkness, *Eloisa* from darkness to light. The thrust of *Eloisa* is thus toward opening a center, again bringing the Paraclete into relation with Hampton Court. The special place that is Hampton is made to bear the knowledge inherent in the elegiac vision at the poem's close, so that Hampton is penetrated by the one signification of nature it had sought to exclude. Eloisa's darksome round is another center to be opened, but with a difference. To open this prison-house into a marriage bower is an awakening into the consciousness of life-in-death, exactly contrary to Belinda's enforced recognition of death-in-life, the meaning of setting suns.

The relation between nature and grace is somewhat analogous to that between the immediate temporal present and historical time as that relation is set forth in the *Temple of Fame*. In time present, the domain of the goddess Rumour, the valuations of Fame are obscured or deformed. The more that the present moment is dominated by Rumour the more the past closes and ceases to be available as a goal or measure of the contemporary imagination. Similarly, in *Eloisa*, when nature is given over to the ''jealous God'' (81), the meaning of nature *sub specie aeternitatis* contracts or closes, and as this happens the relation between nature and grace is progressively denied. The result of this process is that nature assumes an independent existence to the unimaginative man (blind to the meaning of grace) who lives within it. As God is expelled from nature, Satan enters into the now vacant space. Thus one way to understand Eloisa's situation is to recognize that her passion for her lover is justifed by her vision of nature, for she sees nature as an autonomous realm acting according to its own self-generated laws. Nature contains within itself all that Eloisa loves, or—perhaps the better way of stating it—nature justifies her passion in much the same way that people commonly refer their desires to a source of authority beyond themselves and say that it is *natural* to do or to behave as they do. Eloisa's initial condition is essentially no different, except that the object of her passion has been brutally removed from her, so that she has been denied the full participation in nature that, to her, is largely the meaning of loving. All of this being so, the nature she clings to is now "rebel nature" (26), a nature that will not capitulate to another reality that is seen as hostile and antagonistic to it. Her passion is now (so she thinks) informed with a heroic component, and to behave as she does is a measure of the greatness of her love. She becomes therefore the classic type of the alienated, and her idea of her passion passes beyond the personal into the phenomenal, which is to say that it takes its authority from the fact that passion is part of nature and nature wronged.

This is the usual motive for rebellion, and it affiliates with Belinda's usurpation of nature's power ("Rival" to the sun). Belinda's act is informed by her sense of superiority to the male and hence to marriage, which she views and is encouraged to regard by the sylphs as threatening to her autonomy. Eloisa's rebellion is informed by her sense of the superiority of *love*, the autonomy of which has been denied and negated. When this happens, the nature that was to cherish and contain Eloisa is not merely reduced but transformed. It now becomes a darksome round, a place of sterile and repetitive actions unilluminated by the principle of love. Something analogous to this sequence occurs when the ruling passion is transformed from a grace within being into an idée fixe, an obsessive and self-destructive habit of mind. Love, which was to be the fulfillment of Eloisa's identity, instead possesses it, so that she acts and has acted under the aegis of the jealous god. The worship of this god, she tells us, prohibits marriage, which merely means that the god denies all laws except his own ("Curse on all laws but those which love has made!"[74]). Eloisa's god of love sponsors what seems like freedom but is really enslavement, for this god is jealous and "when we profane his fires, / Those restless passions in revenge inspires" (81-82).

Eloisa is thereby enlisted under the governance of a tyrant, or of nature devoid of grace, only another form of the tyrant's identity.[19] To her way of thinking, nature and grace have nothing to do with each other, and to think in this way is to live within the fires of passion or, those passions deprived of their immediate object, to be consigned to the cold, loveless round she inhabits at the beginning of the poem. Once we put things in this way we can see the appeal of the subject to Pope's own imagination. Love is a reality that has been emptied of divine content and exists independently by a self-generated authority. This authority is seemingly formidable, for what the god of love promises Eloisa is "bliss (if bliss on earth there be)" (97), but such bliss is subject to violation as once again the garden of delight is invaded and "A naked Lover bound and bleeding lies!" (100). The invasion of the garden correlates with various despoliations we have already witnessed elsewhere, and the predatory theme resonates, however faintly, in the mutilated and bleeding Abelard.

Eloisa's retrospection tells us that she has experienced the age-old violation of the pastoral dream, the bliss without end. Though such a recognition should awaken her to the limits of nature's sufficiency, it in fact does not. On the contrary, she sees her subsequent profession of the novitiate's vows in sacrificial terms: "Canst thou forget that sad, that solemn day, / When victims at yon' altar's foot we lay?" (107-8). As the garden closes to Eloisa, the sacrificial altar opens to her consciousness (as it does to Belinda's; the difference being that others, not she, will be the victims): "Not on the Cross my eyes were fix'd, but you" (116). The recurrent image ("fix'd" eyes) implies a continuity of contexts; paradoxically, Eloisa is to Abelard as Belinda's admirers are to her, and the obsessional image enforces her role as victim, again suggesting that Pope is coming at a similar problem from different angles. The power of self-devotion and the power of the self's devotions are equally demonizations of identity. Such propositions givern his perception of Eloisa's predicament and provide the terms for our reading of the poem. The "darksom round" that will become "roseate bow'rs" (317) suggests the distance to be travelled, defines the metamorphoses to which the circle is subject.

The falsely dedicatory altars of the *Rape* re-emerge in *Eloisa* in two ways. First, the altar at which Eloisa professes herself is seen as a sacrificial altar, which it is not. Second, the jealous god

of love has his own altar that she rightly but unknowingly associates with enslavement. She is "Confess'd within the slave of
love and man" (178); consequently, "Love finds an altar for forbidden fires" (182). Within the slave mentality fostered by the
jealous god, the *fires* she endures are the measure of her torment
and her passion, and it is almost needless to remark on the
recurrent significance of the ambivalent word "fire" within the
extended Popeian text (the canon). The round is thus a place
and a state of mind, the damnation of erotic torment. Therefore
the "bliss" promised by the god is actually a hell, and Pope
gives that hell a precise content some fifty lines later when he
describes it as a nightmare of sexual desire in which the beloved
is illusorily present and withdrawn:

> I hear thee, view thee, gaze o'er all thy charms,
> And round thy phantom glue my clasping arms.
> I wake—no more I hear, no more I view,
> The phantom flies me, as unkind as you.
> I call aloud; it hears not what I say;
> I stretch my empty arms; it glides away.
>
> (233-38)

Within this general context, however, Eloisa envisions her
deprivations not as service to a cruel god, but as a martyrdom.
Unlike Belinda self-deified as "Goddess" of love, Eloisa is
love's saint, possessed of a heroic capacity for suffering in the
service of her god. Thus her "gushing eyes o'erflow" (35),
"Tears still are mine, and those I need not spare" (45), and Abelard is enjoined to "give me all thy grief" (50). Within this
drama of heroic passion Eloisa is the leading actress of her own
theater: "Should at my feet the world's great master fall, / Himself, his throne, his world, I'd scorn 'em all" (85-86). Retrospec-
tively, she proclaims her innocence at love's shrine: "Thou
know'st how guiltless first I met thy flame, / When Love
approach'd me under Friendship's name" (59-60). Love's
assumed identity initiates a concern with right naming that will
open into the central problem of the poem and be re-created
over and again within Pope's texts. His imagination (not

Eloisa's) remains concentrated on the fact of duplicity and on those strategies of usurpation by which a thing masquerades as that which it is not. To my mind, the political bearing of this awareness permeates the poetry, revealing the sort of caution-ary intelligence that renders the nature and trappings of power a central subject. *To name* thus becomes a major preoccupation of the poet, and false and true naming, as *Horace, Imitated* will later make even clearer, a principal obligation of the satirist's job. Here, love's identity bespeaks a concern with naming that func-tions obsessively within Eloisa's imagination, and Abelard's name is another manifestation of the word that enfolds and pos-sesses. She speaks initially of "kiss[ing] the name" (8); it is a "Dear fatal name!" (9); she seeks to avoid writing it but the "name appears / Already written" (13-14); she wishes herself mistress to the man she loves: "If there be yet another name more free / More fond than mistress, make me that to thee!" (89-90). Her imagination collapses "father, brother, husband, friend . . . / . . . all those tender names in one, thy love!" (152-54). To name rightly and to speak the right name are functions of right knowing, as the *Essay on Man* repeatedly insists, whereas Abelard's name obsessively binds her to the darksome round, as prohibitively imprisoning as the Paraclete itself.

"Name" is reiterated throughout the text, but Abelard is called *by* name eight times. Eloisa is not only "I," "me," "my," but also "her," and sounds her own name six times. We are drawn into a consciousness obsessed by the drama of "I" and "you," a consciousness that here can escape its own intensities only by burying "each hapless name" in "one kind grave" (343). Eloisa's struggle seems almost to become that of freeing herself from the compulsive and reiterated agony of *name*, of escaping a present obsession by the immediate expedient of envisioning her own and Abelard's death and memorializing their names ("And graft my love immortal on thy fame"[344]).[20]

What Eloisa is setting out is the story of her love for Abe-lard, its commencement and tragic conclusion. Yet all unknow-ingly she is putting forth the history of her service to the god in a way that recalls the narcissistic moment in *Paradise Lost* when

Eve returns to view her image in the mirror of the lake. Pope is at pains to keep this allusion before us, although he alters it so as to give it another bearing. As Eloisa says, "Back thro' the pleasing paths of sense I ran" (69). To return along that path is to descend from "Mind" (Abelard viewed as "Some emanation of th' all-beauteous Mind"[62]) to sensation, which is what "sense" means here. In Eloisa's case the return signifies a collapse of the meaning of love, a contraction to the irreducible essence of sensation. And this is also what she means when she states: "Dim and remote the joys of saints I see, / Nor envy them, that heav'n I lose for thee" (71-72). In itself it is another occasion of martyrdom but equally a paradox. It is not the flesh she abandons but the spirit, and in dying to the spirit she lives to the flesh. This peculiar kind of sainthood continues to enforce what is at the center of Pope's vision here: the god of love as the antithesis to the Christian God, and Eloisa's heroism is demonized to the extent that her rebellion seems to her the measure of her own greatness, another *rising* to another occasion sponsored by other *fires.*

This is merely a further variation of the selfhood engendered by the cruel god. For this reason the generative basis of love sponsors the freedom of the "I": "Curse on all laws but those which love has made!" Her apotheosis is to make love a world, and she, like Belinda, is at the center of her own construction. Yet nothing could be clearer than Pope's irony: "Oh happy state!" she says, "when souls each other draw, / When love is liberty, and nature, law" (91-92). The obvious comment to make is that when love is liberty, nature cannot be law, for law is abrogated in the freedom (however delusory) that love bestows. On the contrary, such freedom is slavery, which is the only law of the jealous god. These are the entrapments of Eloisa's passion, an intellectual muddle that is another counterpart to the darksome round.

Even more so than in the *Rape,* Pope here keeps insisting upon the betrayals implicit in a misreading of the language of love. Eloisa's ingenuity is employed in opening the word, in discovering a synonymous reality inhabiting it (love equals liberty, nature equals law), and her passion is fueled by a linguistic facility predicated on the fact of identity of meaning. Insofar as her monolog is based on the word *love,* her argument is really about the meanings of the word, those licenses it justifies and the liberations of the self with which it is consistent. Pope's perspective imposes upon the reader an awareness of the self-deceptions the word engenders. In this sense, language constitutes the "I," for self-identity is comprised of those investments that the word is made to bear. Something very similar happens in the *Rape,* wherein honor is the public reality, albeit private mask, of the coquette, and the relation between private and public selves is at the heart of Belinda's lament concluding Canto IV. I find these concerns inexplicable without reference to the liberating engagement with language in the *Temple of Fame.* The more we examine this subject the more we encounter that peculiarly pervasive relation between power and knowledge in the extended Popeian text. Eloisa's effort to invest "rebel nature" with the justification love provides is only another and futile attempt to set up a contradiction and imbue it with the authority of law, her own version of the union of power and knowledge.

Her attempt to cut nature off from the divine results only in separating herself from nature. What the rebel is then left with is something that rapidly becomes a hell, a disnatured reality from which the divine presence has been excluded. Into this now vacant space rush the subjective deities that are the furies of the mind. In a much lesser key, in the *Rape* these furies are the agents of Belinda's selfhood, the sylphs, whose purpose is to promote her self-deification and thereby subvert the order of nature. In *Eloisa to Abelard* the immediately resident demon is "Black Melancholy" (165), the *genius loci* or, in conventional eighteenth-century terms, the personification of the darksome round. Her "death-like silence" (166) provides us with the sort of informing content we have been seeking. "Black Melancholy" is the agent of the cruel god, whose intention is to prevent the acts of adoration to which the Paraclete is dedicated. In another sense, "Black Melancholy" is the female deity leagued

to the jealous god (and thus an obscene imitation of the marriage of tutelary deities in *Windsor-Forest*), and the subversion of
a center is enacted under the aegis of the usurping deities who
now possess Eloisa. Her possession defines the terms of her
demonization; enlisted in the service of the jealous god, she is a
votary at his altars. Melancholy is also the deity directly correspondent to Spleen, and each is the psychological objectification
that characterizes, respectively, Eloisa and Belinda. Possessed
by a deity who signifies the *content* of her fall, each woman
assumes that spectral identity by which she is possessed. The
demons are both inside and outside the mind: inside they deter-
mine perception; outside they are what is perceived.

The Paraclete is Abelard's creation, corresponding to Eden:
it is a "Paradise . . . open'd in the Wild" (134). But this paradise
is subject to closure when its own law is violated, and when this
happens, either man may be expelled, or the paradise may simply invert itself to become its own antithesis. Something like the
latter action is consistent with the two meanings of love in the
poem and with the two deities with whom love is identified.
The jealous god of love is the negative form of the Christian God
of love. When God is rejected by the imagination, love does not
simply disappear but turns inside out and presents itself as an
oppression of the spirit, a grief and a burden. This inversion is
precisely what Eloisa experiences, but she conceives of the burden as the measure of her own devotion when it is, as I have
been arguing, the measure of her own enslavement. Instead of
being love's saint she is love's victim, and the distance between
these two realities is that between vision and delusion, always a
difficult distance to measure. But Pope allows us to gauge that
distance by the introduction of "Black Melancholy," in spite of
the fact that Eloisa takes her incarceration as proof of her fidelity
to love: "here for ever, ever must I stay; / Sad proof how well a
lover can obey!" (171-72). And it is thus, to come full circle for
the moment, that "Love finds an altar for forbidden fires" (182):
within the darksome round another altar corresponds to those
other altars existing within Hampton. From another perspective, the Paraclete is a temple of erotic love, which is what Eloisa

has made of it, and in the center of this temple is not a "hallow'd Quire" but an altar to the demon-god.

If we step back from the four poems we perceive that each is about a special place and about those invasive passions that threaten its integrity. We see also that Pope is drawing upon different poetic traditions and driving these into a complex relation; while working within genres familiar to the eighteenth-century reader he is deploying them in ways no one else had envisioned. He is offering his readers what they will recognize as "imitations" and simultaneously creating his myths out of disparate poetic materials.[21] By widening and deepening the terms of his inquiry, he explores a series of related subjects in poems seemingly inconsistent with one another. It is arguable that this procedure is what necessarily substitutes for epic, for the long poem Pope was never able to write. During his life he does not so much change direction as develop what is explicit in the early works, and the gods and goddesses of the later poems derive from those in the early verse.

Eloisa's monolog is concerned with the maintenance of the obsessive "I" at its center, an "I" that resists dislocation and discovers sanctions by which to sustain its devotion to the jealous god. Belinda's dark rejection of what is owing to nature is here transposed into Eloisa's effort to establish the authority of nature independent of grace. Over and again she invokes this authority; what she regards as the unnatural resignation of love is resisted by reference to a context of companionable forms: "streams . . . shine between the hills," "grots . . . echo to the tinkling rills," "gales . . . pant upon the trees," "lakes . . . quiver to the curling breeze" (157-60). In nature there is nothing solitary, except Eloisa herself, and her deprivations inspire a demonization of the landscape, the "Black Melancholy" who "saddens," "darkens," "deepens," and "breathes a browner horror on the woods" (167-70). Her effort is to find the correspondent object in which passion can repose; not finding it she is given over to the compulsive repetitions that bind her freedom (which ironically was to be her reward for service to the god): "I ought to grieve, but cannot what I ought; / I mourn the lover, not lament the fault; / I view the crime, but kindle at the view" (183-85). Such responses provide another occasion of the "round"; in such a context she envisions analysis as an act of self-multilation, another seeming subversion of desire by discriminations she resists:

> How shall I lose the sin, yet keep the sense,
> And love th' offender, yet detest th' offence?
> How the dear object from the crime remove,
> Or how distinguish penitence from love?
>
> (191-94)

The efforts suggest themselves as mutilations of experience and combine metaphorically with the physical act of castration, a violation that lies close to the center of Eloisa's consciousness. Her reluctance to make such distinctions suggests a latent association between discrimination and loss, having its source in her awareness of castration. Thus analysis is deformation, and the association immediately sponsors an appeal to Abelard that also links associatively with the fact of identity predicated on loss: "Oh come! Oh teach me nature to subdue" (203). As Abelard's castration calls attention to the insufficiency of nature, it functions in Pope's imagination similarly to Belinda's rape, with perhaps one important difference. The rape *may* return Belinda to the order of nature; the castration (linked to sacrifice) leads Eloisa to the order of the divine. In each poem an actual and a totemic blood-letting keeps us focused on those alternative, though compatible, realities to which Pope is calling our attention. Yet Eloisa's rejection of moral discrimination is offered as a remarkable imaginative fidelity to the integrity of her experience, which resists any and all surgical operations. That she is caught up in the irony of Pope's perspective is part of the larger point of the scene, and that Abelard, who has suffered the physical dismemberment, is invoked as a pattern for the renunciation is what makes this scene pivotal within the poem. Almost at the middle, Pope is turning the poem toward the terms of redemption.

From such a vital train of association the affinity of Abelard's sacrifice to Christ's sacrifice arises, and it explains the se-

quence by which "God alone . . . / . . . can rival, can succeed
to thee" (205-6). Edwards remarks oddly about the poem that
we "miss the significant shifts of tone made possible by the
superimposition upon the event of a detached speaking voice,"
and "we are not made to feel more than pity for Eloisa's passionate confusion."[22] The observation is useful in a strange way,
for it is not Eloisa's "passionate confusion" that is important
here, but the *passion* of both Abelard and Christ that fuses them
in her imagination, the superimposition of one pattern upon
another. The strategy by which desire is sublimated into adoration is what is at issue. Eloisa's agony in the poem arises from
the necessity to force the soul's datum into a context that strains
its application. To love Abelard and to love Christ are presumably functions of love, yet the separate and hitherto incompatible orientations of nature and grace have existed to her as type
and antitype. *Love*, like *blood* or *rising* or *power* in the other
poems, determines here the crisis she confronts, and the word is
split into its ambivalent and opposed meanings. Love is
opposed by its deceptive simulacrum, in much the same way
that the God is opposed by the jealous god or Fame by Rumour.
Pope's texts are always establishing the grounds for the *wrong*
choice, insinuating the ways in which the simulacrum obsesses
and possesses, and by this strategy mocking the adequacy of
the self's determinations. His imagination is thus always and
ultimately oriented toward exposing the illusions conditioning
the act of choosing, while mocking the "I" constituted by false
choice.

    In order to meet the challenge by which type and antitype
are metamorphosed into typological identity, Eloisa suffers a
dislocation of the "I," the nature of which is explicit in the creation of a second self, the "blameless Vestal" (207), who is an
objectification of her own opposite, an imaginative displacement of the self onto another self. A common strategy draws
power in the *Rape* from its various subversive affiliations, and *love*
in *Eloisa* from the limited and spectral reality into which the
word has been locked. The self cannot be free until the word on
which the self is predicated has been emancipated from the

contexts that contract its meaning. In the *Temple of Fame* the word is known through an encounter with ambivalence that precludes a limited and limiting choice. In *Windsor-Forest* it is redeemed by redirection. In the *Rape of the Lock* it is extricated from the illusory self-reflexiveness on which identity has been founded, and in *Eloisa to Abelard* the word is mediated by a passion that permits the heroine to slide between contexts. Whatever doubt we may have about the success of Eloisa's conversion, the only issue I wish to address is strategic, in order to bring the latter poem into proximity with the others. The relation between Abelard and Christ, and of Eloisa and vestal virgin, is based on the ambiguities of *love*, requiring therefore an opening of the word in ways not previously available to her. The "opening skies" (341) of *Eloisa* and the opening centers of the *Essay* are acts analogous to the poet's own cultural task of opening the word. Pope's act defines the distance between contraction and expansion, between exclusion and incorporation, between the nature that precludes grace and the nature that exists within grace and takes its meaning from it. If Pope forces Eloisa's choice, it is only because her understanding is made correlative with his own, and his use of the word is analogous to hers. Eloisa comes to imagine grace as she imagines nature *because* she re-imagines passion within an expanding typological context, and the identities of Abelard-Christ, Eloisa-vestal virgin, correspond to the ambivalence that now informs the opened word.

Abelard's sacrifice has resulted in a spiritual energy "proportional to the importance of what has been lost."[23] Eloisa's sacrifice is of the same order of magnitude; it turns equally on the paradox of loss and gain, again bringing us round to elegy and to the commemorative moment of purification and release with which the elegiac mode is associated in Pope's texts. In other words, the most intense occasions in that poetry seem to insist upon a death of sorts as the necessary ground of freedom and rebirth. The sacrificial act of the bleeding balm in *Windsor-Forest* is linked, however distantly, to the debt that Eloisa pays to grace. A nature that willingly offers itself to Father Thames corresponds to the passion that freely submits itself to God. *Eloisa* stands as a drama of enslavement and escape, a study of the ways in which nature, seen as self-sufficient and independent, enfolds and possesses. Is it too much, then, to regard the *Essay on Man* as the now obligatory exploration of the ways in which nature under the aegis of the divine assumes its contextual significance for man? I am aware that in raising this question I will perplex those readers who remember my self-imposed obligation to disclose the hidden paths leading from poem to poem. I have no desire to evade this commitment, but only to follow those terms in which inquiry maintains coherence. The 1728 *Dunciad* is amplified by the *New Dunciad* of 1742 and by its addition as a fourth book in the next year. It seems advisable to wait upon the latter event for a full-scale consideration of the four-book poem, while reminding my reader of what he probably does not need to be told. The years intervening between the publication of the *Works* (1717) and the *Dunciad* of 1728 constitute the most intense period of translation and editorial activity in Pope's life. It is not exactly my purpose to argue the specific literary efficacy for Pope of these years, their effect upon and contribution to the creation of the canon, though it seems obvious that without the Homer, in particular, Pope's later and most ambitious poems would lack the allegorical density that the translations of *Iliad* and *Odyssey* nurtured and fostered. The major observation, however, is that the four early poems just discussed provide something of a structure of topics to be transposed and recreated within the poems of the middle and later years. The topics given various form by the young poet were to be re-imagined within the dialectic sustained by the *Essay on Man*, the answering voices of a self alternately responsive to the demonic and the divine. Here again it is the metamorphosis of discourse to which I want to call attention, to a poetic imagination that is equally visionary and re-visionary.

3 The Generic Self and Particular Persons

An Essay on Man

The *Essay on Man* is the greatest philosophic poem of the eighteenth century. It coexists with such other ambitious works as Young's *Night Thoughts* and Thomson's *The Seasons*, and, like those poems in our own time and even through the nineteenth century, it has suffered a vanishing audience and a currency wholly honorific. This is not a peculiar fate for the *Essay*, for it has seemed to many readers a merely obligatory performance, a poem doctrinal to an age, as one scholar puts it,[1] and therefore an excursion for modern readers into an outworn creed. Though it has been brilliantly studied by Maynard Mack, and the historical context of its ideas attentively established by Douglas White,[2] it nevertheless looms in Pope's canon as a forbidding document, lacking both the immediate wit and sparkle of the *Rape of the Lock* and the passionate eloquence of *Eloisa to Abelard*. To its further disadvantage it has seemed oddly abstract, offering little in the way of direct social or political bearing and void even of the sort of nasty trifling that misreaders of the *Dunciad* have always been willing to ascribe to that poem. The most formidable critics of the later eighteenth

67

century, Joseph Warton and Samuel Johnson, disliked it, one is tempted to say, almost heartily, and the poem has attracted to itself the pernicious and deadly label of *unpoetic*. As if all this were not enough, to those who still find an audience for eighteenth-century poetry among university students, the poem proves frequently a pedagogical disaster.

Admittedly, this brief tour of its history is somewhat one-sided. Among Pope's contemporaries there were some to praise it, and it has occasionally found support in unexpected quarters. But the general outlines of the survey are correct, perhaps encapsulated best by Johnson's remark on *Paradise Lost:* ''The want of human interest is always felt.''[3] Yet it is the human interest that compels attention. The psychological myth of the poem internalizes the divine and the demonic as elements of a psychomachian drama, the metamorphosis of the Edenic crisis into its postlapsarian reality. Self-love is opposed by its formidable antagonists, pride and erring reason; together these specters comprise what I have called, borrowing the term from Blake, the selfhood.[4] As in the case of both Belinda and Eloisa, the selfhood obscures the reality of nature, transmuting it into merely another objectification of the self. When this happens, the divine is closed to the imagination, and the selfhood creates the diabolic entities it then worships. In this way the jealous god of love is born and the sylphs are objectified as the instruments of Belinda's desires. The *Essay* thus recapitulates by assimilation and recreates by transposition. It could be written only by a poet who has already taken possession of the field and now builds his greater edifice upon it.

Within the psychoanalytic reduction that the *Essay* embodies, the assault by pride upon reason is a refiguring of the seduction practiced by Satan upon Eve, the consequence of which is the separation of reason from self-love and the creation of erring reason as the newly articulated companion of the demonic subverter. On one level the assault is a violation of the female by the male intruder; the challenge to self-love is presented at the deepest levels of instinctual response, the catastrophic seduction of the companionable female. From this episode is engendered what Pope calls the "family of pain," "Hate, Fear, and Grief" (II, 118). The female has been corrupted by pride's possession of her, and the holy child that is the master passion of God's bestowing falls into the service of pride. The ultimate blasphemy transmutes God's gift into man's curse, and Pope does much more than merely glance at the transformation of the passion into pride's creature, the obsessively degenerate form of the "strong direction" (II, 165) with which God has initially endowed self-love and reason.

My earlier arguments concentrated on the ways in which the word enfolds and possesses, that as *love* in *Eloisa* is opened to an ambivalence incorporating Christ *and* Abelard (grace and nature), *power* in the *Rape* is purged of its perverse association with error and pride, resulting in the assimilation of the word *honor* into the reformed relation between *power* and *knowledge*. In a way that strikes me as provocatively analogous, honor is to power and knowledge much as the ruling passion is to self-love and reason. The self that in the *Essay* discovers its own ambivalence, discovers also the ways in which that passion becomes the instrument of pride and erring reason. Thus the dualism inhabiting the word is consonant with a self-consciousness that perceives in terms of self-love and selfhood. Such a perception initiates the encounter with ambivalence at the heart of the *Essay*. The redemptive engagement with such words as *blood* or *rising* in the early poems now shifts to another form of engagement with the self, and the word redeemed from its possessive simulacrum corresponds to a self-love that defeats the shadowy and usurping agency of selfhood.

This, briefly, is the dramatic content of the *Essay* into which I intend to inquire. Another way of viewing the text, however, is to suggest that Pope re-creates the theme of predator and prey by re-envisioning that relation as pertinent to pride and reason. The action of pride upon reason results therefore in the formation of the selfhood; the union of self-love and reason is the opposing agency within being, a familial unit that fulfills human possibility and bears within itself the continuing evidence of man's fidelity to God. In this respect, it is useful to recognize further that pride creates what Blake calls *Emanations,* the source "of a continuously tantalizing and elusive torment," which in the fallen state "is conceived as outside" of man.[5] Pride's intention is thus to inspire the familiar terms of revolt, to suggest that all the various objects of perception are reducible to the terms of desire and possession. To "Ask for what end the heav'nly bodies shine / Earth for whose use?" is to be answered by pride, " 'Tis for mine" (I, 131-32). Insofar as this context derives from the Miltonic pattern, it assimilates the Miltonic argument in which divine interdiction is presented not merely as a prohibition but as a grace. Concealed knowledge of the future, which reformulates the taboo imposed upon the Edenic tree, is "kindly giv'n" (I, 85), and God's mercy is equally implicit in the restriction of human faculty. If touch were "tremblingly alive all o'er," man would "smart and agonize at ev'ry pore" (I, 197-98). If smell were keener, he would "Die of a rose in aromatic pain" (200).

Pride emerges as the familiarly insinuating seducer, the persuasive agent of power, but emerges also as consigned to that self-destructiveness definitive of its own doom of nonsense. And if Pope moves to establish one of the *Essay's* paradoxical axioms, that to be more is to have less, he moves equally to create the terms of a psychomachia in which pride is not only a rebel against justice, but, like "rebel nature" in *Eloisa,* is an agent of cruelty acting in ignorance of the laws it despises. The Edenic garden being once more displaced, the displacement functions here as an internal fact, and since tempter and tempted coexist within, man, like that nature in which he finds himself, is a "mighty maze! but not without a plan" (I, 6). Pride is not the guide through this labyrinth, but merely another and greater adversary. Thus Pope's first act in the *Essay,* which will later identify Bolingbroke as his "guide," is to warn against the false guardian, pride, a greater and more formidable demon than those who have yet appeared. Once we put things in this way we can perceive that the *Essay* elaborately encounters those oppositions existing within man, thereby translating and re-creating the dramas of internal subversion characteristic of the *Rape* and *Eloisa*. And such an encounter requires the energy of awakened resistance, a demand implicit in Pope's first charge to Bolingbroke, "Awake, my St. John!" (I, 1).

Recent attention to the *Essay* has been provocatively addressed to the "I" and the "you" of the poem. Brower seems responsible for initiating this concern, but Paulson and Griffin build on it to develop the proposition that the distinct identities, "virtuous teacher and erring student, are warring impulses within Pope, and the poem a kind of psychomachia."[6] The bearing of this observation on my own position, that a psychological myth is at the center of the *Essay*, perhaps requires no extended commentary. Yet the relation between the self and the "other" is a consistent feature of Pope's compulsive psychologizing. The gradually existent other is built up by Belinda's cosmetic arts until she beholds her divinity in a glass. The other that she desires to become is invoked by Eloisa as sainted "sister." The other may be a desirable entity or not (depending upon the perspective of actor and/or poet), but in any event it exists as a constituent element of identity to be conjured (the *Rape* and *Eloisa*) or vituperatively banished (the *Essay*). As a simulacrum, it suggests here the sort of shadowy interior identity that opposes self-love and provides further evidence of the critical metaphor, metamorphosis, in Pope's imagination. Paulson notes that Pope's "earliest translations and imitations were of Ovid's *Metamorphoses*, and in *Windsor Forest* the georgic readjustments are posed in terms of metamorphosis. The central one is of Lodona, fleeing from Pan, transformed into a river, her flight into a smooth-flowing contemplative mirror of nature, as war is transformed into peace."[7]

This is true enough, though I have in mind specifically an objective identity always in danger of breaking down, of metamorphosing into its antithesis, an instability which must partially account for the particular vilification lavished upon the "you" of the *Essay*. It would seem that one function of Pope's satire is to advise this "you" to keep its distance; although the relation between "I" and "you" may be objectified into a discourse ("virtuous teacher and erring student"), it exists far more potently as an internal dialogue or constituent feature of the psychological myth. The question of course bears on how long the "I" can sustain itself, pressed from within by its own simulacrum, which promises a greater "I" than that already known (yet glimpsed and imagined). What I am addressing now is a persistent problem of identity and growth in Pope's poetry and in romantic poetry as well. To what extent does growth confirm an already known identity, or, on the other hand, threaten it by breakdowns of one kind or another? The latter possibility seems to furnish the occasion of persistent fearfulness in Wordsworth's verse. Do "I" continue to incorporate within "me" what "I" once was, and if "I" do not, what then have "I" gained and lost?

Weiskel puts this concern neatly by speaking of the "distance . . . between the intentional, subjective, 'I,' which is confined to the *now* and is the ultimate locus of the signified, and the objective 'me,' or identity, which is imaginatively predicated across the moments.'"[8] One way of looking at the *Essay* is to suggest simply that its metaphysic is designed to pacify any irresoluteness about the world that may invade the "I" of the poem. Another and related way is to argue (as I have been doing) that the "I" is militantly on guard against its own internal subversions (which are designed to produce a "you"). In one sense therefore the "you" of the *Essay* is the selfhood rampant, unconstrained and free, a distorted mirror image of the "I" in much the same way that the goddess in Belinda's glass is another such distortion. These ideas, in turn, produce a battery of questions about the sources of the self's stability. Satire cannot flourish unless the questions are both urgent and answerable, and it is difficult to think of a historical moment when more answers were furnished: nature, wit, judgment, decorum, self-love, ruling passion, etc. What perhaps we have not quite understood is the essential quality of "Augustan" anxiety, which in Pope's texts seems commonly to take the form of some sort of adversary relation (even when the poem, as with the *Essay* or the *Temple of Fame*, is inconsistently satiric). In any event, the *family* within the *Essay* is one way in which the "I" is incorporated into a "we" (self-love, reason, and ruling passion). The other way involves the relation between Bolingbroke and Pope. And one might well argue that the construction of a plural identity is mandated by the opposing multiple selves that at all points threaten identity. It is possible to extend this reflection to include the *Epistles to Several Persons,* to Martha, Cobham, Bathurst, and Burlington, who serve as aggregate elements of a "we" (socially defined) that can resist the incursions of opposing identities.

Pope's texts are especially alert to the breakdown of socially or psychologically determined units. "*Wit* and *Judgment* often are at strife, / Tho' meant each other's Aid, like *Man* and *Wife*" (*Essay on Criticism,* 82-83). Or the companionable relation between self-love and reason is subject to internal subversion. Or, conversely, a malformation imposes a duplicitous and malign union upon the world: "Inseparable now, the Truth and Lye; / The strict Companions are for ever join'd" (*Temple of Fame,* 494-95). At the risk of overstating my case, the marital unit seems a keystone for the edifice of *relation,* ultimately the radiant habitat that is nature. This may be why Eden, now displaced into Windsor/England, is presided over by Father Thames *and* great Anna. The monarchical metaphor is equally a critical one (wit and judgment), a psychological one (self-love and reason), a series of reflective displacements of the Ur-myth (Adam and Eve). Of course what I am addressing is how a poet organizes his thought, disposing its law within his various texts. Marriage is the metaphor to which Belinda will not submit, the law Eloisa disdained: "How oft', when press'd to marriage, have I said, / Curse on all laws but those which love has made!" (73-74). I am inclined to read this passage as alone offering sufficient evidence of the satirist's presence glimmering through the text, another example of the hidden god (the poet) mocking his creation, or, simply, of Eloisa invoking false knowledge ("law") in the service of "Love." Eloisa's "law," originating in "rebel nature" ruled only by itself and therefore existing independently of subordination and integration, violates society's law.

Thus in the *Essay* Pope's address to Bolingbroke: "Teach me, like thee" (IV, 377) to know "our Knowledge" (398), a knowledge that animates a plural identity, the knowledge that makes a "we." Broadly conceived, this is the law of the self, motivating the principle that self-love is social (III, 318), spanning the distance between an "I" and a "them." Knowledge that perverts or escapes the irreducible design of sacramental union is thus not knowledge at all. The bearing of these remarks on the union of pride with erring reason and the power of knowledge and the knowledge of power that such a union inspires should be obvious.

Man is "in doubt to act, or rest, / In doubt to deem himself a God, or beast; / In doubt his Mind or Body to prefer" (II, 7-9). Contrapuntally, the first word of Epistle II is "Know." The relation between *to doubt* and *to know* suggests the extremes of human comprehension, even as God and beast, mind and body, establish an unmediated dualism. The reach of this dualism spreads like a stain throughout the opening lines. Man "thinks too little, or too much"; he is "confus'd" by "Thought and Passion." He is "abus'd, or disabus'd / Created half to rise, and half to fall; / Great lord of all things, yet a prey to all" (12-16). This sort of provocative ambivalence is the rocking horse of perception, alternative motion without a point of rest, and man the being who shuttles between the terminal points of self-reflexive definition. Such a being is, in a word, Pope's *adversarius*. If he is one whose ambition is to "mount," to "soar," to "teach" (19, 23, 29), he is equally one whose invariable fate is to "drop" (30), in this case into himself, where he is a fool. The rise culminates in another fall, a Daedalian disaster, itself a consequence of the flight, an extreme calamity that is a function of extreme ambition. And when Pope restates this matter he does so in terms of opposites that habitually defeat each other's ends. Thus "What Reason weaves, by Passion is undone" (42). The argument implies of course that "thyself" (30) is a compound of irreconcilable antitheses, that man's compulsive act is to create and uncreate, and that the definitive quality of human nature is an

internal antagonism. The result of Pope's subsequent anatomi-
cal directive, presumably to the "you" of the epistle, to "strip"
science and "lop th' excrescent parts" (44, 49), leads back again
into a dualistic consciousness of time past and time future:
"Then see how little the remaining sum, / Which serv'd the
past, and must the times to come!" (51-52).

Therefore we have initially a series of oppositions. They
comprise mind and body, reason and passion, God and beast,
time past and time future, and they lead directly into "Two
principles . . . ; / Self-love to urge, and Reason to restrain" (53-
54). It is thus the formulaic significance of the epistle's opening
that compels attention and dictates a particular kind of argu-
mentative strategy. If we are left momentarily with another pair
of antitheses (to urge and to restrain), it will subsequently
become the burden of the epistle to establish these apparent
contraries as in fact confederate, as constituting a "we" that
deliberately invokes the Miltonic context by assimilating
Milton's male and female into the shadowy agencies of self-love
and reason. I am of course now proposing that the garden is
transposed into human form, that the collaborative relation
between self-love and reason recreates man's loving dependence upon God or, that relation violated, his fall into demonic
possession. For this argument we need to understand something more about the interaction between abstractions, self-love
and reason, and their dramatic identities.

"Most strength," says Pope, "the moving principle
requires," but "Sedate and quiet the comparing lies, / Form'd
but to check, delib'rate and advise" (II, 67, 69-70). Yet, at the
same time, presumably because it does not and should not act,
reason is a "weak queen" (150). Pope encourages us to think of it
as a "guard," but not a "guide" (162), confiding its perceptions
to self-love.[9] Into this context he had earlier introduced instinct as
a faculty correlative with reason, yet distinct from it: "Twixt that
[Instinct], and Reason, what a nice barrier; / For ever sep'rate,
yet for ever near!" (I, 223-24). It later appears that instinct is the
"acting" power, reason the "comparing" (III, 95); where in
the former "God directs," in the latter " 'tis Man" (III, 98).

When reason acts, it is liable to blunder ("Entangle Justice in her net of Law,"[III, 192]), which suggests that it in turn has usurped a power that belongs properly to instinct, and that as a peculiarly human faculty, reason "may go wrong" (III, 94). This is so not only because of man's fallen nature, but because reason is inherently fallible, whereas instinct is not. This is an especially complex position as it bears upon the generic definitions of reason and instinct. We require something of an analogy here to Milton's description of Adam and Eve, as his rendering bears on their distinct capacities. "Hee," says Milton of Adam, was formed "for God only, she for God in him" (*Paradise Lost*, IV, 299). Insofar as Pope defines instinct as the sensible evidence of a divine datum, shared disproportionately by man and brute, we may very likely recognize instinct as Milton's "Intuitive" reason (*Paradise Lost*, V, 488) or "Spirit of Truth" (*Paradise Regained*, I, 462) returning upon us in another guise.

When Raphael explains the distinction between angelic and human reason, he suggests that reason is the soul's being, though manifest differently according to the *degree* occupied by angel and by man. Thus reason is "Discursive or Intuitive; discourse / Is oftest yours, the latter most is ours, / Differing but in degree, of kind the same" (*Paradise Lost*, V, 488-90). Through instinct man participates in the Miltonic intuitive reason, but discursive reason, that which is "oftest" his, is what Pope means by reason in the *Essay*. This argument provides the foundation for his description of reason as a "weak queen," a companionable monarchical power leagued to self-love, but distinct from and inferior to it, in that the latter power participates more directly in intuitive reason.[10] Instinct is a datum given to save man from the pride of erring reason, from the seductions to which reason is inherently liable, and something like a secondary line of defense is organized against the selfhood. If Pope is, as I believe, following Milton in contextualizing the relation between self-love and reason, he necessarily departs from Milton on the issue of the ruling passion, yet even this departure will lead us back to the myth. The companionable relation between self-love and reason is subject to the further violation that the passions may occasion. Pope says that these are "Modes of Self-love" (II, 93), yet "List under Reason" (98). This is not a contradiction but a confirmation of the equivalent relations the passions maintain to each. Like man and wife, like wit and judgment, self-love and reason are meant to be each other's aid, but their own efficacy is enhanced by the help of the master passion that assimilates all other passions into itself. Yet this passion is both a "peccant part" (II, 144) and the "Mind's disease" (138), and, as it is both, the passion is vulnerable to the deformations of purpose imposed upon it by pride and erring reason.

What man is trying to create is the total form of his identity, in which he is aided by the divine datum. The form of himself that man is engaged in making requires the cooperative enterprise of self-love, reason, and master passion, which occasions the advice that reason "treat this passion more as friend than foe" (II, 164). Though enough has been said already concerning Pope's dubiety about reason, the subject recurs and sustainedly reminds us of the elusive vagaries commensurate with reason and with the peculiarly capricious behavior that characterizes it. Under the aegis of pride and erring reason, the fall of the master passion is equivalent to a further subversion of the human estate, one result of which is to bring about another closure of the divine and thus another creation of the darksome round. When this happens, the jealous god is enthroned as the object of veneration and man is well on his way to the evocation of, and service to, a god similar to that of the *Dunciad*. In other words, the subversion of reason by pride sponsors a further corruption in which the master passion is enlisted in a rebellion, and the Christian God is conceived as a tyrant who cruelly imposes his law upon man and arbitrarily forbids him access to the instruments of his greater power. As the divine datum within man (the ruling passion) is transformed into an obsession, the divine reality in which man is located is denied, and the closure to which I referred earlier occurs. This situation parallels those of the *Rape* and *Eloisa*.[11] When reason separates herself from self-love to fall under the suasive power of pride, the result is the formation of the demonic family in which the master passion becomes now the agent of the selfhood. It is for such reasons that the ruling passion is a dangerous gift.

Pope details this consequence more fully toward the close of Epistle III. The sacrificial acts in which the "Flamen tasted living food" and "his grim idol smear'd with human blood" (265-66) imply the primitive venerations of the selfhood sustained by another blood-letting, the result of which is the creation of a rival deity whose nature is cruelty and whose murders are erected on the basis of a mystery religion. Moreover, as the master passion organizes all other passions in its service ("One master Passion in the breast, / Like Aaron's serpent, swallows up the rest," [II, 131-32]), that passion perverted is enlisted under "Superstition" (III, 246) and now draws to itself the darker passions released from the governance of self-love and reason. Thus:

> Fear made her [Superstition's] Devils, and weak Hope her Gods;
> Gods partial, changeful, passionate, unjust,
> Whose attributes were Rage, Revenge, or Lust;
> Such as the souls of cowards might conceive,
> And, form'd like tyrants, tyrants would believe.
>
> (III, 256-60)

Speaking of Blake, Frye observes that the "leading motive of sacrifice is the Selfhood's desire to do what the imagination wants to do, enter into communion with God; but the Selfhood's god is Satan or death, and it can only make that god appear by killing somebody."[12] The selfhood makes its gods in its own image. "Zeal" (III, 261) is now the form devotion assumes, an inversion of reason that, Pope says, reminding us of reason's earlier function, "became the guide" (261).

Once we set out the terms of this conflict, we can further map the territory of the mighty human maze. Self-love and reason preside over the master passion, though "Nature [is] its mother, Habit is its nurse" (II, 145). At any moment pride's assault upon reason may dispossess self-love, and as this action occurs the ruling passion is directed toward the ends of the newly confederate family of pride and erring reason. The demonic family includes rage, revenge, and lust, weak hope, and fear. The virtuous passions are displaced by the vicious, now ascendant, which become in effect modes of pride and list under erring reason. In defining the ways of subversion, Pope invents a psychology that depends upon metamorphosing the Edenic context: Milton's actors gather as the prototypes of Pope's abstractions.

Within this general context the function of instinct is to alert others to the subversion that has taken place, so that "All join to guard what each desires to gain. / Forc'd into virtue thus by Self-defence" (III, 278-79). All of this would be somewhat easier to recognize had Pope's antitheses been more clearly defined. As a comprehensive term, self-love is inadequate, if only because it does not permit a proper distinction between incompatible agencies. Pope seems to recognize a distinction between self-love and selfhood in his reference to "mean Self-love" (II, 291), but a clearer understanding requires our acknowledgment that the way of self-love is that of the new Adam, responsive to the God within (and without). As such it embodies the hope that culminates the vision of futurity in the closing books of *Paradise Lost*. From Milton's Satan derives the other way, the way of the predator and subverter, thereby keeping alive in Pope's poetry a consistent fascination with the terms of predatoriness and despoliation. Thus it is that Pope's *Essay* opens into an allegory of the new Adam and the old Satan, and the superimposition of the demonic family of pride, erring reason, and master passion, now divested of its divine significance, re-creates (negatively) the superimposition of identities evident in *Eloisa to Abelard*.

The obligatory performances of self-love and reason exist within a context of internal threat, and the consciousness of fall remains as a penitential reminder of the result of dereliction. The internalization of Milton's myth imbues the *Essay* with a dramatic context that exacts from us a recognition of its affinities with the early works and those yet to come. It re-establishes the drama of type and contrary, submits the warring antagonisms of the sexes in the *Rape* to the internal conflicts of the *Essay*, and presents again in an alternative form the conflict between nature and grace within *Eloisa*. Moreover, it rehearses at length the sustained conflict between power and knowledge, identifying "pow'rs" (l, 178, 180, 232, 241, etc.) only to drive them into an accommodation with the knowledge the *Essay* recommends. But because Satan has taken up residence within man, because the innocent intercourse between self-love and reason has been already once violated, and because the dark usurpation by pride has once before occurred, reason cannot be the privileged faculty of the *Essay*, but only a weak queen. It has fallen once and is liable to fall again.

The *Essay* points to what Blake calls "opening a centre."[13] In effect, man is "open" when the familial center is disposed beneficently to those larger contexts in which man acts and has his being. Instead of opening a center, however, pride and erring reason conspire to close it, and to do so is to create a habitat for the selfhood. In the *Rape* the same process is signified by Ariel and the sylphs. The rising of the underworld upon Belinda and Hampton Court from the Cave of Spleen, by way of Spleen's bag of "Sighs, Sobs, and Passions, and the War of Tongues" (IV, 84), precipitates the frenzy of the selfhood when its obsessive ends are frustrated. In the *Dunciad,* Dulness is what man makes of nature and of human nature, a false kingdom of desire and energy, a place where men and women enact the opposite of the sacred marriage, the copulative revel. And all of this explains why Pope comes very close to defining self-love and reason as parents, and the master passion as the holy child of God's bestowing, which, incidentally, explains Pope's image of the miracle, of that passion, "Like Aaron's serpent, [that] swallows up the rest" (*Essay*, II, 132).

Mack has observed that "Pope's 'creation' of Twickenham constituted an act of the mythopoeic imagination and . . . a 'composition of place' without which he could not have written his mature poems as we have them."[14] It is a nice point, but *place*, as such, is a recurrent element within Pope's imagination dating from the early poems, from which, one might say,

Twickenham itself derives. The special place in the *Essay* is both nature and human nature, and all the contention within the poem concerns whether man will make of either a wild or a garden. Without pushing the matter too far, I want to make it apparent that Pope is doing here in his own way what Blake was to do more than a half century later, that is, returning upon the available myth re-created in *Paradise Lost*. The *Essay* is not an "imitation" of Milton's epic. Much more than being an abiding allusion, it is an adaptation of that poem to the service of Pope's own. The *Essay* is contextualized within that myth, its conflicts not merely validated in this way, but informed with a dramatic significance they could in no other way possess.

Addison had earlier spoken of those "antiquated Romances" that "bring up into our Memory the Stories we have heard in our Child-hood, and favour those secret Terrours and Apprehensions to which the Mind of Man is naturally subject."[15] If Addison opens the way to romance, Pope turns from such dark implausibilities to recover from epic its latent psychological and allegorical properties, the kind of allegorical license that is so consistent a feature of his own Homeric translations. On this basis he rejects the credulity Addison recommends. The distinction between the fabulistic and Pope's chastened allegory suggests a special burden of his own poetic: the necessity for a rigorously disciplined accord between the demands of the probable and the marvelous. Not incidentally, Milton's epic is *true*; Pope's redaction of it permits the same claim, and his psychological myth is informed with the validity of Milton's Christian epic. The *Essay* brings Milton's epic forward in time, establishes its postlapsarian facticity in the Augustan context, and thereby roots its meaning firmly in the historical present.

Obviously, the *Essay* is a philosophical poem, possibly founded on the Lucretian model, as has been frequently proposed, but even if this is so the *De Rerum Natura* is another paradigm serving other purposes. My interests, however, have little to do with the philosophic content of the poem, but focus instead on the constituent elements of opposition and collaboration. The rebuke persistently administered to the objective "you" is the same rebuke visited upon the internalized "you" of the poem, the selfhood. It is for this reason that Pope's initial task is to define the pretender, pride, whose characteristic state of mind is jealousy and whose habitual act is appropriation. The "Right" (I, 294) of the *Essay* is thereby established as a critique of the adequacy and nature of knowledge ("And all our Knowledge is, Ourselves to Know" [IV, 398]). For the selfhood is always plotting the death of nature, but Pope shows us that nature's death is equivalent to the death of the self. The illusion of freedom, the unchecked sufficiency of the self, is the dream of the egotistical sublime (as with Belinda and Eloisa), but structure (law) is the reality. In "spite of Pride, in erring Reason's spite, / One truth is clear, 'Whatever is, is Right' " (I, 293-94).

The burden of Epistle IV is to translate the psychological myth from the theater of the mind to the theater of man in the world. Pope's opening address here to St. John relocates the individual within the context of his kind. The substance of Pope's argument is *contemptus mundi*, which itself functions within the tradition of *ars moriendi*, suggesting again the recurrent tension in Pope between the active life and the retirement ideal, the georgic repudiation of the greater world in the cultivation of the interior garden. That the last epistle dismisses human claims upon the things of this world, that first riches are rejected, then greatness, then fame, implies the progressive obliteration of the false lights of the selfhood's egotism, reminding us of another and different negation in *Dunciad* IV. The poem that begins with Bolingbroke ends with him, and the adversary relation between the "I" and the "you" of the text is displaced by the newly articulated "you" of Bolingbroke, the mentor and "guide": "Tell (for You can) what it is to be wise?" (*Essay*, IV, 260). St. John is man finally and fully awake, purged of his own malaise: "Self-love but serves the virtuous mind to wake" (363). From himself he proceeds outward until "Heaven beholds its image in his breast" (372).

Milton's vision is the history of the Fall; Pope's is the redaction of that vision to a myth of man within the continuing

context of *fall*. At the close of *Paradise Lost* what is *in* Adam are
Satan's works, and the meaning of history is the protracted
effort of man to extirpate those works, to free himself from the
domination of a "you" that has taken up residence within him.
The relation here is that between a vision and a dialogue, and
yet, as Paulson observes of Pope, "they usually join; the latter is
often a frame action for the vision."[16] Pope's frame action is a
dialogue; within the dialogue occurs the contextualizing of the
Miltonic myth, a large part of the poem's envisioning action.
And, finally, the *Essay* concludes with the awakening of
Bolingbroke, a casting off of the powers that trammel up self-
love and deny its guidance. The delusive sublimity of the selfhood—its desire for autonomy—is rebuked by the very act that
defines self-love as social, the relation between Pope and
Bolingbroke. If power, as I have just previously suggested, is
merely the goal toward which an illusory freedom aspires,
benevolence is the reality of self-love, which reveals in its action
the ways man binds himself to the world and moves within the
medium of time itself.

   When Hartman comes to speak about Wordsworth's
dream in *Prelude* V, and the pursuing flood culminating the
dream, he suggests that it signifies "Wordsworth's recognition
of a power in him (imagination) which implies and even prophesies nature's death."[17] The inversely correspondent image is of
Bolingbroke's "name," which "along the stream of Time . . . /
Expanded flies, and gathers all its fame" (*Essay*, 383-84). Behind
this ship of passage, Pope's "little bark attendant sail[s]" (385).
The poet's imagination moves on its progress within the chan-
nel of time, following its guide, the one greater man. The power
in Pope is not a flood, a nightmare in which the self is drowned
by the power it evokes, but a vehicle proportionate to the
medium ("stream of Time") in which man lives and has his
being. In Hartman's reading of Wordsworth's dream, the Bedouin is the

   initiation-master, who guides the poet, but only to a more radical
   loss of Way. His symbols, the emblems of the human spirit, of

revelations achieved by man himself, suggest two *akedot*, or fundamental ways in which man binds the world to himself. They exalt not only the human mind but also nature, and are therefore both nature-things (stone, shell) and mind-things (books). Poetry paradoxically forsees a destruction of these bonds.[18]

Like Wordsworth's Bedouin (but with a difference), Bolingbroke is Pope's "initiation-master." As a guide his name is both the word and the way. Spoken by the poet at the end of his poem, it is the crown of a performance leading from "sounds to things, from fancy to the heart" (392). For Pope's allegory has been about the ways in which man clasps the world to himself, sees into the heart of things, and, escaping from the self-enclosing center of the temporal moment, opens that center to its meaning in eternity.

When therefore Pope turns round on the subject of fame, as he does in the fourth epistle ("What's Fame? a fancy'd life in others breath, / A thing beyond us, ev'n before our death," [237-38]), it seems at first a repudiation of the "hallow'd Quire" in the *Temple of Fame*. On the contrary, what immediately appears as fame's contracted center ("All that we feel of it begins and ends / In the small Circle of our foes and friends," [241-42]) opens into the recognition of what "future age[s]" shall bestow upon "this verse" (389). What happens here is what happens in the earlier poem. The "honest Fame," acknowledged by the narrator at the close of the *Temple of Fame* (524), defines an alliance between fame and virtue related by analogy to the poet's hope for his own poem under the guidance of Bolingbroke. Because of the tutelage of this master, Pope's fame is absorbed into or, following his own image, drawn in the wake of that greater power signified by his "guide, philosopher, and friend" (390). Pope's power of naming (which in the *Essay* is the power of calling things by their right names) is here transposed into the power of Bolingbroke's name, and as "guide" Bolingbroke is both the namer and the knower. To submit therefore to his *name* is to invoke a power greater than the self, and the uneasy correlation between the world and the ideal, adressed in the *Temple of Fame,* is here settled more firmly within the context of expanding time, over which the presiding word is not fame but virtue.

If the *Temple of Fame* thus incorporates a rejection of the temptation to embrace the fallen form of the goddess as she is manifest in the world—the immediate temporal context of a man's life, the *Essay* restates that rejection while simultaneously affirming Fame's only true context and that greater deity to which she is herself subordinate. Paradoxically, in thus binding himself to time the poet denies its delusive temptations, its immediate seductions, as in fact nothing other than an agency of the selfhood. The *Temple of Fame* makes clear through "Lust of Praise" (522) that Pope is thinking in exactly these terms. Equally, in the *Essay,* "Wit's false mirror" (393) is the glass not in which the self is deified (as with Belinda), but in which Pride is obliged to read the significance of the temporal under the aegis of the divine. As nature reveals the divine, time discloses its corresponding reality, and both nature and time viewed as expanding structures in this way give up their meaning to man. Unlike Wordsworth's terrible dream, the imagination here yields its priorities, submits to what it embodies. It does not fear "its power to do without nature,"[19] but joys in the recognition that its power derives wholly from the divine and is returned to that source.

The alternative identities of Belinda as goddess and Eloisa as heroic lover are here intensified in the specter of the selfhood and opposed in another key by Bolingbroke. The narcissistic sublimities of self-defeating desire are resisted by the grace inherent in self-love. The *Essay* expands the topics of the earlier poems while maintaining the "composition of place," the controlling metaphor of circle or circumference, and repeats in another key the conflict between type and antitype. To follow Pope's own images, the *Essay* is a charting of his own terrain or an attempt to locate the sources of the floods of passion that have occupied his imagination from the beginning.[20] My argument has obviously focused on the relation of the poem to that imagination. If the epic was closed to him, and if romance offered a critique of origins too darkly implausible to be accepted, Pope's mythmaking nevertheless found its acceptable form in a "science of Human Nature."[21] To many readers Pope's allegory has never declared itself, has never seemed to be quite *there*.[22] A critic deep in the misassessments to which the *Essay* has been subject would have no difficulty exhibiting a choice collection. And if the *Essay* were the only issue it would perhaps not be worthwhile. But even our most advanced and perceptive critics keep forcing upon our notice presumed failures in eighteenth-century poetry of a most aggravated sort. Fletcher, for example, states that "Besides defining beauty, the aestheticians of the eighteenth century adduce the two rubrics of the sublime and the picturesque. These terms name the direction taken by allegory after 'the breaking of the circle.' The process of breakup had shown no catastrophic, clearly discernible moments at which we could say, 'Now the springs of allegorical poetry will have to be renewed.' "[23]

The point is, however, that the deployment of meaning across the extended text suggests an imagination that strategically recomposes its various (and related) fictions in changing contexts. This activity is less than purely allegorical (how could it be otherwise in work that has only an implied narrative status?), but more than what one recent student of allegory is willing to allow: "the aims of Swift's and particularly Pope's works are satirical, and so they criticize what is, rather than attempt to lead the reader through an examination of what is to that sacred otherness implicit within it."[24] This familiar statement minimizes the allegoric and fictive tendencies within Pope's imagination, reductively constraining him to his "Augustanism," to the presumptively limited enterprise that is satire. Much of what I am doing here is an effort to open such a pervasive and time-honored judgment to the kinds of scrutiny that an examination of multiple texts provides, and thereby to break down, at least where Pope is concerned, a too exclusively categorical judgment. Empson suggests that "Part of the function of allegory is to make you feel that two levels of being correspond to each other in detail and indeed that there is some underlying reality, something in the nature of things [i.e., a "sacred otherness"], which makes this happen."[25] What occurs when we read the *Essay* is that we are continually being recalled to a drama that exists both inside and outside the mind, that in fact is inside because it was at some moment in pre-history outside the mind, and the event has been recomposed as an act *in potentia* within being. We have thus a context to understand Pope's aphorism about the proper study of mankind. Such a study does not disavow myth (for it could not), but indicates where myth begins, as an objectification of mind in narratives of origins and endings, narratives that are translations of Empson's "underlying reality" into patterns of action.

To examine this idea further is to perceive that Pope's mock-epic (the *Rape*) is correspondent to his miniature epic (the *Essay*), in the precise sense that the latter rationalizes the action of the former. The *Rape* is explicable as a tale of demonological possession, but such possesion has been naturalized (not fantasized) by the psychological myth of the *Essay*. Belinda's absurd cosmos is (in fact) rooted in the nature of things, and it is kept comic (mock-epic) only because Pope is not yet ready to surrender that cosmos to its full potential of terror. The *Essay on Man* tells us that it need never be so surrendered; the *Dunciad* tells us what happens when it has been.

Epistles to Several Persons

No work by Pope is closer, chronologically and thematically, to the *Essay on Man* than his *Epistles to Several Persons.* Throughout the early 1730s Pope was writing the *Epistles* as he was composing parts of the *Essay,* and they were to constitute a volume complementary to it, "Ethic Epistles: The Second Book." Much of the history of composition and publication is detailed by Leranbaum. On thematic grounds, she especially associates *To Cobham* with *To a Lady,* the last epistles to be completed, and connects them through the theme of the ruling passion. Obviously, the subtitles of each work, "Of the Knowledge and Characters of Men," and "Of the Characters of Women," suggest that the poems are companion-pieces. Likewise, the two earliest published works, *To Burlington* (December 1731) and *To Bathurst* (January 1733), are affiliated by a common concern with the use of riches. "There is every reason to see both the *Epistle to Bathurst* and the *Epistle to Burlington* as a pair expressing the rewards and happiness associated with the right use of riches and the virtues of benevolence."[26] And, as Wasserman reminds us, *To Bathurst* is occupied with "liberality," *To Burlington*, with "magnificence": the "two poems, taken together, constitute Pope's satiric adaptation of Aristotle's analysis of the ethics of wealth."[27] Moreover, all four poems find explicit relation to the ethical interests of the *Essay*.

Yet the relation of the *Essay* to the *Epistles* remains somewhat vexed. It is clear from Pope's 1734 Index that *To a Lady* and *To Cobham* are intended to correspond to the dominant concerns of Epistle II of the *Essay*, whereas *To Bathurst* and *To Burlington* bear specific relation to Epistle IV. On the other hand, there is significant evidence to indicate that even as late as 1735 Pope was not certain of the extent of the projected *opus magnum* or of what epistles it was to be comprised. What we can be sure of is that the composition and publication of the *Epistles to Several Persons* are closely related to the composition and publication of the *Essay*. It is equally evident that Pope thought of *To a Lady* and *To Cobham* as companion-pieces and that he thought the same of *To Burlington* and *To Bathurst*. The precise relation of these two sets to each other was to be further based on their relation to the ethical topics of the *Essay*. What in fact happened, however, is that the full-scale plan for the "Ethic Epistles: Second Book" was not completed, so that Pope's projected arrangement was not satisfied.

I will not be much concerned here with the ethical formulas of the *Epistles* but with an overview that keeps the work in proximity to the allegorical plan of the *Essay*. In order to link the epistles more closely with one another it is necessary to recognize that the affiliations usually set forward between the first two epistles and the second two are subject to more complex interpretation. It is a commonplace of critical observation to remark that the "inconsistency of the feminine character . . . is the subject of the *Epistle to a Lady*,"[28] but the case is clearly not so simple. *To a Lady* is occupied with, among other topics, the related themes of power and authority, and with the evocation of the demonic element associated with power, of which money is one manifestation. The theme of moral and financial corruption is given perhaps its most extended treatment through the character and parable of Balaam in *To Bathurst. To Burlington* is most immediately occupied with the theme of magnificence, yet it also explores the relation between "taste" and "sense," the latter offered as analogous in its mode and operation to that of the ruling passion in the *Essay*. In *To Cobham* the same dominant agency within Pope's psychology is reintroduced and examined as a paradox within character.

The presence of related subjects makes it necessary to establish cross-relations between epistles not normally considered companion poems. But what we require most urgently is an overview linking the *Epistles* with the principal conflict of the *Essay*, that between the claims of selfhood and self-love as they are set in relation to the master passion. Moreover, as we read Pope we are continually being redirected to earlier contexts. *To a Lady* concludes with the artful compliment to Martha Blount upon the gift of the "gen'rous God" (289), who gave her "Sense, Good-humour, and a Poet" (292). "Sense" keeps *To a Lady* in proximity not only to *To Burlington*, but also to the *Essay on Criticism* (wherein "sense" is a recurrent term) and to the *Rape of the Lock* (through Clarissa's advice to Belinda). The close of *To Burlington* must also remind a reader of the imperial theme concluding *Windsor-Forest*, as both poems celebrate the magnificence attendant upon imperial destiny. Recognitions of this kind impose a significant burden upon the reader of Pope's poetry, which is both highly allusive and cross-referential, so that, as some scholars have found, it is not only impossible to limit the extent of allusion, but equally difficult to chart the intricacies of internal reference.

Of Pope's characters in the four epistles, the most memorably pejorative portraits are those of Atossa *(To a Lady)*, Wharton *(To Cobham)*, Balaam *(To Bathurst)*, and Timon *(To Burlington)*. Each is in turn opposed by one principal actor. Correspondingly, there are Martha and the various persons to whom the poems are dedicated, also perhaps including the Man of Ross, who seems a more notable figure than Bathurst. It becomes mandatory also to examine the related terms linking the first four characters and then to compare these terms with those linking the second group of four. Each of the negative portraits is a further revelation of what the selfhood entails, and each is opposed in turn by the contrary portrait of one who fulfills the meaning of self-love.

One of the governing principles of *To a Lady* involves the same exploration of extremes that we find in *To Bathurst.* As Wasserman remarks of that poem, "the ethical principle of the mean between vicious extremes determines . . . [Pope's] system of portraiture." He makes much the same observation of *To Burlington,* wherein of "the two extremes of magnificence—shabbiness, or deficiency of expenditure, and vulgarity, or tasteless extravagance—Pope's poem concerns itself with the latter."[29] The principle itself functions in relation to the portraiture in *To a Lady:*

> How many pictures of one Nymph we view,
> All how unlike each other, all how true!
> Arcadia's Countess, here, in ermin'd pride,
> Is there, Pastora by a fountain side.
>
> (5-8)

The conception governing the inconsistency of the female character implies an adaptation of the "Aristotelian ethical tradition of *mediocritas,* or the definition of virtue as the mean between opposing vices."[30] " 'Most Women have no Characters at all' " (2) precisely because they have too much *character.* As the center of virtue is defined by the principle of *mediocritas,* the center of identity depends upon a harmony of extremes or oppositions.[31] And this principle is itself consistent with the psychology set forth in Epistle II of the *Essay:*

> Love, Hope, and Joy, fair pleasure's smiling train,
> Hate, Fear, and Grief, the family of pain;
> These mix'd with art, and to due bounds confin'd,
> Make and maintain the balance of the mind.
>
> (117-20)

To a Lady reconstitutes the divisiveness between the sexes that rules the *Rape of the Lock,* and re-attributes that division. Belinda's desire for power is now reformulated as the desire for power that follows upon the feared loss of pleasure, and the disjunction between "Nature" (211) and "Experience" (213) reveals the familiar discontinuity between states that are harmonious by design, yet subject to violations of one kind or another. It would be excessive to say that *To a Lady* re-creates the *Rape,* transposing it from mock-epic to Horatian mode, yet it is not too much to remark that *To a Lady* continues to comment on the *Rape* and on the issue of sexual warfare. And this issue in turn affiliates with the blood-letting of *Windsor-Forest,* so that each of these poems keeps us focused on the subject of predator and prey, itself a function of sexual warfare (even as the hunt in *Windsor-Forest* incorporates the relation between Pan and Lodona).

Those females in *To a Lady* who "conquer with so wild a rage" (221) are nothing less than the aggregate identity of Belinda, but in the later poem we are suddenly invited to consider them from a wholly different temporal perspective, that is, to see them as they were in youth and as they are in age: "Beauties, like Tyrants, old and friendless grown" (227). Folly, as the collective identity of woman, is urged to its extreme manifestations, and the identity that Folly assumes follows upon Belinda's in the *Rape;* that is, the "fate of a whole Sex of Queens!" (219) is the prophetic, albeit collective, fulfillment of Clarissa's warning to Belinda. In *To a Lady,* Pope urges his earlier subject to its calamity, dispossessing that subject now of its mock component and compelling it into the full futility of sexual warfare: "Still round and round the Ghosts of Beauty glide, / And haunt the places where their Honour dy'd" (241-42). The demonic element persists in the vision of Sabbath-holding

"Hags" within their "merry, miserable night" (239, 240). The poet has inverted transcendence, Belinda's ascendant lock, into its cognate, the demonic sublime or gothic mode. Yet the summoning of Martha ends the cycle of pleasure and power by enclosing Martha within the meaning of "softer Man" (272).

Pope's avowed purpose in the poem is to "paint" Folly when she grows "romantic" (16). The various female exempla he summons serve as manifestations of the abstraction they collectively represent; they illustrate what the abstraction *means*, and it means the incorporation of extreme modes of behavior ("sinner it, or saint it," [15]). The reduction of the characters of women to those dualisms that overdetermine their responses suggests the method of caricature, and while some of the portraits refer specifically to particular people, in the aggregate they serve to flesh out a complex abstraction called Folly. Fletcher argues that caricature is "allegorical in essence, since it strives for the simplification of character in terms of single, predominant traits."[32] Atossa, for example, is a grotesque, an epitome, which is precisely what Pope calls her ("all Womankind!" [116]). This method of characterization prepares us to regard Atossa as a component of the collective portrait, an element within the complex personification, Folly. Equally, it prepares us to view Martha as the alternative to the individual portraits of women and to their identity as Folly. Pope does not incorporate Martha within a personification, but it is obvious that the complexity of her character opposes the simplifications inherent in the poem's other females. For this reason she is not presented as a caricature but as a portrait of the "softer Man." If Fannia, Rufa, Sappho, Silia, and Papillia suffer from the same defect of sustained incongruity, Martha benefits from the paradoxical coalescence of male and female qualities within herself. This seems to me a highly allegorical method in which the redemptive figure of the female (Martha) is opposed to the aggregate portrait (Folly). Chapin remarks on Addison's contribution toward a theory of personification, noting that the "figure is associated with poetic 'fiction' as opposed to prosaic 'truth,' with the unreal as opposed to the real."[33] It would seem apparent that Pope's method dissolves this sort of opposition between fiction and truth, rejecting as well Addison's commitment to the "fairy way" of writing and to the imaginative investment in fictions that such a way requires.

In creating the personification, Pope endows it with various moral and intellectual perversities that require for their realization a sustained darkening of the female type and lead inevitably to Atossa. Thus Folly is divisible into its parts, those separate females who comprise the personification and are the very reality of it in the world. Having made the division, he re-animates the collective portrait as a "whole Sex of Queens!" now demonized as "Hags [who] hold Sabbaths, less for joy than spight." The portraits thereby serve the purpose of evoking an *idea* of woman possessed by the dualisms that constitute her as having "no Character," and subsequently require from Pope a portrait of that woman whose concordant contradictions sum up the ideal female.

Such an opposition furnishes the dramatic context of *To a Lady*, and into this context are assimilated the key terms, *power* and *pleasure*, here re-created as the pervasive or dominant dualism hopelessly dividing a woman's life. The fact that these terms recapitulate while varying the conflict within the *Rape* should suggest to us how close Pope remains to the earlier bases of his thought. Atossa and Thalestris are merely manifestations of the same sort of subversion, which produces the same "warfare" (118) that is the primary impulse of each character. *To a Lady* arbitrates the relation between power and pleasure, and each passion is conceived as a motive leading to hostility between the sexes. Pope tells us that the "Love of Pleasure, and the Love of Sway" (210) are "almost" (208) the only ruling passions in women. Yet if women seek power they do so because they are by "Man's oppression curst" (213). So women become tyrants to avoid becoming victims, and the presumably endless alternation between one state and another is definitive of their cyclical adventuring in the fallen world. In these terms the poem sustains the sexual conflicts of the *Rape*, another rendering of the warring antagonism between men and women. The "Worn out'' (229) females emergent in Pope's collective portrait (''a whole Sex of Queens!'') leave the reader's mind divided between sympathy and repudiation, very likely Empson's state when he remarked that Pope ''finds himself indeed hag-ridden by these poor creatures; they excite in him feelings irrelevantly powerful, of waste, of unavoidable futility, which no bullying of [the] object can satisfy.''[34] The operative terms are ''irrelevantly'' and ''unavoidable,'' and we must shortly recognize the bearing of these on Pope's argument.

Since the love of pleasure comes from ''Nature'' and the love of sway from ''Experience,'' Pope seems to be defining in the latter a dark aspect of social determinism, as inevitable as that which comes from nature, and may justify Empson's use of ''unavoidable.'' In any event, the recurrent predatory passions reappear in man and woman, and the poem re-envisions (with a difference) the relations between Pan and Lodona, Baron and Belinda. If, alternately, women are oppressed and oppressors, such oscillations only re-introduce another unmediated dualism, making for one more in a series of oppositions: women are discordant beings, men and women are warring opposites, nature and experience are irreconcilable. The poem that begins lightly concentrated on female inconsistency develops a radical opposition between the sexes that is itself founded on the radical discontinuity between the innocent passion, pleasure, and the passion that is the immediate fruit of knowledge, power. The female who passes from innocence to experience ontogenetically recapitulates the stages of the Fall, passing from innocence (231) to power, to futility.

This progress is the ultimate consequence of sexual divisiveness, the distant fate of Belinda, had Pope urged his mock-epic beyond its comic resolution. In *To a Lady*, he brings us to the very brink of fatality, to that seemingly ''unavoidable futility'' noticed by Empson. But it is against this background that Martha is summoned, and the poem's dialectic undergoes another transformation. The oppressive tyranny of beauty ''Flaunts and goes down'' (252), and another sun sets, again by association summoning the elegiac mode of the *Rape*'s close. Here Pope says, "So when the Sun's broad beam has tir'd the sight, / All mild ascends the Moon's more sober light" (253-54). This light moderates the extremes of brilliance and darkness, as Martha herself arbitrates the antithetical qualities that distinguish each sex and is that rare creature, a "softer Man." Within the epistle time reveals a second stage, a displacement from the oppressions consonant with "glaring Orb" (256). Within the second stage, Martha's virtues "grow" (251). So that what may appear initially as loss (given the fact that the woman is forty-four years old) is redirected into the terms of gain, even as the inconsistency of the female character is, re-applied to Martha's character, a concordance of antitheses: "Reserve with Frankness, Art with Truth ally'd, / Courage with Softness, Modesty with Pride," etc. (277-78). At the beginning of the *Elegy to the Memory of an Unfortunate Lady*, Pope asks the crucial question: "Is there no bright reversion in the sky, / For those who greatly think, or bravely die?" In *To a Lady* he poses essentially the same query, and the bright reversion in the sky is the serenely ascendant majesty of Martha's growing "Charm" (251).

The night of those women who "would be Queen for life" (218) is a "merry miserable Night." Martha's night is informed with heaven's "last best work" (272), in one sense the moon ascendant above the dying sun, and in another the redeemed female who is the softer man. If we reverse Pope's terms, the tyrannical female is the stronger woman, the sustained elaboration therefore of petulance and vanity, a continued manifestation of oppression and victimization. Against Martha's concordant contradictions are set the discordances that bind Atossa, who is "By Spirit robb'd of Pow'r, by Warmth of Friends, / By Wealth of Follow'rs!" (144-45). Obviously, the poem does not cancel its leading proposition ("Woman's at best a Contradiction still," [270]), but transmutes the contradiction into a *concordia discors*. Equally important is the way it projects the antitheses of the female character in Atossa and Martha, signifying thereby the redemptory promise of the new Eve as she emerges redeemed from the contradictions that limit and defeat Atossa, a negation of "pow'r" consistent once again with the failure of self-knowledge. Much the same strategy governs Pope's perception of beauty's "Ghosts" (241), the futile relics of a solar tyranny over whose "Night" Martha presides in "Virgin Modesty" (255). The ascendant moon draws us from the demonized places where aging beauties, like hags holding sab-baths, are constrained to repetitive and darksome rounds ("Still round and round the Ghosts of Beauty glide," [241]) in the ser-vice, I am reasonably tempted to say, of the jealous god of love.

Martha's rising negates the re-emergent "end" of "Pow'r" (220) earlier associated with Atossa and here conjoined to that "whole Sex of Queens!" Her rising is the exercise of another and different power, one that in turn "raise[s] the Thought and touch[es] the Heart" (250). *To rise* and *to raise* are actions reformulated within the allusive context provided by the sociality of self-love, a power that is equally self- and socially reflexive, and that points toward a newly articulated subject-object relation. *To raise* is the action of benevolence within the world. In *To Bathurst,* for example, Oxford and Bathurst "raise the sinking heart" (244). The Man of Ross teaches the "heav'n-directed spire to rise" (261). Those who raise others do so within a context that forces the reader's reconsideration of the alliance between power and knowledge. Yet it is equally true that the larger associative context resonates with the significance of *fire* and *flaming,* even if these terms are only implicitly present in the text. Thus Martha's ascendant moon is crossed by the descen-dant "glaring Orb," and the earlier ambivalence within *rising* (*uprising*) is restated as a function of the poem's imagery.

The relation between these heavenly bodies also bears back upon the *Essay on Man* and serves Pope's allegory. The sun's reflected light illuminates the otherwise dark body of the moon as the Godhead is the light irradiating the human estate. Man cannot possess this source for it exists beyond time and nature, both of which contain its embodiment in a way appro-priate to their own mutability. By the same token, the moon is an emblem of the relation in which man stands to Godhead. Insofar as Martha participates in the meaning of this emblem, she fulfills the anagogic meaning linking moon to sun. But those queens who, like Belinda, have usurped a power that can never belong to them are condemned to the fate of that power within time. While the sun is an image of Godhead, the "glaring Orb" is a deceptive semblance of that same Godhead, a malign simulacrum emblematic only of the selfhood's aspirations. The situation here is analogous to others we have witnessed. What pride sees when it views the sun is a divine power it wishes to make its own. Any attempt to possess this power is frustrated by the fact that only its semblance can be appropriated, which means in effect that the attempt to rival the sun results in the return to that temporal order from which pride had sought to escape. Possession is thus an illusion, and instead of grasping the sun it captures only its fate in time. Instead of finding eternal life, pride finds only death. Martha's moon is a light owing nothing to pride's orb; instead, like that moon with which she is linked, she moves within her own subordinate sphere deriving her light (power) from the Godhead itself. It is thus that Martha rules according to those principles of suasion given into her own keeping, as lines 257-68 suggest. And the backward glance at the *Rape of the Lock* ("Mistress of herself, tho' China fall" [268]) tends to confirm our understanding of the proper sphere of a woman's action.

From the standpoint of the selfhood the sun is an emblem of power. From the perspective of self-love the sun is an emblem of Godhead, and the effort to rival or appropriate its power is a blasphemy. Consequently, Martha's moon has both a natural and an anagogic significance. It is a softer light moderating the extremes of glaring orb and individual darkness, the extremes to which the selfhood is inevitably committed. It is equally the redemptory promise of a second birth that uniquely irradiates, under the guidance of the divine, the unvarying journey toward death. Between the extremes of folly and tyranny, between abject submission and oppression, between thoughtless youth and futile age, Martha mediates the previously unmediated extremes that characterize most women. And this points also to the efficacy of what Pope means by "Sense" (292), an intuitive discernment that, unmethodized, reformulates the meaning of

softer man. Martha's light is, in a further extension of the
metaphoric relation between sun and moon, a reflection of the
intuitive reason that informs the male principle, and so it links
her more firmly to the power of the Godhead invested in man.
By subtly refashioning the fallen form of woman, Pope raises
her into the newly companionable ideal of male and female. As
Martha is linked by analogy to reason in the *Essay* she fulfills the
terms of guardianship characteristic of that agency. This is the
allegorical interpretation of her suasive power. As woman, her
ruling passion is a datum that sponsors benign concordance and
saves her from the vicissitudes of pleasure and power that otherwise enclose her sex. No longer cursed by man's oppression
within the recurrent hostilities of male and female selfhoods,
she is consistent with that reason she embodies and is newly
confederate with the male principle. The close of the poem is
thus a prophecy of the marriage, more properly a re-marriage,
of self-love and reason, and of that new Eve who is no longer a
"weak queen" but now a newly brightened articulation of her
own opposite and thus a "softer Man."

Fletcher suggests that the "typical agent in an allegorical
fiction has been seen as a daemon, for whom freedom of active
choice hardly exists. This appears to have a major correlate in
the theory of compulsive behavior, where it is observed that the
mind is suddenly obsessed by an idea over which it has no control, which as it were 'possesses' the mind."[35] Such is precisely the point of the darksome round both here ("round and
round") and in *Eloisa*. Compulsive behavior is the negative form
assumed by the ruling passion when that passion is undirected
by the cooperative union of self-love and reason, or, more especially in *To a Lady*, by *sense*, an intuitive recognition of ordered
relations among the parts comprising a whole. This is the value
Pope gives the word in *To Burlington*, where he advises: "Still
follow Sense, of ev'ry Art the Soul, / Parts answ'ring parts shall
slide into a whole" (65-66). Sense, along with "Good-humour"
(292), the sociable grace that attends it, is the constituent psychological element making available the free play of the mind,
its ability to attend sensitively to what is outside itself. Such a

freedom is a primary necessity enabling the mind to pass beyond its own subjective concerns into the larger sphere that sympathy and benevolence afford. Indicating the absence of such freedom is another way in which Pope signifies possession by the selfhood. This at least partially explains why obsessive behavior is a recurrent feature of his various portraits, and why it seems oddly linked to insatiate behavior, a frenzy that Pope embodies in such actors as "Zeal" or such acts as "hecatomb." The immediate point, however, is that obsession is joined invariably to the demonic element as a structural feature of Pope's psychology: Satan possessed by an idée fixe is committed to a mode of behavior that limits freedom while providing the illusion of it. Pope can never quite disjoin folly from villainy; if the latter is an addiction, the former is its lesser weakness, a "whim" (58). When folly grows romantic it grows whimsical, which means that it seeks various mirror images of itself. And this is why, "How many pictures of one Nymph we view, / All how unlike each other, all how true!" (5-6). The ultimate whimsicality of the "I" produces "no Character."

The result, as Pope makes clearer in *Dunciad* IV, is to make self appear while making God disappear: "Oh hide the God still more! and make us see / Such as Lucretius drew, a God like Thee: / Wrapt up in Self, a God without a Thought" (483-85). When this happens, to cite Fletcher again, "daemonic influence so limits and simplifies character that character in the normal sense no longer exists, and the possessed man plays a role constricted in the very manner we have already discussed."[36] Or, in the terms I have been specifying, the selfhood occupies the interior space within that is vacated by self-love, nature turns inside out, hell rises and heaven disappears.

Fussell comments on the humanist definition of the "one great crime against human nature—the transformation of man into automatic machine."[37] This sort of reductionism is the counterpart to demonic possession, the surrender of the "redemptive will" (Fussell's chapter title) to those obsessive drives that dehumanize character. Folly, as we have seen, is the allegorical embodiment of psychological extravagance, a simplistic demon with "no Character" who is analogous to Dulness, the goddess of no mind. If therefore *To Cobham* is the companion poem to *To a Lady*, it is so on the basis of those comparable simplicities that invade the characters of men. The result is the transformation of character into caricature, another over-determination of action predicated here on the deformation of the ruling passion, the metamorphosis of a direction into an obsession. It is thus that *To Cobham* permits Pope the exploration of a subject that lies close to the center of the *Essay's* myth: the effect upon behavior when the passion is subverted from its true ends and enlisted in the service of pride and erring reason. *To Cobham* offers various examples that illustrate a humoral compulsion.

Leranbaum observes that in the poem Cobham "is (prophetically) praised for dying words which will surely do him credit, in distinct and unique contrast to other characters whose dying words reveal them as consistently and ignobly self-centered."[38] She has in mind such dim figures as the "rev'rend sire," "Helluo," the "frugal Crone," "Narcissa," "sober Lanesb'row," the "Courtier smooth," and "old Euclio." All of these are guilty of the same sort of degeneration in which the automatism of desire records a kind of negative creation, an act of moral isolation and alienation, which seems always the result of a reductive tendency in man, a desire to be rid of the burden of the complex self, the arbitration among opposing tendencies that "Make and maintain the balance of the mind" (*Essay on Man*, II, 120). The balance of the mind always requires a harmonizing of extremes that does double duty as an ethical and psychological principle, and, under the rubric of *concordia discors*, returns to serve as a constituent of Pope's metaphysics. Thus "self-centered" describes exactly that closure the *Essay* addresses, which in *To Cobham* is presented as the ultimate reduction of the divine datum to its grotesque or parodic semblance.

The assault of pride upon self-love and reason is always presented in the name of freedom, though freedom is merely the disguise power assumes, a reflection that returns us to *Eloisa to Abelard* and to the illusory freedom bestowed by the jealous god. In *To Cobham,* the related issue of right knowing is darkened by the partiality that the ego inevitably bestows upon its own judgments (''To observations which ourselves we make, / We grow more partial for th' Observer's sake,'' [11-12]), and by the likelihood that knowing cannot be dissociated from the chance perspective that determines what it is we do know. In one sense the issue of *To Cobham* is the obscurity that envelopes the ''I,'' severing action from motive (''Oft in the Passions' wild rotation tost, / Our spring of action to ourselves is lost,'' [41-42]), and thereby subverting the very basis of self-knowledge. Yet it is against this despair that Pope launches his own version of determinism. Whatever license the selfhood claims, it is always and invariably restricted by the nature of the divine datum, which, inducted into the service of the selfhood, is metamorphosed into its opposite. The ruling passion cannot be other than what it is, by which I mean only that the freedom assumed by the selfhood necessitates the inversion of the passion. It turns inside out and becomes its own opposite. Wharton's ''Lust of Praise'' (181) is the inversion of a particular celebrity, achieved in the service of an admirable ambition, into the unselective desire for ''gen'ral praise'' (196). Wharton, who could have been ''great,'' ends as merely ''flagitious'' (205). The moral imperative of the ruling passion becomes the immoral compulsion of an idée fixe. God's grace becomes man's folly and love becomes lust. The selfhood correlates with an erroneous reading of the passion, evidencing again Pope's description of it as a ''peccant part,'' and the agency that was to allay anxiety instead generates it. This is the selfhood's freedom, a doom of folly. Wharton's life constitutes a tyranny and a rebellion (the terms are Pope's and point back to the earlier poems), resulting in an ambition for praise that confuses and contradicts purpose. The selfhood's victory is employed by Pope as an occasion of irony at its own expense.

The good of the divine datum cannot be accommodated to the desires of the selfhood; rather the passion is the instrumentality by which its purposes are frustrated. This is the nature of the ironic vision in *To Cobham.* Here again, Pope seems to isolate a particular aspect of the *Essay's* myth and to elaborate on it within the contours of a discrete poem. He makes his argument by obviating the second principle of the *Essay* (reason). Though Leranbaum notices the omission, she accounts for it by distinguishing between the intentions governing Epistle II and those manifest in *To Cobham:* "where a dominant aim of the *Essay* was to urge man to redirect his attention from vanity, pride, and egotism outward and upward to a sense of participation in a divine and beneficent universe, the *Epistle to Cobham* considers man, not as he ought to be, but as he is: restless, obstinate, contradictory, perverse."[39]

The point, however, is that the action Pope describes here depends upon the prior subversion of reason, and upon our recognition of this fact as a determinant of Wharton's behavior. Not to understand this situation is to lose allusive contact with the *Essay's* myth. Wharton returns to us as another version of the "you," the presumptuous being whose internal subversions have made him what he is. As a realistic critique, *To Cobham* provides a living example of possession and metamorphosis, evidencing the man who empties the ruling passion of its divine significance and fills it instead with anxiety and illusory desire. If in the *Essay* Pope defeats the specter of the selfhood, in *To Cobham* the selfhood defeats itself. Wharton's performance is simply another in the continuing drama of fall, and of "honest Nature" (227), which can be truncated but cannot be re-created by its subverter, for the plain reason that the selfhood has no creative power at all. The ruling passion "sticks to our last sand" (225) as the pathetic evidence of what man has made of grace.

In that *To Bathurst* treats of riches it is a companion poem to *To Burlington;* in that it deals, in Wasserman's words, with the "paradisiacal pre-economic state,"[40] it creates through its mythology another link to *To Burlington* and joins further with the *Essay on Man.* In recent years there has been some effort to read *To Bathurst* as a poem advocating Christ-like virtues. The

Man of Ross has been the central figure in this mode of interpretation. Wasserman's reading provides the *locus classicus* for this endeavor: "the essence of the wifeless, childless Man of Ross's portrait is that beneath the surface language is a current of references to Christ's life and miracles."[41] This view is sustained by Edwards, who finds also that the Man of Ross "re-enacts, with his dependents and with the landscape, the loving dealings of God with nature and of Christ with man."[42] And the notion has gained further support in Erskine-Hill's remark that "there is a certain harmony between Kyrle's life and the great doctrines of the Christian religion."[43]

As with *To Burlington, To Bathurst* seeks an ethical resolution to extreme modes of conduct in moderate or normative behavior, in this case in liberality as the mean between the extremes of avarice and prodigality. But *To Bathurst* differs notably from its immediate companion poem in terms of its prevailing mythos. In *To Burlington* Pope focuses on the re-created garden, on man's loving care for the goddess, and on the fecundity which is the reward she bestows upon him. In *To Bathurst,* equally an "ethic epistle," the principal subject is rebellion, and it is Pope's consciousness of Satan that grows in the poem. Undoubtedly, this awareness summons the Man of Ross and endows him with the Christ-like qualities that others have noticed. It is not an unlikely conclusion since it fulfills again the conflict between type and opposite we have almost everywhere observed. Though the poem is crowded with specific persons, who provide positive or negative examples of Pope's ethical theme, they are set against the background of a familiar conflict. In the portrait of Ross and in the emergent figure of Satan the drama of self-love and selfhood is once more enacted. Thus we need to concern ourselves with the apparent presence of Satan in the poem, and in this regard Wasserman may be of substantial help. He observes that the opening of the work allusively offers, through the image of gold flaming forth as "rival to, its Sire, the sun" (12), the concealed myth of Phaëthon. And he further suggests that "Phaëthon's ambitious attempt to usurp his father's place was Christianized as Lucifer's revolt against

God."[44] Equally, however, *rival* allusively summons Belinda's impiety, reminding us of the modal variations to which the complex word is subject in the extended text.

We should find that the paradisiacal pre-economic state alludes more nicely to Lucifer's fall than it does to Phaëthon's, and does so with the precise economy for which sensitive readers of Pope have always valued him. The myth of rebellion, which will end with Sir Balaam, begins with reference to gold and to nature ("as in duty bound," [9]), which "Deep hid the shining mischief under ground" (10). "Man's audacious labor" (11) is glossed by Wasserman to mean that "man's unnatural ambition has released Pride itself into the world."[45] It is of course the obvious point to make, and implies immediately the death of that prelapsarian state through the sin of pride, and calls also to mind the cardinal instigator of human audacity. Man's impertinent labor releases gold and Satan into the world. That God immediately counteracts this folly through the action of *concordia discors* ("Then careful Heav'n supply'd two sorts of Men, / To squander these, and those to hide agen," [13-14]) is very much to the point of Pope's theodicy. But we are looking for a way to read the epistle, and thus looking for a system of signals linking the misusers of riches to their Satanic prototype. Something of this is evident in the reference to riches, which are "Giv'n to the Fool, the Mad, the Vain, the Evil, / To Ward, to Waters, Chartres, and the Devil" (19-20). The generic terms correspond to specific actors and thereby suggest a contrapuntal relation between the one and the other. If "Evil" is not out of relation to fool, mad, and vain, then neither is "Devil" to Ward, Walter, and Chartres.

The device tells us something of the way Pope is thinking here and has thought in other places. His consciousness of Satan grows from an allusion to an identification and into a progress. The *progress* in financial transactions from "bulky Bribes" (35) to "Blest paper-credit!" (69) is entirely an advance upon the means of influence at Satan's disposal. For paper-credit "lends Corruption lighter wings to fly!" (70). It is not reductive, I think, to observe that if Satan begins as a "shining mischief under ground'' (10), he is soon a winged mischief. When Wasserman speaks of the tale of Sir Balaam, locating it within its proper biblical and classical contexts (Job and the rape of Danae), he says that "Pope's artistry of poetic assimilation lies in his telling the story in the terms, not of the myth, but of the allegorical meanings which the original myth concealed, yet without losing allusive contact with the myth.''[46] This is perfectly exact, even down to the distinction tacitly employed between myth and allegory. The growing presence of Satan in the poem depends upon an allusive contact with the myth, but the allegorical significance is primary and immediate. Riches are Satanic; yet it is the burden of virtue to convert this evil into good, and the endless art of transmuting bad to good is not God's alone but man's as well. This, I take it, is the real importance of Ross in the epistle, though Pope is careful not to endow him too liberally with wealth (and therefore is able to preserve the initial doubts consistent with "shining mischief").

The image of "low-born mist" (*To Bathurst*, 140) recalls Satan's entrance into Eden "as a mist by night." His evasion of Uriel and the cherubim correlates with Pope's second reference to "Corruption . . . , / (So long by watchful Ministers withstood),'' (137-38). The action of a mist blotting the sun affiliates with Satan's initial rebellion as "rival to . . . the Sun," corresponding directly to Belinda's own rivalry and to that of the tyrannical females in *To a Lady*. Blunt's "wizard" (136) is obviously a false prophet (as Satan proved to Eve), but the precise counterpart to this passage occurs in the *First Epistle of the First Book of Horace, Imitated* ("Proteus, Merlin, any Witch," [152]). Like Blunt's wizard these are false prophets within an allegory of worldly values envisioned as the ground of enchantment and delusion. Blunt is such an enchanted person; the prophecy he has been given is both true and false. The Fall is predicted within the image of Satan crouching on the perimeter of the garden, though Blunt takes the prophecy to mean that the good is thereby defeated, and by this means becomes an advocate for expediency, the apologist for corruption who chooses corruption as the way of the world.

The relation between Blunt's worldly values and Cotta's mock-monkish abstinence defines another set of extremes, for which Ross's behavior is the mean of virtue. But I am less interested in the epistle's ethical formulas (which have been set out very well elsewhere) than I am in the way the poem reveals the pattern of Pope's imagination. The associational structure, for example, that provides corruption with wings links riches to insects, who "when conceal'd they lie, / Wait but for wings, and in their season, fly" (171-72). Concealment and flight are the terms of diabolic duplicity; inevitably as such they summon another figure from Pandemonium, "pale Mammon" (173), who within six lines is transmogrified into Cotta, and who, like Cotta, "pine[s] amidst his store" of plenty (173). If Blunt is, as Wasserman calls him, a falsely self-conceived "latter-day Noah," [47] as Pope's imagery of impending "flood" and "deluge" suggests, Cotta is equally a latter-day Mammon. The false prophet Blunt and the false god Cotta emerge from their respective typological contexts and necessitate, or at least make plausible, the reading of Ross as the type of Christ.

Surely not far from these actors is Cotta's son, whose prodigality manifested in "slaughter'd hecatombs" (203) looks toward Timon's "Hecatomb" in *To Burlington* (156). Like Timon, whose sacrifices advance his own vulgar extravagance, Cotta's son sacrifices in the name of prodigality, and each is conceived as acting under the agency of zeal ("Zeal for that great House which eats him up," [208]), which again returns us to the *Essay on Man* ("Zeal then, not charity, became the guide," [III, 261]). Timon and Cotta's son both misunderstand their ethical duty, but their misapprehensions are located within a theological context that insists upon the linked relation between theology and ethics. Each figure is an example of the bad custodian, respectively slaughtering and sacrificing, whereas, as *To Burlington* insists, " 'Tis use alone that sanctifies Expence" (179). Within this pattern it may be superfluous to explicate the precise bearing of *sanctifies*, but we might notice that in *To Burlington* "Splendor borrows all her rays from Sense" (180), whereas *To Bathurst* condemns Cotta's son as without the

"Sense to value Riches" (219). Sacrifice and sense bring both poems into proximity, and though Timon sacrifices others to his vanity, to dinners "perform'd in state" (157), Cotta's son simply sacrifices himself to the state ("His oxen perish in his country's cause," [206]). Each act is conducted under the agency of zeal, "not charity," and zeal is the demonic agent that permits us to slide between ethical formulas and theological primitivism.

Charity is of course the Christian virtue, ethical and religious, and as zeal is the theological vice founded on persecution and hatred (in the *Essay*), it is equally the ethical failing founded on prodigality and pride. Charity is thus the antitype to pride, which translates again into the opposition between self-love and selfhood as these epistles move within the context largely defined by the *Essay*. Liberality is a mean between extremes; by definition it is moderate and moderating, even as religious enthusiasm is excessive and vicious. But lest we forget the portrait of Satan in the emergent celebration of the Man of Ross, Pope restores it to us through Villiers. The "alas! how chang'd from him" (*To Bathurst*, 305) has the unmistakable ring of Miltonic allusion, and if the Man of Ross is what benevolence makes of the fallen world, Villiers is what the immoderate man makes of riches, in what I believe admits of a double meaning. Villiers is "lord of useless thousands" (314), whose victory is the defeat of himself ("Victor of his health, of fortune, friends / And fame," [313-14]). His victory is also the ironic triumph of the ruling passion conceived now as dissociated from reason and directed to the ends of vain self-glory. Pope had earlier reminded us:

> "The ruling Passion, be it what it will,
> "The ruling Passion conquers Reason still."
> Less mad the wildest whimsey we can frame,
> Than ev'n that Passion, if it has no Aim.
>
> (155-58)

In Pope's portrait Villiers is that "soul of whim!" (306) who simultaneously defeats the ends of riches and the ruling passion, making the one "useless" (314) and the other "mad"

(331). The two words apply as well to the portraits of Cotta and his son; the avarice of the former is useless, whereas the prodigality of the latter is mad. In this context Bathurst is introduced to teach us that "secret rare, between th' extremes to move / Of mad Good-nature, and of mean Self-love" (227-28). The portrait of Villiers is related to those of Cotta and Cotta's son, and Bathurst's embodiment of the golden mean stands between the ends to which riches are disposed by Cotta and his son. In much the same way, the ruling passion of the Man of Ross (charity) opposes the purposeless passion of Villiers, which conquers reason and himself. On the anagogic level, if Ross exemplifies Christ, Villiers embodies the Anti-Christ.

Pope's negative portraits have been of men in the grip of an obsession or "whim." They have misunderstood their obligation to the ruling passion and misconceived the nature of wealth, which "in the gross is death, but life diffus'd" (*To Bathurst*, 233), and "well-dispers'd, is Incense to the Skies" (236). As a categorical virtue charity participates in the meaning of self-love and the definition of sociality. The man of Ross's charity is a paradigm for the self that loves its neighbor as itself, and benevolence is the virtue that frees man from an obsessiveness in its own right diabolic. If riches in the aggregate are Satanic, charity is the grace within man transmuting evil into good. In other words, benevolence is the art of morality, and man's relation to money in *To Bathurst* is akin to (though not the same as) his relation to nature in *To Burlington*. Timon sees in nature only a gargantuan goddess whom he labors futilely to possess. In the same spirit, Cotta possesses money, not realizing he is possessed by it. The potential good of nature and of wealth is deformed, and the theological context of zeal and selfhood catches up both malpractitioners, associating each equally with the demonic and diabolic. Conversely, Burlington and Boyle, who "grace" and "improve the Soil" (*To Burlington*, 177), are like Kyrle, who acts under the auspices of love, retaining within himself the grace of the ruling passion and directing it under the governance of reason to social and religious ends. In this way wealth "well-dispers'd is Incense to the Skies." It is the debt man pays to his common mortality, the devotional act signifying his retention of grace and fidelity to God.

In this context then, Balaam is one whose wealth drives out grace and transmutes a "Blessing" and "God's good Providence" into "Wit" and "lucky hit" (*To Bathurst*, 377-78), or, within the terms of the epistle, into a *whim* of fortune. Balaam, fallen into mean self-love, falls into temptation. Satan "In one abundant show'r of Cent. per Cent., / Sinks deep within him, and possesses whole" (372-73). The emergent form of Satan, beginning with his own fall and progressing through his winged flight to the garden and his allusive existence within Villiers, culminates in the clarity of his revealed form in the inverted parable of Job. The history of the emergent diabolic in the world, beginning with Satan and ending with his victory over Balaam, is what the poem is about. Yet Satan's victory is necessarily informed with the ironic values of Villiers's victory, and if we read the poem as I am suggesting, Balaam's rape corresponds to Villiers's self-rape. Balaam is raped of "Wife, son, and daughter" and "wealth, yet dearer" (399-400), suggesting again the presence of predator and prey, and reminding us that only the selfhood can defeat self-love, that obsession is the darkness of the ruling passion counteracting grace. Balaam's tempter is the fallen angel inhabiting Villiers's ruin, and the ruling passion becomes the night of the self. Balaam, who "curses God and dies" (402), has recapitulated in his own life the history of man's fall, the conversion of grace into death.

The same enterprise that leads Pope in *To a Lady* to present Martha as woman redeemed, as muse and inspiration, leads him here to create the revealed and degenerate form of the selfhood, man fallen and yet determined to fall again. In the *Moral Essays*, Pope's vision moves between redemption and fall; the myth grows in his poetry, not as a single entire narrative, but redactionally conceived and determining the necessities of his art. His accommodation of "imitations" leads him to a poetry of multiple allusion in which the ethical bearing of his art coexists with classical and Christian allegory. As in the tale of Balaam he fuses the Jupiter-Demon who descends upon Danae with the

Satan-demon who destroys Job's children, so too does he con-
join the derived precepts of the *Nicomachean Ethics* with the sur-
viving tradition of Renaissance allegory. And it is probably
worth making the point, while not insisting upon it, that Satan
as Prince of Air visiting storms upon Job's children corresponds
to the passion-tormented Atossa, whose "Hate" and "Gratitude" are equally a "storm" (*To a Lady*, 132). *Storm* is the literal
and metaphorical manifestation of diabolism, and it seems
advisable to read the portrait of Atossa through the allusion to
Satan's action and also through the correlative allusion to Jupiter, who descended upon Danae in a rain (storm) of gold. *Storm*
links widely divergent portraits and brings them under the scrutiny of a single focus composed of multiple nuances of moral
light and shade. Atossa is not Satan, who is not Jupiter, but
Atossa cannot exist for us as Pope's description demands unless
we perceive the larger composition of which she forms only a
part. Strictly speaking, Atossa is a type of Lamia or Hecate or
Lilith, the terrible female who demands sacrifice, and thus she
affiliates with the sacrifices demanded by Zeal and offered by
Timon and Cotta's son, or, in the *Dunciad*, by Cibber himself.

On the other hand, Blunt's evaluation of himself as the
type of Noah, and hence the type of Christ, follows the pattern
of scriptural exegesis, and that Blunt should so regard himself is
obviously ironic in light of Kyrle's presence in the poem.
Zwicker remarks of *Absalom and Achitophel* that, "read with an
understanding of the typological significance of biblical narrative, the poem unifies history past and present in an eternal paradigm."[48] What *To Bathurst* provides, in Zwicker's words, is a
particular "historicity both of the sign and what it signifies."[49]
Pope's contemporaries are disposed within a figural interpretation linking type to prototype, and thus is set forth an idea of
historical truth that is similar, if not identical, to that presented
in Dryden's work. What we need ask is why Pope does here
what is not otherwise a conspicuous feature of his poetry
(although the Horatian imitations will offer an occasion to recon-
sider the question). The answer may be derived partly from
Pope's need to continue transposing his myth from the theater

of the mind (its psychological form in the *Essay on Man*) into the theater of the world (its historical form in *To Bathurst*). Once we make this connection, we may further establish a requirement of the myth. Though, as Wasserman has observed, the myth is not *told*, its informing allegory is at all points present in the text. (What Wasserman and I are calling allegory, Auerbach and Zwicker would prefer to identify more precisely in this context as figuralism.) But the point is, however, the same point of *Absalom and Achitophel*: sacred and secular history coexist and coalesce. Contemporary history exists within a frame that defines the meaning of that history, and topical actors are disposed within a pattern equally mythical and historical. There is no difference between the one and the other; they mutually reinforce each other and provide a way of understanding what history means.

Thus Cotta is the type of Mammon, Villiers of Satan, Kyrle of Christ; and Blunt and Balaam are the opposites of Noah and Job. These are the meanings of actor and behavior (like Cotta's avarice) that otherwise are explicable only as greed. But greed itself requires a meaning, and because it does we move from ethics to sacred history, to the irreducibility of myth. History informed by the word is therefore analogous to nature informed by the divine, and the pattern corroborates the links between text and sacred text, and further incorporates nature itself as simply another kind of sacred text. *To Bathurst* in this way builds out from the *Essay*, assimilating into itself a meaning of temporality (scriptural history) that the *Essay* does not offer, but which Pope's growing conception seems to demand and is consistent with his own view of allegory:

> I think the forming the Machines upon the Allegorical persons of Virtues and vices very reasonable; it being equally proper to Ancient and Modern subjects, and to all Religions and times: Nor do we look upon them so much as Heathen Divinities as Natural passions. This is not the Case when Jupiter, Juno, etc., are introduc'd who tho' sometimes consider'd as Physical powers yet that sort of Allegory lies not open enough to the apprehension.[50]

The allegory that does lie open enough is not a "remote kind of

Fable or Fiction,'' but the ''sort of Machinery, for the meaning of which one is not at a loss for a Moment.''[51] And that meaning is precisely embodied in Pope's figural rendering of contemporary history.

When in the *Dictionary* Johnson illustrates the meaning of *sense* he takes as one of his examples the lines from *To Burlington:*

> Good sense, which only is the gift of Heav'n,
> And, tho' no science, fairly worth the sev'n:
> A Light, which in yourself you must perceive;
> Jones and Le Notre have it not to give.
>
> (43-46)

It is surprising that Johnson should find his example in *To Burlington* and not in the *Essay on Criticism* in light of the meaning he assigns the word: ''Understanding, soundness of faculties; strength of natural reason.''[52] His definition is consistent with the meaning Pope generally intends in the *Essay*, but in *To Burlington* the word is enriched by its associations with the ruling passion and with self-love. Sense is here a variant of that passion, ''the gift of Heav'n,'' an intuitive faculty consistent with the nature of self-love: ''Still follow Sense, of ev'ry Art the Soul, / Parts answ'ring parts shall slide into a whole'' (65-66). The ''human soul,'' says Pope, ''Must rise from Individual to the Whole'' (*Essay on Man*, IV, 361-62), a rising predicated on obedience to the principle of divine design, and hence an act that glances back to those various and suspect risings of the earlier poems. The good man

> Learns, from this union of the rising Whole,
> The first, last purpose of the human soul;
> And knows where Faith, Law, Morals, all began,
> All end, in Love of God, and Love of Man.
>
> (IV, 337-40)

Something of this same activity is proposed in *To Burlington*, and *sense* is the instrumentality enabling man lov-

ingly to re-create the ordered garden, as well as to distinguish
between the extremes of shabbiness and vulgar ostentation. So
that sense is an aesthetic and an ethical principle, a light within
the self, and simultaneously a source of illumination for that
lying outside the self.[53] The garden objectively correlates to the
moral estate of its creator, and sense, like the master passion,
may be deformed by an excess of vanity or pride, the ethical
consequence of which is vulgarity or tasteless extravagance. In
the *Essay on Man* the perversion of the ruling passion leads to
the selfhood; in *To Burlington* the corruption of sense leads to
Timon, and each figure is identical to the other. Burlington is the
man whose love progresses from self to society, thus serving as
the corrective to Timon and as the form of self-love in the world.
But not all the characters of *To Burlington* are human actors. The
"Genius of the Place" (57) re-creates the *genius loci* of the earlier
poems, a tutelary deity with which man is advised to "Consult"
(57). Leranbaum suggests that as "Good Sense, the 'gift of
Heav'n', is the Light of the soul of Man, so the goddess Nature,
the 'Genius of the Place', is the divine centre of the natural
world."[54] Thus another center opens beyond itself, "scoops in
circling theatres the Vale, / Calls in the Country, catches opening glades, / Joins willing woods, and varies shades from
shades" (60-62).

The collaboration between Burlington and the genius of the
place is the positive form of the negative relation between Eloisa
and Black Melancholy. Equally, the genius mediates between
man and God, even as in the *Essay* nature performs the same
function (the good man "looks thro' Nature, up to Nature's
God," [IV, 332]). As *To Burlington* is occupied with the ways of
loving or abusing the divine center in man (sense), it is also
about the cultivation or perversion of *place* as such actions bear
on man's custodial function. So that while the ruling passion is
the agency through which man creates the total form of his identity, sense in *To Burlington* is the means whereby he cultivates
what is outside himself. As sense is a faculty the *Essay* does not
include, *To Burlington* addresses this deficiency and continues
thereby to chart the mighty maze.

The epistle re-animates the myth of the garden as seeding-place, a center of fertility from which will issue the public monuments that distinguish Burlington's imagination, the "Idea's" (195) of his mind called forth by kings. Thus the poem, about riches, is also about fertility and love, another definition of riches and the condition of their application. The essential act is the awakening of the fructifying female, who will as "laughing Ceres re-assume the land" (176), and the "Deep Harvests" (175) culminate a romance in the metaphor of generation. The comic antithesis is implicit in Timon's own goddess ("Greatness," [103]), a Brobdingnagian female (the image is Pope's). Timon's effort to embrace her defines Lilliputian man ("a puny insect, shiv'ring at a breeze!" [108]) envisioned within an absurdly erotic moment. The degeneration of love is played out through squirting Cupids (111) and a pointless "Fountain, never to be play'd" (121). Potency (power) is a function of *sense* sponsoring both an act of love and a bringing-into-being. Like *To Bathurst, To Burlington* focuses upon the clarification of a form, in this case the female form either lovingly cultivated by sense or deformed by the selfhood that misuses and misreads the datum. The garden as woman is also the garden as seeding-place; beloved by Boyle and Bathurst, she yields her deep harvests: "future Buildings, future Navies" (*To Burlington*, 188). Generation links the fertility of the goddess to the propagation of Burlington's mind, and the allegory of love given and reciprocated—the play between *sense* and *harvests*—issues also in the submission of "dang'rous Flood," "roaring Main," and "subject Sea" (199-201). As in *Windsor-Forest*, the hitherto rebellious elements of nature freely offer themselves.

Beyond this, the epistle suggests further affinities with the *Essay on Man*. Pope characteristically transposes the center of his attack from key to key, sometimes catching up seemingly divergent topics within similar terms of varying intensities. Thus the sacrificial acts of religious Zeal in Epistle III of the *Essay* are parodied by Timon's hospitality. Timon's dinner is a "solemn Sacrifice" (157) as are Zeal's offerings to the gods. It is an act of pride, as Zeal builds "heav'n on pride" (III, 262), and it is performed in a "Temple" (156). Zeal perverts and deforms the ends of religion; Timon's hospitality is of the same magnitude of corruption. Similar terms hedge both figures. We move from religion to hospitality, from the personification (Zeal) to the man, and we move easily between both because they belong to the same general order of misuse. On the other hand, Burlington imagines "Temples," erected by kings, as "worthier of the God" (198). Zeal's temple ("th' etherial vault," [III, 263]) and Timon's are fanatic places of slaughter (hecatombs); Burlington's is restorative of devotion, a fitting habitation for God, the ultimate consequence of the harmony enjoyed by sense and the genius of the place.

Weiskel states that in "the positive sublime, spirit and matter are differentiated in principle but not yet in the fact of perception or intuition."[55] Pope's attempt to convert spirit into matter is increasingly founded on a series of givens (sense, taste, ruling passion, etc.) that demand a fidelity always in danger of breaking down. His chief effort seems concentrated on shoring up those various data, while remaining simultaneously alert to the subversions threatening them. *To Burlington* is an excellent example of Pope's conception of the one life within us and abroad. The genius of the place is *out there,* and the cultivation of the datum (sense) materializes the good form of the goddess, thereby inducting Burlington into the revealed sociality of the role he moves forward to fulfill. Self-love *is* social. But the entire structure rests on an apprehension of the self and its powers that is, at best, psychologically tenuous. There is often no way to tell if a cultivated inwardness is doing its job. This is why the confrontation between the "I" and the "you" always signifies a crisis in the poetry, and it is one of the reasons why Pope is so nervously alert to the ironic moment and strategically presses allusion into this service.[56] Is the "you" a demonic simulacrum of the "I" (as in the *Rape of the Lock*), or is it, as in *Eloisa to Abelard*, the form that the "I" should appropriate? If sense is "A light, which in yourself you must perceive," how do you know whether you have perceived or misperceived it? The answer seems to be that the self knows itself by meditating the grounds of its own authority, but the issue is likely to be referred merely to the success or failure of its own efforts.

Much of the imaginative energy of the *Essay on Man* goes into exploiting the dissatisfactions of the "you" that is always failing to be more than it is and therefore always uneasy and malcontent. Pope's system functions to reveal the "you" as a being badly contextualized, and the fault is not in the context but in the self. Similarly, Pope imports the Aristotelian ethical frame for *To Bathurst* and *To Burlington,* an ideological framework within which the various actors of the poems are disposed, defined, and *known.* Timon's vulgarity is akin to Wharton's "Lust of Praise." The moving down the scale from love to lust is equivalent to moving along the scale from magnificence to tasteless extravagance. Both are acts of lust, as Pope's implicit image of puny Timon and gargantuan goddess makes clear, and Timon's fate is to be contained within a pathetic center from which issues no harvest and which radiates no light.

That Pope is thinking in such terms is commonly evident in his imagery. "Splendor," he says of Boyle and Bathurst, "borrows all her rays from Sense" (*To Bathurst,* 180). Sense as a sun radiating influence recalls the spider living along his line (*Essay on Man,* I, 217-18), the small pebble dropped into the still lake (IV, 364). The relation between sense as sun and splendor as lesser body, deriving its illumination from the greater, doubles back also upon the concluding image of *To a Lady,* and the concord between sun and moon asserts itself unobtrusively in *To Burlington* as a variation of the praise Pope accords Martha. *To a Lady* concludes with an artful compliment to Martha upon the gift of the "gen'rous God," who gave her "Sense, Good-humour, and a Poet." The recurrent *sense* keeps *To a Lady* in relation to *To Burlington,* incorporates Clarissa's advice to Belinda, and further includes the *Essay on Criticism*'s multiple references to the same word. The re-emergent complex word is another aspect of the emergent complex context. The conclusion to *To Burlington* re-imagines the close of *Windsor-Forest,* as both works celebrate the imperial theme and the majestic destiny of *Britannia Redivivus.* As we read Pope we therefore re-read him, and in so doing we witness not only the growth of an ethical system, but the necessities that lead him in *To Burlington* to rediscover the bounties contingent upon the act of well and truly loving.

Like his own figure of the "green myriads in the peopled grass" (*Essay on Man*, I, 210), Pope's verse is crowded with various actors, all of whom are, in one way or another, related to and agents of the central conflict between self-love and selfhood. Burlington is opposed by Timon. Behind both are the allegorical figures of the *Essay* displaced into a new context,[57] and the "sense" with which Burlington is endowed restates the custodial theme. Timon is not merely the bad steward, but the bad lover; his center is inert; he himself is infertile; and he is caught within the poem by the mocking iconography of sterility. Nobody would call forth the ideas of his mind because he has none to call forth. The correspondences between Timon and Zeal (pride, sacrifice, temple, hecatomb) are portended by the re-emergence of the demonic element ("Some Daemon whisper'd, 'Visto! have a Taste,' " [*Burlington*, 16]) and are specifically associated with the misuse of riches, the "pelf" of *To a Lady*. As Pope's texts bear on power, they necessarily incorporate the ends to which money is applied, the works of man including works of adoration, and they rise from the level of worldly purpose to religious devotion. And as the poems gather their energies they gather also the actors who cluster about these powers, directing them to good or evil ends.

Pope's topicality was a subject of considerable interest for eighteenth-century readers and remains today a continuing scholarly inquiry. But it is not difficult to understand his vexation at the identification of Timon as Chandos. Timon is more readily Ostentatious Grandeur than he is Chandos, and *if* Cannons was an example of glaringly bad taste, Timon incorporates the unfortunate duke and all those who share in his aesthetic and moral defects. It makes much more sense to say that Timon is Mammon, the continually recurrent desire to create a false paradise motivated by self-centeredness and envious emulation. Thus Wharton of *To Cobham* and Timon of *To Burlington* coincide if not coalesce. They are variations on a theme—the misuse of the divine datum that drives each further into himself. And the self lost within itself is no longer social, is no longer even an "I," but is markedly and recognizably alienated from an intuitive grasp of its own powers. Perhaps the final ironic assault upon such a self is based on the assumption that it does not know how to appeal to its own powers. Pope couches this reflection in the metaphor of dress ("But treat the Goddess like a modest fair, / Nor over-dress, nor leave her wholly bare," [*To Burlington*, 51-52]), but the hardly submerged erotic element obviously signifies a sexual economy that is being addressed by the poet under the rubric of an aesthetic principle. Knowing involves knowing how to awaken one's own pleasures, which therefore involves self-knowledge as a function of the power over nature. This is what those who are lost within themselves have lost, and their appetites are discharged in various sorts of adventurings designated as rape or lust, or in the comprehensive metaphor of predator. And the observation again reminds us how deeply Pope's fear of the primitive penetrates his text, for the primitive is always mere power, or power without knowledge, and hence it is destructive and self-destructive. This is to a large extent what a poetry of civilization is all about.

4 The Self-Regarding "I" and the Egotistical Sublime

Horace, Imitated: First Satire of the Second Book,
Epistle to Arbuthnot, and *First Epistle*
of the First Book

Subjectivism seems to originate as a reaction to institutions no longer doing their job. This explanation has been frequently offered to account for the emergence of what was at one time called "preromanticism." And we have seen Pope's poetry warn over and again of the consequences when the sacred is displayed in favor of the merely visionary, a function of the expansionist ego, the sublimity of the "I," as Pope rightly recognized. Such is the essence of the Satanic temptation, the promised promotion of the self in the scheme of things. But what happens when Pope comes to regard himself, when he occupies the center of his own stage, and becomes his own subject? This is the question that interests me here, and it requires some extended attention to three poems commonly defined as Horatian imitations. Most scholars concerned with *Horace, Imitated* have noticed that the various poems offer "a much more central concern with the role of the poet and a clear sense of the poet in *propria persona*." Yet their incipience is not uncharacteristically referred to a *jeu d'esprit*, a "relaxation from the greater moral seriousness demanded by the *opus magnum*."[1]

Are we to give credence to the idea that these works arise from Bolingbroke's hint to Pope, or would we be better advised to look for their importance in relation to concerns already defined in these pages? Insofar as the *First Satire of the Second Book,* the *Epistle to Arbuthnot,* and the *First Epistle of the First Book* turn Pope's vision upon himself—and the poetic act itself—they set before the reader a definition of the poet and the man. They seem, that is, to be the glass in which Pope regards himself in a manner appropriate both to his personal identity and to his vocation as poet. And as this is so, his poetry moves within concentric circles almost simultaneously constructed. The *Essay on Man* is an exploration of generic identity; the *Epistles to Several Persons* inquires into the behavior of particular men and women in the world; and the *Imitations* serve to permit the satirist to observe himself. Nowhere in Pope's work is the social function of the satirist's role better or even as well set forth. If we think of his poetry in the terms I have just been suggesting, we see that the *Imitations* complete a process in the observation of humankind extending from man's relation to the divine to one man's special notice of himself. These poems seem to leap from his pen in the early and middle years of the 1730s, the most sustainedly productive years of his life, and the types of the *vir bonus,* Bolingbroke, Bathurst, Oxford, the Man of Ross, yield now to Pope himself.

The three poems in particular that I have specified clarify Pope as poet and as man, incorporating him therefore within a context of other lives and other performances. Obviously, the *Imitations* provided him with various opportunities: for political and social commentary, for a direct engagement with contemporary life. The *Imitations* offer something more, noted by Griffin as the possibility of seeing the self "more fully . . . in the presence of the antiself."[2] And Griffin plausibly poses Hervey and Walpole as Pope's antiselves, even as Timon is the opposite of

Burlington, Martha the antithesis to Atossa, and Cibber the contrary to Bolingbroke. Such a setting up of self and antiself is a characteristic Popeian strategy, and there is little reason to deny its continuity within the *Imitations*. But my more immediate interest is to suggest the relation between a historical and a personal identity. However flawed Alexander Pope may have been—and have known himself to be—the historical identity of the poet, and his public vocation, are what saved him from himself. These remarks merely signify that I am coming round on my argument from another perspective, and that the *Imitations* offer another justification for the familiar Popeian recourse to the historical context. Over and again, identity has been the complex issue. Who is Belinda or Eloisa and what is the nature of their self-betrayals? What saves us, or does not save us, from ourselves? I find these concerns central to the *Imitations*, to the effort to locate once again the humanist context, the reclaiming historical identity that is a stay against personal misadventure.

To *Arbuthnot* is therefore a key document, for it is uniquely a poem about Pope and about the vulnerabilities of the man himself. Against this document play the *First Satire of the Second Book* and the *First Epistle of the First Book*; self-preservingly they define the man emergent in his historical role. They imply the immediate practical bearing of the ruling passion as it directs and determines a life, and they demonstrate the historical validity and contextual utility of the satirist's calling. In this regard, Griffin's optimism exceeds my own. He remarks that "the private and public selves may only appear to be antithetical."[3] I think, rather, that we approach à crisis here in Pope's vision of the human estate, and that the nature of this crisis extends beyond the oppositions apparent within one man to embrace the universe of type and antithesis. A Cibber does oppose a Bolingbroke, and the abiding question bears on which of the two will prevail. Because this issue is so central to Pope's imagination, it dictated the creation of both the *Essay on Man* and the *Dunciad*. And, because it is equally vital to his sense of himself, it required another and different forum that the *Imitations* provided. There is consequently a certain heroism evident in these poems, an effort to bring the greater subject down, as it were, to Pope himself, and to leave the issue, as I believe he leaves it, in doubt. Perhaps this is finally why one cannot speak convincingly of Pope's humanist optimism or pessimism. There is too much evidence on both sides of the question, too much historical reality informing that knowing intelligence. And from this line of reasoning I gather further support for the urgencies informing Pope's mythopoeic imagination: the haunting and persistent reality of the Fall not merely as a present condition with which man lives, but as a threat portending another and more disastrous fall.

To preserve the residue of grace that makes the middle kingdom habitable or to lose it entirely are the large-scale polarities of Pope's greater subject. If in the *Imitations* he comes round on himself, it is only to drive the question home. Yet it had been there from the beginning: in Pope's own ambitious candidacy for celebrity evident in the *Temple of Fame*, and in the personal wisdom that leaves him attendant upon the one greater man of the *Essay on Man*. Now, however, the topic shifts slightly, and it is not a question of the divine pattern but of historical patent, of an intelligence seeking to verify its chosen role and assessing the obligations that pertain to it. That this should be his intention here is consistent with Pope's earlier efforts. From the small center of himself that he gives us in *To Arbuthnot* we move outward to the enlarged identity of the guardian poet, the man who merges with his role to be more than he would otherwise be. This effort, I take it, springs from a fundamental habit of mind, which tests the various impulses of the self against its derived ideals, and in turn provides the only legitimacy the self may claim.

What will emerge here is not new to our reading of Pope; it merely refocuses our attentions upon a context compatible with other contexts we have so far explored. Pope's imagination seems never to take eccentric passages, seems never to be deceived by subjects irrelevant to his main design. Because this is so, we should be more wary of the notion currently growing in our scholarship that Pope's chief poetic pattern was in some way broken or aborted. Whatever the fate of the projected *opus magnum,* there is another and larger design within his work that does not suffer the frustrations of intention or execution that supposedly vitiated that program. There is little sense of a radical incompleteness as, say, with Coleridge, equally little evidence that his sources of power fell away, as with Wordsworth. There is, rather, the evidence of steady progression of the sort we now associate with Milton or Blake, but yet seem to deny Pope. In the 1730s, Horace offered him what others had offered him earlier: models for fulfilling the larger design. And if we reflect that he is one of the most assimilative of English poets, there is no question of an alteration of purpose or direction in these works of his last full decade. For Pope, it was always a matter of taking what he needed from a widely diversified literary past to further coherent and complexly compatible goals, to compose his perceptions into the unity that is the very substance of imagination's figure.

The *First Satire of the Second Book* was published in February 1733; it identifies Pope as both guardian of the realm and good friend at Twickenham to those who, like himself, have performed serviceable acts within the state. The satirist's classic complaint is that his verses are received as "too bold," not "complaisant enough," "too rough," or "weak" (2-5). Beat about by various charges, he seeks "Council learned in the Law" (8). Fortescue advises flattery or at least discretion, but the particular terms of Pope's response, following Horace, suggest that satire is both a pleasure and a self-revelation: "In me what Spots (for Spots I have) appear, / Will prove at least the Medium must be clear" (55-56). Thus it is an "impartial Glass" (57), an instrument in which "my Muse intends / Fair to expose myself, my Foes, my Friends" (57-58). Satire is set over and against the law, a reflecting eye that without bias detects folly, an honest judicial medium ensnaring those like Mary Howard, Lady Mary, Walter, and Chartres, rogues normally exempt from effective legal retribution. Under the governance of the muse, satire is a divine gift, the satirist's vocation a dedication, a ruling passion. Horace serves as bardic prototype for Pope, even as

Boileau and Dryden figure forth the satirist within kingdoms that respect and protect his role.

Pope's attacks on the various antitheses of the satirist, the libelers Delia and Sappho, the cheats Walter and Chartres, bring forth the clarified form of the poet. Blackmore and Budgell, the unhappy contemporary equivalents of Virgil and Pindar, are rejected as poetic models. Maresca notes that Pope's "lines about Dryden and Boileau (111-14) are based upon Persius's description of the satire of Horace and Lucilius. . . . And shortly before this, in lines 105-6, Pope has echoed Dryden's translation of Juvenal's appeal to the precedent of Lucilius."[4] It is apparent that Pope locates himself within a context of classical and modern satirists in order to elucidate a bardic identity and the tradition to which he now elects to belong. In the *Temple of Fame* he had found four poets in the "Centre of the hallow'd Quire." If in his commitment to the epic tradition he had previously found his model in Homer, he here discovers it in Horace, in those "grave *Epistles,* bringing Vice to light" (151), which are not to be confused with "*Libels* and *Satires!* lawless Things indeed!" (150). The guardian of the realm is thus an exponent and champion of "Virtue" (105), a defender of "Her Cause" (109), and entitled to the protection of church and law. And Pope's obligatory performance is directed against those who " 'scape the Laws" (118). Within the misapprehensions that beset his identity and confuse his purpose, he derives a historical weapon superior to the uncertain and tenuous retribution of the law. Fortescue's good-natured exoneration of "grave *Epistles*" is a concession to the lawfulness of satire, but the mockery and ridicule it provokes are above legal jurisdiction ("My Lords the Judges laugh, and you're dismiss'd" [156]).

The devolution of Pope's identity from its public into its private form, in which as retired poet he offers retreat to Bolingbroke and Peterborough, is an expression of the *contemptus mundi* animating the benevolent man. Bolingbroke's restorative "Feast of Reason and . . . Flow of Soul" (128) and Peterborough's orderings of Pope's garden define the self harmonized within its own acts of peace. Guardians of the realm

and custodians of the garden, Pope and his friends cultivate an
order within the self, a temporary georgic repudiation of strife
that is itself an eduction of communality superior to what the
world can offer. Much more emphatically than Horace, Pope
turns from the present moment to clarify the resources of the
self and to discover its patent in the historical community of
satirists and in the contemporary fellowship of men greatly
good. The poet poses himself between the world and retirement
from it and contemplates the uncertain justice of the former. It is
clear that the *type* of the satirist wins his case: in common judgment he may be flatterer or libeler, a discordant creature within
the body social; but the long perspective of history vindicates
him even beyond what the *adversarius* can grant. The accordant
selves, private and public, define him as enlisted in the impartial
service of the muse. His satiric performance is thus a persistent
manifestation of justice or virtue, his ''Glory'' a ''Moderation''
(67) of partisan callings, his identity an ''honest Mean'' (66),
momentarily returning us to the ethical formulas of the *Moral
Essays*. The poet as scourge of virtue, bringing vice to light, is yet
the occasion for the laughter of good men.

This is the burden of the *First Satire*. The succession of satirists is a grace within time, a visionary profession that mocks
human institutions (''Hard Words or Hanging, if your Judge be
Page''[82]), and speaks in defiance of the poet's particular fate.
Pope's poem is of course coupled to its model, but it moves well
beyond the limited Horatian context to define a justification of
the satirist more personal and more convincing than any other
similar statement by him. The poet seeks his freedom and dedication within the urgencies of history, and, obedient to the
necessities that have summoned him, he confirms and enacts
the prototypical performance. In the final analysis, the antidote
to the poisons and corruptions of Delia and Sappho, Walter and
Chartres, is the bardic vision of virtue that the presence of evil
makes necessary. Pope's argument is a variation of the *Essay*'s
derivation of good from ill, an exploration consistent with the
bases of his thought, but here employed to explain the urgencies
compelling the poet. At the beginning of the satire he asks

"Advice" (10) of Fortescue; what he gives in return is an insight into the persistently emergent form of the poet as satirist.

As the satirist's patent is derived historically, his act is a guarantee of historical veracity. Pope does more than glance at this idea in his reference to George II: "And justly Caesar scorns the Poet's Lays, / It is to *History* he trusts for Praise" (35-36). But the satirist's judgment informs history, and the issue focuses on Pope's ironic deployment of "justly." The justice "Caesar" expects is one in which he will be disappointed, for a justice that he scorns is being prepared as decisive. Brower notices that "there is a degree of personal seriousness in Horace that Pope rarely ever reaches in his *Imitations.*"[5] Pope's special performance drives the personal into the general and plays off two articulations of justice within time and society. Fortescue's advice ("Better be *Cibber*" [37]) is another bad suggestion, prudent perhaps, but irrelevant to what is the burden of the poem, the emergent identity of the satirist. Pope's immediate response is to cite his ruling passion ("Each Mortal has his Pleaure" [45]), but it is subsequently quite clear that such pleasure involves the correspondent risk of self-revelation: "In me what Spots (for Spots I have) appear." The point is of course that "the Medium must be clear," and again one revelatory medium (satire) is posed against another (law). Satire is thus a grave charge ("Satire's my Weapon, but I'm too discreet / To run a Muck and tilt at all I meet" [67-70]). This is precisely what he will do in the *Epistle to Arbuthnot*, but that poem reverses the terms of the *First Satire* and moves toward a "personal seriousness" exploited by Pope as a personal comedy.

The legitimate power of scribal succession is designed to resolve the discontinuity between the word and the world addressed in the *Temple of Fame*, and thus to constitute a historical continuum acting under the conjoined aegis of church and state. If in the *Essay on Man* nature is the window through which man looks upward to God, satire is the glass in which man looks backward into history, which means, in effect, upon his own image. As in the *Essay*, satire is "Wit's false mirror," now held up not to nature's light, but to history's. In the *Rape of the Lock*, "A heav'nly Image in the Glass appears" (I, 125). In the *First*

Satire, satire is an "impartial Glass." Belinda's glass is the instrument by which the "other" is appropriated, animistically embodying those powers she desires and reflectively confirming them. That Belinda "bends" (126) to the glass suggests that her sovereign is the power she has assumed. Pope's glass is impartial; that is, the appropriation of its power carries with it the correspondent risk of self-revelation: "In me what Spots. . . ." This peculiar kind of priesthood confirms the (literally) visionary profession, but entails equally the risk of self-knowledge, meaning that the text in which one reads history is also the text in which one is read. Pope's image forces a reconsideration of the price of power and knowledge exacted by the quasi-divine instrument he employs. His allusive contact with his own earlier poem displaces the meaning of knowledge from its mythic context into the texture of history, transposing (metamorphosing) forbidden knowledge into the revealed truth that legitimizes a high cultural enterprise. The single metaphor of *glass* brings the *Rape* and the *First Satire* into proximity, offering alternative commentary on the relation between illusion and revelation as each is alternately served by the medium in which each appears.

The self that appears to Belinda is a variation of the *Essay's* "you," now appropriated by the self as constitutive of its "I." The self that appears within the envisioning glass of Pope's *First Satire* enforces recognitions inconsistent with "Cosmetic Pow'rs" (*Rape*, I, 124), providing thereby a variation on the motif of disguise or dissemblance. Sappho "at her toilet's greasy task" is inconsistently Sappho "fragrant at an ev'ning Mask" (*Epistle to a Lady*, 25-26). The absurd disjunction between one identity and another indicates the distance between artifice and art, between false and true naming (libels, for example, and satire), analogous to that between the ludicrous and despicable "Temple of Infamy" and the *Temple of Fame*. The made *thing* that is Sappho is sister to Belinda conjured under the rubric of "Cosmetic Powers." And this correspondence admits the introduction of another between Eloisa and the "other" she invokes, the sainted sister and vestal virgin enjoined to save her from herself, to metamorphose her identity from the "you" she has become into the "I" she desires to be. Obviously, this is a strategy susceptible to substantial variation, to be played now one way and now another. In the *First Satire,* the made *thing* is not the self, but the potentially self-betraying instrumentality wielded by the poet. Only by these means can satire be justified, for only in this way can it be secured against effective appropriation by the selfhood, the internally subversive and power-seeking "other." On the contrary, it is the component reality of the "other" that satire reveals, the "other" that eludes the punitive retribution of the law.

As a poem about art and history, the *First Satire* gathers the shadowy identities of the *Essay on Man,* reconstituting the interior drama of that poem into one of contemporary personages disposed on the historical field. Simultaneously, the poem is an apologia for the purposiveness of the ruling passion, disposing its similar manifestations within the continuum of a bardic tradition. At this late stage it seems unnecessary to emphasize again an allusive mode that sustains complex relations to an unfolding body of poetry, Pope's own. The *First Satire* does not violate Pope's design; it merely transposes its elements from one plane to another, another act of metamorphosis that may be equally characterological or formal, a principal of behavior or genre. This fluency bespeaks the coherence of an imagination that posits the totality of its meanings as a function of a complex symbolism, organizing its various structural principles so as to drive his poems into various contexts, and thus to break them down and recreate them again. It is a continual process of reformulation, analogous perhaps to the making of a long poem by combining its discrete parts into one entity. But reformulation itself posits process, disintegration and reintegration, mythologizing and demythologizing, and posits the terms in which categorical absolutes (nature, history, etc.) are validly recomposed as we move from one dimension of meaning to another, from one poem or set of poems to another. The object of this method is to guarantee veracity; crudely put it is an intellectual *system.* More nicely, it is the result of an "inner logical discipline" that creates the genuine "language of allegory."[6]

And it is within this general context that the self-exposing-
ly ironic comedy of *To Arbuthnot* takes its meaning, demanding
from us a recognition of Pope's identity transposed, from the
poet to the man, and requiring our acknowledgment of the self-
revelatory veracity of the medium itself. The relation between
the *First Satire* and *To Arbuthnot* is that between a public and a
private self, between history and autobiography, between poetry as a social institution and the poet as a man. As such the
relation tends to confirm Pope's habit of dialectic, of playing off
against each other two opposing perspectives that, taken
together, constitute a new and larger entity. This is the method
of the *Essay on Man* and the *Dunciad,* of *To Burlington* and *To
Bathurst,* of *To a Lady* and *To Cobham,* and even of the *Rape* and
Eloisa. It would be an overstatement to insist upon this kind of
activity as a perfectly consistent methodological principle governing Pope's poetry, but it is not, I think, unreasonable to propose such a procedure as a function of an imagination that
conceives in terms of thesis and antithesis, and builds its larger
structures on the basis of elaborately designed tensions beween
opposing principles.

On the other hand, as I have suggested, Pope defines his
concepts within related dramatic contexts, so that the exploration of *nature* within the *Essay on Man* is leagued to the variant
inquiry of *To Burlington,* and both poems are linked to a comparable study of the same term in *Eloisa* and the *Rape.* As a poetic
method it makes critical control over any single work nearly
impossible, for it requires the reader to continually re-encounter
Pope's poetry as an accretive and cumulative text, and not
merely as a documentary index to moral or conceptual values,
the method, by and large, of nineteenth-century Pope criticism.
The priority of *nature* (with its particular associations) in the *Rape*
blends with the meanings of *nature* in *Eloisa.* No meaning
assumes any special priority independent of its context, and
each context qualifies the other in relation to such contingent
values as devotion, love, and sexuality. We tend, that is, to discover that what we may wish to take as absolutes are always
slipping into the status of relative propositions, and that the

dramatic situation retains thereby its priority. I propose this argument only as a rather belated rejoinder to the Arnoldian critique, which was rhetorical rather than Aristotelian. A truly dramatic criticism applied to Pope would, I trust, reach some of the same conclusions about him that I have reached in this study.

The *Epistle to Arbuthnot* is not, strictly speaking, one of the Imitations, though Butt refers to its "easy Horatian talk."[7] Pope was busily writing it in 1734, while Arbuthnot was dying, and its employment of Arbuthnot as interlocutor differs significantly, say, from the use of Fortescue in the *First Satire*.[8] Moreover, *To Arbuthnot* answers the other work in a very specific way: the poet as heir to the past yields to the poet as man besieged and confounded by the present. In the one poem the poet's passions are lawful, historically justified by the satirist's traditional role; in the other his passions are comedic, tumultuous, justified by nothing more than his own failure to control the fools and knaves who rush upon him. If, then, the *First Satire* moves toward the delineation of the ordered and pellucid poet, *To Arbuthnot* rushes toward picturing the disorder and confusion of man trapped in the moment, a victim of those seeking fame and himself a victim of his own. Following the bardic vision of the *First Satire*, *To Arbuthnot* is the comedy of the performing self of the poet.

Aden remarks that "a case can be made for Warburton's procedure in giving some of the speeches to Arbuthnot in the 1751 edition of the *Works*."[9] I believe so too. There is no need to review the evidence for the poem as verse dialogue. Aden sums it up briefly, noticing among other things Butt's hedging on the subject: "The change from epistle to dialogue may be the work of Pope."[10] Our evidence can be derived internally, from the nature of the speaker and the dramatic situation Pope presents. Knoepflmacher comments on the "speaker's brilliant self-definition of his role as satirist."[11] It is a good place to begin, for it immediately poses *To Arbuthnot* against the *First Satire* and raises questions as to the differences of self-definition evident in each poem. Initially, Pope is a reasonable man besieged by fools: "All *Bedlam*, or *Parnassus*, is let out" (4), and his complaint about the reality from which he has fled is that it is random and inconsistent. Beyond this objection, the argument suggests that he is without a principle by which to discourage, or a desire by which to accommodate, the demands made upon him. In the putative *real*—the poem's fictive situation—the poet cannot function as a poet. He must, that is, behave as a man, and it is in this way that he is most vulnerable. From the outset the poem dramatizes the inadequacies of the speaker to control a situation that will not submit to his defensive stratagems. He does therefore what all men do in comparable circumstances—falls back upon his virtues and offers them as the cause of his misfortunes.

The long apologia beginning with line 125 and continuing until the Sporus portrait (305) is both autobiography and self-justification. Its bathetic self-dramatizations are equally rhetorical poses and self-revelations, insofar as the poem plays out the comedy of the performing "I" at its center. Ehrenpreis attacks the rhetorical analysis of persona in *To Arbuthnot* as it separates speaker from author, observing that once "this split is accomplished, the connection of the poem with history is destroyed."[12] But we are spared this conclusion by returning to the fictive situation. The poem is about Alexander Pope, but it is also by Pope. We need not destroy the autobiographical accuracy of the text to remark on the context within which the autobiography exists, that of verse dialogue. By anybody's account, an interlocutor speaks at least five times in the poem, although the 1751 edition also gives the last two lines to Arbuthnot. On each occasion except the fifth, he counsels prudence, advises restraint. His last interjection, at line 390, is the briefest of all: "What Fortune, pray?" It occurs while the speaker is in full career celebrating his parents' virtue, and if Pope cannot be silenced he may be encouraged in the harmless random discourse honoring father and mother. And if he cannot be checked, he can be mocked. Pope's *adversarius* here is not a Fortescue, and Pope is not a satirist *in the poem*. He is a man irritated by attack and demand, and although speaker (Pope) and author (Pope) are the same person, they are different figures at different times and in different roles. In other words, *To Arbuthnot* is a poem about Pope; its autobiographical veracity need not deflect us from the bathos informing the poem. That we should not be so deflected indicates Arbuthnot's purpose here. The poem provides sensible evidence of the dissociation of besieged speaker from author, and sufficient confirmation of that control exercised by the poet behind the poem, yet unavailable to the principal actor within the poem.

To avoid this conclusion we must argue, with Ehrenpreis, that the work's intention, grounded in fact, is "pseudo-rhetorical," a "conventional means of giving life to the speaker-poet's expression of his own views."[13] The other alternative is to suggest that the bathetic self-dramatizations are masks of the poet's own devising, personae chosen by him. Ehrenpreis's essay is directed against this latter position. But neither argument contends with the role of Arbuthnot, with an *adversarius* who is honored (and with good reason) far more than Fortescue. And it is through Arbuthnot that Pope, as author, communicates his distance from his speaking self. On this evidence we can build a case for a sustained complexity: the poem is poetic autobiography of a peculiarly witty sort, a structure of self-revelations in which speaker can be distinguished from author, though both are ultimately one. We shall shortly need to ask why Pope would want to write such a poem, but for the moment it is enough to notice that a complex authorial consciousness carries on relevant levels of awareness, self-justifying and self-mocking, and in the process pays tribute to Arbuthnot. If we then bring this work into relation with the larger context, it is evident that Pope is again constructing a performance of the self who is self-victimized, and the satirist self-satirized merely rings a variation on a pervasive theme.[14]

If the *First Satire* defines the emergent identity of the poet as satirist, and appeals to history to legitimize that role, *To Arbuthnot* focuses not on history but on man in the present moment, and man enmeshed in the moment is the world's

victim and his own. It is a fine Popeian thrust, and *To Arbuthnot*
brings it neatly home. The two works enforce Pope's characteristic act of coming round on his subject again. They illustrate an
ironist's state of mind, a skepticism that compels the linking of
radical alternatives to which a subject is made to submit. *To
Arbuthnot* looks back upon the *First Satire* and qualifies our
expectations of the poet who is also a man. Satire is an "impartial Glass," Pope warned, in which "what Spots (for Spots I
have) appear." *To Arbuthnot* demonstrates this truth while
admonishing the ego militant in its claims against the world.

Through Arbuthnot, Pope mediates the element of *play* in
the *Epistle*. Pope is and is not the one who knows, is and is not
his own subject. In another play, Arbuthnot is the glass in
which the reader reads Pope, even though Pope, in the poem,
refuses to read himself in the same glass. Yet at the same time
the poem is a glass through which we look back to the securely
self-justified author, now withdrawn and leaving us with his
"other," while enjoying the play he has initiated. It is another
sort of god-role, though obviously one with sufficient mind, and
it allows Pope to objectify the "other" and thus to undemonize
himself. The poem reveals Pope's "Spots," as the *First Satire*
told us it must, but such a ritual revelation (the act of writing
satire) again establishes the poet as knowing the price of knowledge and being willing to pay it. Nothing is more dunciadic than
paying the wrong price for the wrong knowledge, and it is this
mock that echoes within the *Rape*. In *To Arbuthnot*, self knowledge is antithetical to the mere factuality of the autobiographical
mode. Pope's speaker knows everything there is to know about
himself, yet the play of the poem is to withhold from him the
redemptive self-knowledge held within the poem's glass. It is
into this glass that he refuses to look. Here again a single metaphorical principle sustains a protracted meditation on *knowing*
and doubles back on the excoriations of the *Essay*'s "you," the
mon semblable of the poem's "I."

In *To Arbuthnot*, Pope is himself a variation of the hidden
god whose simulacrum within the world's body is all that can
ever be directly declared or apprehended, and whose presence

is behind those texts that are themselves manifestations of his knowing. One may guess at how such a recognition served the interests of a poet whose constant revision of his private self, in the letters, was a major occupation. All of this suggests a very perverse play on the sociality of self-love, which, it would seem, is inconsistently committed to public declaration, if only because such declaration must be mediated by various acts (texts) which simultaneously reveal and conceal, unhappily inviting and necessitating misreadings. And obviously it raises questions about the incoherence of the self and about the artistry that preserves the representations of the self and passes on an identity to posterity. Clearly, however, such reflections bear on Pope's occasional georgic temptations, to leave the world that is a diminished thing to the diminished things who act within it, to cultivate, for example, a single determinate meaning such as Twickenham, a text and a context of another kind.

The ironic mode of the speaker's vauntings thereby balances us between kinds of knowing. Pope, we say, is speaking the truth about himself, but truth has assumed the status of an idealized image of the poet and of the self who fulfills it. In other words, the poem details a vexatious relation between the selfhood and self-love, between the poet's investment in the pride of self and that true recognition of his function that is the legitimate purpose of his calling. Because of the ironic mode we recognize a distance between, say, Pope and the Sensibility poets. Weiskel observes how these later poets are tempted ''back into the safer, regressive precincts of narcissism, the renunciation of the gloomy egoist devoted to Solitude, Contemplation, or Melancholy.''[15] Such dark deities of the narcissistic sublime are courted by the poet seeking new sources of power and vision. Pope's own dark divinity in *To Arbuthnot* is pity (self-pity), the inversion of pride and thus another adjunct to the selfhood. In terms of the psychological myth informing the *Essay*, Pope's self-pity is an attempt to justify what he would have his auditor understand as a proper self-love. But if we are reading the poem as I suggest, that definition is one Arbuthnot refuses to accept.

It is also true that what the Horatian poems offered Pope

was a historical analog to his own role as satirist, and Horace functions as another source of authority for a poet vitally interested in such sources. The "Advertisement" to the *Imitations* makes this clear:

> The Occasion of publishing these Imitations was the Clamour raised on some of my Epistles. An Answer from Horace was both more full, and of more Dignity, than any I cou'd have made in my own person; and the Example of much greater Freedom in so eminent a Divine as Dr. Donne, seem'd a proof with what Indignation and Contempt a Christian may treat Vice or Folly, in ever so low, or ever so high, a Station. Both these Authors were acceptable to the Princes and Ministers under whom they lived.[16]

If the *Imitations* provide Pope with a center of personal authority, they also permit him, sheltered under this authority, to speak of his own anxieties both as poet and as man. The poems define another contest of alternative *voices* (*First Epistle*) similar to the alternative identities that in the *Essay* contend for mastery and dominance. In sum, the dialectical principle that poses the *Essay on Man* against the *Dunciad* (and self-love and selfhood in the *Essay*) is sustained within the *Imitations*. Clearly, the contest between Montaigne, Locke, Aristippus, and St. Paul, on the one side, and the dark powers represented by London and the voice that whispers "Be but Great" (101), on the other, is the humanist contest between authoritative history and the self that seeks its authority in itself (confirmed by the voice of London). These dark powers are the equivalent to mid-century solitude, contemplation, or melancholy, the voices solicited by the self in isolation, the voices of the gothic mode. What happens at mid-century amounts almost to a reversal of the humanist position: the dark powers are invoked as sources of energy, a kind of Faustian courtship of the demonic for the sake of appropriating (or realizing) proscribed powers (proscribed in the special sense of being antisocial). This line of inquiry allows us to glimpse the prophetic tone in Pope's poetry, and to understand how lucidly the conflict between alternative powers is set forth. The poets of mid-century who have escaped the containing formulations of Pope's *nature* and *history* seek for the source of their visions in those feelings that the greater writers before them (Spenser, Shakespeare, Milton) felt. The mid-century transmutes these early writers into the context of primitivism. When Weiskel discusses Collins's *Ode on the Poetical Character* he notes that ''Milton represents a poetic potentiality prior to the alienation of the divine and the natural, but this possibility is just now closing for the aspiring poet.''[17] Exactly, but the observation points to the essential difference between Collins and Pope, and virtually defines the premise on which the *Essay* is written.

For Pope, closure is a function of the will to power; to recognize this truth is the burden of the *Rape*, even as the relation between desire and closure animates Eloisa's despair in her poem. There the problem is focused on the relation between physical and spiritual love. Later the subject becomes self-love and social love. When we approach Pope in these terms we get the right sense of an extended subject, which, in the *Dunciad*, is metamorphosed into various corruptions of sexuality, including the lingering and abiding oedipal fantasy that distinguishes the relation between Cibber and his ''mighty Mother.'' Much of the *Dunciad*'s comedy is invested in the farcical behavior of the body: the duces are forever losing their footing, falling, slipping, diving, etc., as though they are in a crazy-house of their own making (which in fact is precisely where they are). And this crazy-house of nature incorporates and requires a perverse sexuality as the inevitable antithesis to the relation between man and nature specified in *To Burlington*. Pope is highly consistent in exploring the varieties of love, throughout his poetry, though we seldom think of him in these terms. What kinds of love are yet possible in the fallen world? And what kind of self-love, to come back to *To Arbuthnot*, is a form of self-betrayal? *To Arbuthnot* addresses this question, and in doing so its comedy borders the far darker comedy of the *Dunciad*. But another problem also arises, and this bears on the extent to which the poet may be tempted to ally himself with his own selfhood, to take himself, in other words, at his selfhood's evaluation. Arbuthnot is in the poem to prevent this occurrence, to permit Pope to explore his own susceptibility to self-pity without running the risk of being ensnared by it. If we think again of the *Dunciad* we may recognize that to some large extent it is simply a story of the kingdom of antipoetry that Cibber brings into being, the tale of the poet who chooses and is chosen by that kingdom in despair of the true realm of poetic vision.

Differently from the *Essay on Man*, but in a way that bears comparision, the *First Epistle* dissolves an illusory idea of priorities. The excitement of the work arises as we conceive of Pope listening to the various voices of the poem. To be kept from himself (41) suggests a discord in search of a principle of concord. And those who best release him to be himself are the spiritual doctors, Montaigne and Locke, Aristippus and St. Paul. To be oneself is to be free (''Sworn to no Master, of no Sect am I'' [24]), yet such freedom is qualified by ''Life's instant business'' (42). If the ''blood rebel[s] . . . / With wretched Av'rice, or as wretched Love,'' there are ''Words, and Spells, which can controll / (Between the Fits) this Fever of the soul'' (55-58). Such words are spoken by virtue, wisdom, and philosophy. They are opposed by ''London's voice'' (79) and one ''who whispers, 'Be but Great' '' (101). Yet the court and the people are enthralled: ''a King's a Lion'' and the ''People are a many-headed beast'' (120-21). To be under a spell is to be subject to ''some whimzy, or that Dev'l within / Which guides all those who know not what they mean'' (143-44). And the dark night of the mind is signified by ''Proteus, Merlin, any Witch'' (152). Rich and poor, king and people, eunuch (literally) and Sir Job are transformed beings, and such transformations are the fevers of the soul, the self enmeshed in its own desires. The drama of contraries embraces spiritual doctors and witch doctors, and the *First Epistle* is an allegory of the material world envisioned as enchanter,[18] the world realized as Circean transformer of man into beast. Not to know what one means is an abuse of the ruling passion, a failure of self-knowledge, a denial of God's datum.

The *First Epistle* is thus concerned with an exploration of those duplicities inhabiting self-consciousness, and though not exactly a psychomachia it leagues with both the *Essay on Man* and the *Dunciad* as it is attentive to the emergent powers within the self that usurp purpose and distort coherence. This is the fate of all those "who know not what they mean" or discover for themselves "how ill I with myself agree" (175). The determining ideas of the *Essay* are re-examined and re-applied to the special case of the poet. The myth of the concordant being self-orchestrating his ruling passion breaks down. He is a "Demigod" except when clouded by a "Fit of Vapours" (188). Both glory and jest, he recapitulates the indeterminateness of human nature, and the imagination becomes the instrument for creating fictions of identity. Horace says: *"Quo teneam vultus mutantem Protea nodo?"* (With what knot can I hold this face-changing Proteus?) Pope says that no knot can hold him (or Merlin, any witch), for these magicians are not eccentric to us but exist within, and if they are to be bound, it is with "Words, and Spells."

It is a question of who binds whom. To "lock up all the Functions of my soul" (40) is to transform the radiant center of human identity into a prison-house. To resist the demon within, however, is to enclose him within incantations that spring from the poetic word and its informing humanist wisdom. The *New Dunciad* is anticipated on the level of personal violation, and the poet's quest is for a lost but native nobility that the one greater man, Bolingbroke, is again petitioned to provide: "my Guide, Philosopher, and Friend" (177). Pope's tale here is of the self lost within itself ("That keep me from Myself" [41]); its ruling passion controverted by the devil within, a latent self-duplicity to be opposed by the evocation of the clarified self: "That Man divine whom Wisdom calls her own" (180). The struggle for the soul of man is what the poem is all about, and as it is so the conflict shifts from the *Essay's* generic inquiry into a more immediately personal drama. Yet the psychomachian elements of the *Epistle* require that we view Pope as a figure assisted in his struggle against evil on earth and in his own mind, and thus as a variation of the pilgrim-knight as poet, aided by the chevalier Bolingbroke, himself a variation of the grace-lending Christ.[19]

Earlier I noted how a unit like *glass* functions to keep some texts in proximity to one another. *Whispering* is another element of the same kind, reducible to a particular mode of address that keeps the larger mythic context before the reader. In Belinda's "Morning-Dream" a "glitt'ring" youth "Seem'd to her Ear his winning Lips to lay, / And thus in Whispers said, or seem'd to say" (I,25-26). At the close of the *Temple of Fame* "One came, me-thought, and whisper'd in my Ear" (498). Here, in the *First Epistle*, "A Voice there is that whispers in my ear" (11). What do we make of this whispering if not a sensibility alert to its own intuitions, and yet at least on one occasion equally alert to the psychic subversions that such intuitions may signify. G. K. Hunter makes the interesting remark that Pope "believed that the Frame of Order should not be accepted passively; it requires its martyrs and witnesses to demonstrate against any betrayal of standards . . . , and for Pope the basis of this witness must always be the individual sensibility of the poet, which gives him access to truths which are concealed from others by the disorders of real life."[20] But surely the matter is not so simple, for what happens to the poet when he becomes involved, as in *To Arbuthnot*, with the disorders of real life? And, moreover, what happens to anybody, Belinda included, who becomes so involved? How does one then bear true witness, maintain a cause, attack an enemy, judge between a truth and a falsity *whispered* in the ear?

To my mind such queries point toward the problem inherent in self-knowledge, the basis of true speaking and true hearing, and return us to *To Arbuthnot*, wherein true speaking simply cannot be heard for what it is. I believe this situation always has within it what Tuve signifies when she says that "the large literature of virtues battling with vices, which we are accustomed to think of solely as a great tableau of the psycho-machia we call the moral struggle, had running through it another kind of image as well—the spirit's quest for a lost but native noblesse."[21] On the one hand, this quest seems always on

the brink of giving up the world, abandoning it to its own inera-
dicable subversions, and thus permitting the self's orientation
towards its own acts of soul-making and soul-saving. On the
other hand, self-love *is* social. I find these separate topics subject
to endless re-orchestration in Pope. They seem always to invoke
a variation of the same quest for significant data, the evidential
basis of action, which again must remind us of the word opened
to the alternatives it conceals, of the self opened also to the possibilities inherent within it. Thus the ruling passion is a "direction," instinct another datum, sense an intuition. The "Frame
of Order" may require its martyrs, but it may also indifferently
accept the sacrifices of its fools. How does one finally arbitrate
the difference? Pope's quest seems remarkably innocent of an
itinerary: "As drives the storms, at any door I knock, / And
house with Montagne now, or now with Lock" (24-25). Very
good, but on the principle of any port in a storm, what then?
"Back to my native Moderation slide, / And win my way by
yielding to the tyde" (33-34). Is moderation experientially
derived, or is it what it seems to be: "native" and thus another
datum? The poem keeps positing the possible coalescence of a
"me" and a "Myself," now subversively kept apart, that
requires what for its unity: a *Nichomachean* mean, a *concordia discors*? The incompanionable reality of a "me" and a "Myself"
restates the internal betrayals of the *Essay*, the subversion of a
"me" akin to that which threatens reason. If the defilement of
the "I" is at the heart of things, no wonder then the self's anxiety about who speaks the privileged and whispered word.

    In the fifth book of *Paradise Lost*, Eve wakes to tell her
Satan-inspired dream to Adam:

> Close at mine ear one call'd me forth to walk
> With gentle voice, I thought it thine; it said,
> Why sleep'st thou *Eve?* now is the pleasant time,
> The cool, the silent, save where silence yields
> To the night-warbling Bird, that now awake. . . .
>
> (35-40)

Just previously, Adam, "her hand soft touching, whisper'd

thus. Awake" (17). And again: "Such whispering wak'd her" (26). The voice close at her ear and Adam's voice seemed to her one voice, having the same purpose, to "wake" her from sleep. In Pope's text, *whispering* is the unit that recapitulates or, more exactly, summons division, the normal state of the Popeian hero.

If it is to the resolution of division that the *First Epistle* is addressed, we might expect the poem to continue to play upon the issue by inquiring into causality. Thus the question: "Say, does thy blood rebel, thy bosom move / With wretched Av'rice, or as wretched Love?" (55-57)." Like rebel nature of *Eloisa*, rebel blood is a unit in the figuration of the myth and an occasion of division. Pope's text (not Horace's) continues to elaborate just what division involves, and it involves the separation of the self into its warring components, a conversion under the aegis of an internal voice that whispers its subversive doctrine. Wretched avarice is a lust, as, I presume, is "as wretched" love. These passions are unhappily companionable in a misreading of the divine datum or a willful perversion of it. We might want to say that love is as wretched because it has fallen to the condition of avarice, and thus suffers a dislocation, that each is overly fond of its object and, being obsessed by the object, can be said to lust after it. For such reasons the lines draw in their wake the un-Horatian reference: "Slave to a Wife, or Vassal to a Punk" (62). I am reading this line as further explication of "as wretched Love," of the consequence of uxoriousness, and I wish just narrowly to resist re-allegorizing avarice and love as the fallen companions in the fallen garden.

I am not quite sure what the text licenses at this juncture, though it is obvious that the poet who knows the redemptive word ("Know, there are Words, and Spells, which can controll / [Between the Fits] this Fever of the soul") is about to speak (whisper?) it: "All that we ask is but a patient Ear" (64). The poetic vocation is listening to the word and speaking of it. Surely, Pope's text is here playing upon the Edenic myth, recapitulating it, as it were, yet within the Horatian frame, an overwriting placed upon the Horatian text correspondent to the loosely formulated eighteenth-century notion of "imitation." We fall through Horace's text into Pope's more profound text, and the sort of action I am describing here correlates with the transposition of the *Rape* into the Horatian mode of *To a Lady*. In this regard, much of Pope's writing is actually a re-writing of other texts, either his or, as here, Horace's (the Latin poet's *Epistle* into Pope's *Epistle*). This sort of imaginative enterprise tends to provide, within Pope's canon, a body of homologous texts.

When Barthes explores the Racinian hero he asks the primary question: "Who is this Other from whom the hero cannot detach himself? First of all—that is, most explicitly—it is the Father. . . . The Father is the Past."[22] In Pope's texts we have seen various versions of the "other." In the *Essay*, the "other" is the resident "you," the dark primordial interloper and seducer whose purpose is to estrange reason from self-love, and to displace the latter by an*other*. Yet the "other" is equally the father figured as "Guide, Philosopher, and Friend." Hence Bolingbroke, whose admonitory presence in the text is first seen as an intrusion: "St. John, whose love indulg'd my labours past / Matures my present, and shall bound my last! / Why will you break the Sabbath of my days?" (1-3). The question is designed to remind us of the unwelcome presence of the "other" as the self prepares to elude judgment and thus escape its eye: "ah let me hide my Age!" (5). It is not the voice of this "other" that Pope wishes to hear, for he knows that it will urge upon him the relentless duty to which he has responded over and again in the past, but from which he now wishes to claim the right of surcease, to inhabit "Life's cool evening satiate of applause" (9). Thus, in the Barthesian sense, the father is the past, but what is equally the past is the original divisiveness from the father that continues to inhabit the present. And what is being asked for is the freedom to serve no master: "Sworn to no Master, of no Sect am I" (24). So that the father is imaged exactly as he appears to the poet: a task*master* who binds the son to his authority. This is to re-imagine the master-slave relation of *Eloisa*, the difference being that Eloisa's master is a tyrant to whom she willingly enslaves herself, whereas Pope's is the father he would deceive. Thus Pope's claim to arbitrate his own duality, to distinguish the identities of his voices, is another claim to freedom consequent upon self-knowledge.

He must therefore in his own text demonstrate the talismanic power of the word he wields, which is his ultimate claim to authority. Yet it would seem that the word can only recapitulate the antitheses inherent within it: " 'Tis the first Virtue, Vices to abhor; / And the first Wisdom, to be Fool no more" (65-66). True enough, but how does one avoid washing one's hands with Pilate? I take it that in the *First Epistle* self-knowledge continues to be the issue, a knowledge that derives its authority from the divine design of the *Essay on Man* now displaced onto the *Epistle*. To break faith with that design is to be invaded by "some whimzy, or that Dev'l within / Which guides all those who know not what they mean" (143-44). To know not what you mean is to re-create the internal subversions of the *Rape* or *To Bathurst* or the *Essay*, for self-knowledge compels the figuration that Pope transposes from text to text. This activity by the poet seems the only way to posit its inexhaustible vitality, its endless pertinence. A coherence invades the text that will not let language slide into the mere relevance of moral admonition, or lodge final authority in the individual sensibility of the poet. Thus, in one sense, the *First Epistle* is an act whereby the poet self-consciously dispossesses himself of his power, claims almost to have no power, and calls upon Bolingbroke to lend his grace to end the ceaseless cycle of ascendant and descendant voices, imaged in the poem as yet another variation of the darksome round: "I plant, root up, I build, and then confound, / Turn round to square, and square again to round" (169-70). And he solicits the power of a "Guide, Philosopher, and Friend" who is himself a *maker*: "Who ought to make me . . . / That Man divine" (179-80). Finally, Pope's imperative ("ought") is justified by the knowledge (self-knowledge) of an abiding duality resolved only in the grace-lending charity of his initiation-master.

What does this say, then, about the "individual sensibility of the poet"? As I read the three Horatian imitations, they express a very substantial dubiety about that sensibility, show how at any moment it may be betrayed by the very principle of subjectivity on which it resides. Thus Atossa, for example, or Villiers and Timon. Hence the appeal to a heraldic tradition, or to an authority outside the self that must come to discipline that sensibility to an order not of its own making. Perhaps this very authority principle is what the Wartons sensed as a diminishment of what they also sensed as their own humanity, a pre-Blakeian "hardening" of the laws governing human nature. Yet one of the crucial questions is why Pope should return to the *Dunciad* years after its three-book form had been completed. It seems to me that the return is made mandatory by the very betrayals to which a sensibility is subject and despite the various data (sense, taste, ruling passion, etc.) that Pope summons. If Pope reads Satan as a fable of that sensibility possessed, as I am inclined to believe he does, then it is precisely what cannot be constrained by the wisdom (the *voices*) immanent in history. Satan, in sum, is not a good listener; in Bloom's terms he is too strong to be schooled. This awareness necessitates Pope's strategy in the *Essay on Man*, a kind of bullying of the "you" by an elaborate rhetorical attack upon it. But the *First Epistle*'s ironic concession is that "Words, and Spells . . . can controll / (*Between the Fits*) this Fever of the soul" (my italics). Clearly, "Fever" signifies the irrationality of the sublime moment, and "Words" a forcible restraint, the white magic of spiritual doctoring. Pope's image is of Satan as the powerful sick man of the self, whose sickness is his greatness, fevered by the conviction that what is offered as the law is merely a trick by which power perpetuates itself, sustains its authority, compels submission. This was, after all, Eloisa's view of things. Pope seems never for a moment to have doubted his understanding of Satan, but he may very well have come to feel that he had never rationalized it within a suitable vision, and hence the return at the end of his life to the *Dunciad*.

Yet a not incidental purpose of the *Epistle* is to set the satirist in relation to the man, an act of soul-making, a dedication to spiritual doctoring that takes its inception from Pope's reference to the "Sabbath of my days." The sabbath is at once a respite and a dedication, a turning from the world to return to the world. *To Arbuthnot* bespeaks the sentimental language of the besieged poet; the *First Epistle* bespeaks an encounter with the "Functions of my soul," and continues thereby to orchestrate a relation between the private and the public man. There is surely something to Hunter's idea that the *Imitations* "involve primarily a substitution of the order of the individual mind for the Order of the external world . . . as a basis for belief and action, a substitution of subjective evaluation for the traditional acceptance of received values, objectively justified."[23] Yet there is only *something* to it, for Pope's spiritual doctors are themselves the voices of a sustaining wisdom, one that looks from the world's body to the human soul. The man who hears the voice of the selfhood (" 'Be but Great' ") is abandoned to his own subjectivity, to a center that turns out once again to be a trap in another variation of the prevailing metaphor of center and circumference. The obligatory task here is that of focusing attention inward, of listening with the unsectarian ear, and "Late as it is," of "put[ting] my self to school" (47).

I earlier cited Angus Fletcher on the subject of demonological possession and referred his remarks to the *Epistle to a Lady*. The Horatian *First Epistle* brings us round again to the demonic voices that are themselves the disguised agencies of the selfhood and thus to the delusions that arise from subjectivity. Following this reflection, we can return to the ambiguous valuation of *blood* in *Windsor-Forest*, and to the working out of the addiction to blood-letting that the poem dramatizes. It seems equally necessary to recognize that Pope's obsessive or addictive being is what the sublimity of self comes to: in effect, the closed circle of being, a kind of hell, which in turn determines another fall and another imprisonment. When the self falls, it thinks it has risen, and this misperception determines its blindness to the inverted reality that has come into being. The head is now the foot, the bottom become the top. The world turns upside down and hell is heaven. Pope signifies as much in the *Dunciad* by a kind of comedy of the body referred to earlier. Within the crazy-house of nature we "reason downward, till we doubt of God" (IV, 472) because the mind is deluded and its normal actions are inverted. When this happens, everything else is predictable: "Virtue [is] local, all Relation scorn" (IV, 479). Pride, confederate with erring reason, is now enthroned, and man's imperial faculty, will, is literally mystified: "Of nought so certain as our Reason still, / Of nought so doubtful as of Soul and Will" (IV, 48-82).

The relation between body and soul is equivalent to that between nature and grace and informs the *Epistle to Burlington.* The good gardener is there instructed to "treat the Goddess like a modest fair, / Nor over-dress, nor leave her wholly bare." The care of the body is extended into the treatment of the specific place, wherein the good gardener "varies shades from shades," etc., and is advised to "Still follow Sense, of ev'ry Art the Soul." From the relation between soul and body is born those "Idea's" that distinguish Burlington. And we may further trace this conception into the *Essay on Man:* "All are but parts of one stupendous whole, / Whose body Nature is, and God the soul" (I, 267-68). Similarly, Pope employs the idea of the displaced or usurped body in the *Epilogue to the Satires, Dialogue I,* where "pale Virtue [is] carted in . . . [Vice's] stead!" (150). The fallen body that is virtue intrudes within the anarchic disorder of England. Beyond such substitution, the body is vulgarized by being "all liv'ry'd o'er with foreign Gold" (155). This sort of action is figured in the *Rape of the Lock,* and Belinda's excessive adornment of body is a reflection of the corruption of soul it signifies. In itself the idea has a long history of which Fletcher reminds us by commenting on Hugh of St. Victor's *Soliloquy on the Earnest Money of the Soul:* "The whole Christian life-pattern is set forth here in cosmetic terms, even to the mirror (the *speculum*) in which the lady examines her adorned self."[24] And by this route we may return to the *First Satire,* to Pope's description of satire as a "Medium" or "impartial Glass" in which the "Soul stood forth."

Beyond this immediate context, Pope's dualism bears on the critical precepts of the *Essay on Criticism.* There it is said that

> *Art* from that Fund [of Nature] each *just Supply* provides,
> Works *without* Show, and *without Pomp* presides:
> In some fair Body thus th' informing Soul
> With Spirits feeds, with Vigour fills the whole,
> Each Motion guides, and ev'ry Nerve sustains;
> *It self unseen,* but in th' *Effects,* remains.

(74-79)

The art of critical explication is the reduction of the body to its informing principle, the revelation of an irreducible and determining "Spirit" that permeates the text and makes it what it is. Pope's metaphors of body and soul, surface and essence, extend to include the distinction between "Expression" and "Thought" (*Essay on Criticism*, 318) and compel a sense of his own poetic. For what is contained within the texture of language, its enveloping network, is the mind at the center. Translated within the terms of my own argument, Pope's text is the expressive form for the subject at its center, for the protean reality of the myth which demands its various embodiments, yielding finally to a holistic imagination. The Popeian virtuosity is, then, a product of a lifetime's assessment of the body of literature, its treasury of historically recoverable forms that fulfill variously the complex ideational reality of the myth. Body and soul thus dance within the multiple harmonics of form and idea, and as that dance unfolds before us, we witness the myth disposed into the various generic patterns that now invoke Milton or Homer and again Horace or Ovid. It is difficult to imagine a more complex poetic enterprise or one that more greatly tests the resources of a literary imagination. It should give us, however, some extended sense of what history and nature mean to Pope and of how his texts assume that burden. And because all of this is true, the *Dunciad* could never be trifling of any sort, could never be merely *satiric* in the limitedly topical application that word occasionally assumes.[25] However sprightly the *Dunciad* may be, it is the most tragic utterance of which the eighteenth century was capable, the final frightening creation of a body without a soul, a god without a mind.

The Dunciad

If the *Essay on Man* illuminates the meaning of self-love at the center of that poem, the *Dunciad* reveals the figurative identity of Dulness as the triumph of the selfhood. The latter work takes us back to our beginnings in Pope, to the goddess Rumour and her kingdom in the world. Dulness is Pope's last version of his enslaving deities, those obsessions of the mind that haunt the mythopoeic imagination and are as evident in Pope as in Blake. Like the *Essay on Man*, the *Dunciad* has itself suffered from misapprehensions, but where the *Essay* has seemed to many readers both abstract and uncomfortably chilly, the *Dunciad* has presented itself as a sort of "nasty trifling," and has contributed more than its share to the once prevalent fiction of the "wicked wasp of Twickenham." Johnson gives the poem short shrift, pausing only long enough to debate the morality of Pope's motives and impale them upon the lance of one of his more pejorative judgments: the *Dunciad* "affords perhaps the best specimen that has yet appeared of personal satire ludicrously pompous."[26]

If we do not share Johnson's opinion, much of the credit goes to the excellent studies by Williams, Sitter, and others. But it is true that for many readers the *Dunciad* warms the imagination only in comparison to the *Essay*, and Pope's largest and most important works have seemed not merely unrelated to each other, but unhappy examples of extreme tendencies within his imagination. Yet everything within Pope's works leads, as I have been arguing, to these poems, and everything also leads from them. The *New Dunciad* incorporates little that has not been in Pope's texts from the beginning, but it does capaciously bring into existence the divinity that rules the selfhood, and defines the immanence of that goddess as fully as the *Essay* reveals the God within man. The usurpation of Britannia, with which the first book begins, is the debauchery of Albion, the evocation of the false form of the generative mother, and Britannia's "sleep" (7) is the nightmare of England. Book I signifies the reversal of the envisioned future that concludes *Windsor-Forest*, the union of Anne and Father Thames, and it reverses as well the laughing Ceres's re-assumption of the land that culminates *To Burlington*. The first book is not only a demonic invasion of Britannia, but a figuring of the form that invasion takes, and it is therefore a copulative fantasy, a salacious night of the mind. Britannia's sleep correlates inversely to the awakening of Bolingbroke in the *Essay on Man*, and the one greater man is here displaced by the one lesser man, by Cibber the votary of darkness. The *Dunciad* is the *Essay* inverted, for as the latter speaks to the creative action that makes man what he can be, the former addresses a nature whose origins have been obscured and whose reality is appropriately veiled. For all of its local and topical satire, the *Dunciad* details the displacement of the divine that is at the heart of pride's usurpation in the *Essay on Man*. Cibber's demonization is the corruption of the ruling passion in action, and the polity of fraud, obsession, and denial that pervades the kingdom of mind and the extended realm of human culture is causally related to the psychological myth disposed across the pages of the *Essay*. Though I have chosen to treat the *Dunciad* last, and as a complete work, I by no means wish to dissociate it from its legitimate place in the progress of Pope's imagination. Through the reiterated theme of predator and prey, explicit in the relation between Cibber and his "mighty Mother," to the motif of closure and confinement in Book IV, the *Dunciad* echoes and restates the major preoccupations of early and later works. Thus the generational heats of Book I, the obscenity of fructification, recall the prolific confusions of Rumour in *The Temple of Fame*. Answering Cibber's prayer, responding to the "hecatomb" that is, like Timon's, his offering to her, the "mighty Mother" chooses her son and consort.

The word *hecatomb*, repeated now and again in Pope's poetry (and at critical places in the text), suggests itself as another figurative unit within the myth. The meaning of hecatomb as a great public sacrifice, and thus an element of primitive religious ritual, is a recurrently morbid component in the myth of selfhood, a primitivism that Pope persistently isolates as an object of revulsion. The relation between hecatomb and the demonic

enlarges our context, so much so that we should be able to propose a cluster: selfhood-hecatomb-demonic. Any one of these
three will summon the others or stand for them. Pope's 1735
note to line 155 of *To Burlington* comments on his textual reference to hecatomb: "The proud festivals of some men are here
set forth to ridicule, where pride destroys the ease. . . ." His use
of "proud" and "pride" suggests the point I am making. The
myth of the selfhood (pride and erring reason) requires the unit
hecatomb. Commonly, also, "temple" or "altar" will be linked
to it. Thus in *To Burlington*, "No, 'tis a Temple, and a Hecatomb" (156), and in the *Dunciad*, "These an altar raise: / An
hecatomb of pure, unsully'd Lays / That altar crowns" (I, 157-
59). When Belinda invokes her own selfhood, she does so at an
altar (I, 127), and what is sacrificed are the various goods of the
world ("Unnumber'd Treasures" [129]) enlisted in the "sacred
Rites of Pride" (128). Thus the cluster: rites of pride-selfhood-
altar (temple)-hecatomb-demonic. These units, certainly not
exhaustively listed here, suggest the association in Pope's imagination between myth and ritual, and the sketch I have made
should help us to understand the relation between satire and
myth in the *Dunciad* and in the *Rape*.

However absurd and trivial Cibber may be in himself, and
however inconsequential the affairs of a London coquette, Pope
is not merely writing satire. He is demonstrating Cibber's and
Belinda's relation to the myth of selfhood, and his language consistently invokes the myth. We cannot avoid it any more than
his characters can escape it; they are not only caught within it
but composed of it. Equally, their freedom is compromised by
the actions they are self-condemned to choose. On the other
hand, self-love is social, meaning, in effect, circles opening
beyond circles, a series of related structures that depend upon
one another and yet escape one another. This figure is the form
that freedom assumes in Pope's imagination: variation within
unity.

Dulness's action is to impose a regressive infantilism upon
the body of Albion, to "suckle Armies, and dry-nurse the land"

(316). In Eden, however, there "is no Mother-God. . . . Mother-worship is womb-worship, a desire to prolong the helplessness of the perceiver and his dependence on the body of nature which surrounds him."[27] This "body" is another "jetty bow'r" (II, 335), a place of illusory sexual bliss over which the "Mighty Mother" (I, 1) presides, and is simply another version of the fool's paradise or "darksom round." Within this new special place, sexual expression finds fulfillment in generic confusion: "Tragedy and Comedy embrace; / . . . Farce and Epic get a jumbled race" (69-70). The noble line of poets is progressively degenerative and Philips follows Tate, whereas Eusden succeeds Blackmore. In this context, frenzy begets on folly, Bays's breast breeds monsters, and Cibber's works are the "Fruits of dull Heat" (126). Cibber is surrounded by "Embryo" and "much Abortion" (121), "Sinking from thought to thought," falling into the "vast profound!" (118). As he spirals downward he is seized by Dulness at the level of unconscious life, which is what embryos and abortions obviously signify, and what Cibber's existence as "Bug" (130) further establishes. His fall is not precipitated by Dulness, but is the occasion for her to build her kingdom in the world, for Dulness cannot act upon the world unless the selfhood grants it access and this Cibber's prayer permits. His "altar" (159) raised to her is very much like Pope's other altars and has much the same effect. In the parodic inversion of the *Essay*, Cibber is not the prophet of Dulness, but is himself prophesied by Tate and Philips and others like them. He is the Anti-Christ or the negation of the Word, and he comes to establish the kingdom of Dulness on earth.

If we step back from the first book, we witness an aging and idiot goddess seeking a mate. Her intended mate is also her disciple, son, and consort, and he worships her with works "born in sin" (225). The reward for his devotion is to be graced by the "ample presence" (261) of the goddess (an allusion to, though also a parody of, Fame's swelling size), and to be conducted to her "sacred Dome" (265), where Dulness "plann'd th' Imperial seat of Fools" (272). The revelation of her mysteries

("Here to her Chosen all her works she shews" [273]) precedes the announcement of Cibber's kingdom and of her desire to propagate her image through the land. As the vision consolidates, it takes the form of a coronation and forecasts Dulness as the nursing-mother of England. It is Cibber's task to render her meaning incarnate, and the figural reality of his appearance has been implicit in the line of prophetic descent, that "sure succession down from Heywood's days" (98), that runs from Pryn to Defoe, from Blackmore to Eusden, from Tate to Philips.

These remarks bear on Pope's reasons for rewriting the 1728 *Dunciad*. In the earlier version of the poem, there is no reference to Britannia, to Dulness as nursing-mother, to her daughters, Bawdry and Billingsgate, to Theobald's works as prostitutes, or to works born in sin. Perhaps the most notable change is from "Books and the Man I sing" (A, 1) to "The Mighty Mother, and her son . . . / I sing" (B, 1-3). All these changes enforce the figurative meaning of Cibber, emphasizing the disordered state of sin preceding the coming of the mighty mother and the typology of the prophetic line. As Auerbach explains, a figural analysis

> establishes a connection between two events or persons in such a way that the first signifies not only itself but also the second, while the second involves or fulfills the first. The two poles of a figure are separated in time, but both, being real events or persons, are within temporality. They are both contained in the flowing stream which is historical life, and only the comprehension, the *intellectus spiritualis*, of their interdependence is a spiritual act.[28]

In the *Essay on Man*, God is within temporality, manifest in the ruling passion, the grace within being that is evidence of his continuing presence in the world. So too is Dulness within Cibber, the precise content of the selfhood, and if we look to the changes Pope made in the 1743 text we notice that most of them intensify the poem's theodicy. Cibber's prayer concludes with a fatherly benediction upon his own works:

> O! pass more innocent, in infant state,
> To the mild Limbo of our Father Tate:

Or peaceably forgot, at once be blest
In Shadwell's bosom with eternal Rest!
Soon to that mass of Nonsense to return,
Where things destroy'd are swept to things unborn.

(237-42)

Cibber's limbo is the figural reality of the Cave of Poverty and Poetry, its "spiritual womb and tomb."[29] In the A version of the text, Theobald's works were conceived in an alehouse and will end there; they are merely "Unstall'd, unsold" (A, 198). Cibber's works are "born in sin"; their "smutty sisters walk the streets" (B, 230). Thus Pope's pun; they will be sold in the streets and end in hell, whereas those works "purify'd by flames" (227) will return quietly to that non-existence that is their fate. The tear that steals from Cibber upon conclusion of his prayer is a "portentous sign of Grace!" (243). Pope nods in the direction of *Eloisa:* "Devotion's self shall steal a thought from heav'n, / One human tear shall drop, and be forgiv'n" (*Eloisa to Abelard*, 357-58). But Cibber is not devotion's self and he shall not be forgiven. The additions of sin, prostitution, and limbo imply a developed perspective that looks beyond the comedy of bad writing to the latent figural reality, thereby explaining the judgments passed on bad writing and those guilty of it:

> The world beyond . . . is God's design in active fulfillment. In relation to it, earthly phenomena are on the whole merely figural, potential, and requiring fulfillment. This also applies to the individual souls of the dead: it is only here, in the beyond, that they attain fulfillment and the true reality of their being. Their career on earth was only the figure of this fulfillment. In the fulfillment of their being they find punishment, penance, or reward.[30]

The reality of Cibber's works in time is that of *fallen* children of a sinful father. Their misspent lives will be judged in relation to God's design, and for this reason they will be returned to that "Chaos dark and deep, / Where nameless Somethings in their causes sleep" (55-56), or consigned to that limbo "Where things destroy'd are swept to things unborn." Cibber's perversion of self-love is a violation of grace, and Pope drives home his tear as a calculated irony. Occurring at his ''altar'' to Dulness, it gathers into itself the references to devotion in the earlier poems. In place of the *genius loci,* who in *To Burlington* is the ''Genius of the Place,'' in *Windsor-Forest* is Father Thames, and in the *Temple of Fame* is Fame herself, is substituted the obscure mother whose mystery-temple is the ''sacred Dome'' to which Dulness conducts Cibber.

To understand the dome it is necessary to return to the Cave of Poverty and Poetry. Taken together, they are a miracle of rare device, a single unified reality, and thus the negative form of the holy structure made by the true poet. The cave and dome comprise the cosmogony of the *Dunciad,* and Cibber's movement is from the underworld of cave to the upper world of dome, itself a parody of the epic hero's progress or, as in the *Divine Comedy,* of the visionary's journey from lower to higher. But the cave and dome are also the completed body of the egg, that ''new Saturnian age of Lead'' that Dulness will ''hatch'' (28). Once we put all this together, we see the action of the first book. It is the movement from an underworld to an upper world, in the course of which the revealed form of the goddess is made apparent to the hero, and the consummation of the book is the making of the holy structure that is the goddess's egg. Cibber is the initiate into the mysteries of universal design, the hero worthy of becoming the consort (''monarch'') to Dulness, and joining with her in dominion over the leaden age about to be hatched.[31] The selfhood, embodied in Cibber, summons the jealous god, Dulness, who veils the reality of the divine presence and takes possession of the human kingdom.

Much has been said about the ''excremental vision'' of Book II, and most scholars have felt with Brower that it does not offer ''a truly heroic measure of the little world of the poem, or a sense of a more complex evaluation of any sort.''[32] There is some reason for feeling this way. The urinating contest and the tapestried reminder of Curll's ''fresh vomit run[ning] for ever green!'' (156) seem to lack any special significance, though the covenantal meaning of ''Jove's bright bow'' (173) keeps us focused on the inversions of the Christian context and reminds

us allusively of parallel Homeric and biblical texts. Yet the urina-
tors and the disgorger link associatively with the "lake" (69)
deposited by Curll's Corinna, with Cloacina's "black grottos"
(98), with the "silver flood" (274) fed by the "disemboguing
streams" of Fleet-ditch (271), and with the "jetty bow'rs below"
(335), wherein Nigrina and Merdamante vie for the love of
Smedley. Pope's symbolism is by no means applicable to all the
"high heroic Games" (18)—the flattering and braying contests
stand outside it—but it points to an underlying reality of sexual
prowess or fertility and rebirth. From Corinna's lake into which
Curll falls, he rises (after Cloacina's intervention) "Renew'd by
ordure's sympathetic force, / As oil'd with magic juices for the
course" (103-4). From "th' effluvia strong" he "Imbibes new
life" (105-6). But the new life is a delusion within other delusions. His victory is the empty image of the poet prepared by
Dulness, "the tall Nothing" (110); he stretches after Gay, "but
Gay is gone, / He grasps an empty Joseph for a John" (127-28).

Corinna's "lake" and Cloacina's "nether realms" (101)
participate in the excremental vision, though that in itself is not
of particular importance unless we give that reality a content. It
begins to be apparent that its content is not the revivifying
waters of rebirth, but is instead linked associatively with both
treachery and death. That is, Curll's "Vaticide" (78) involves
the dissolution of poetic identities, a kind of murdering of Swift
and Prior in which they are usurped by Cook and Concanen
(138). More importantly, the image of waters signifies two
opposed realities: life and death. Curll is not reborn, unless he is
reborn as vaticide, which seems to me the significance of his fall
(76). In a poem dedicated to inversions of one sort or another,
the image of the fructifying waters of life is inverted first as
excrement (the dead matter of the body), and second as the
death that metamorphoses Curll into vaticide. The nature of his
creative act, under the auspices of Dulness, is to create copies of
the true poet and to impose these illusions as the reality. This is
the power over knowledge he appropriates, and it explains his
fall. As Dulness says, "And we too boast our Garth and Addison" (140). Another way of making the same observation is to

remark that Curll is demonized by his fall, enlisted as an agent of Dulness, who is herself manifest in the separate individualities of Corinna and Cloacina. The former's lake and the latter's nether realms are early manifestations of the jetty bowers of the mud nymphs, the filthy yet enticing haunt of the deceptive female. That the early images of foul water expand to such bowers provides a focus for the action of the second book. And these reflections in turn lead to the falsely convenantal significance of Osborne's urine and to Curll's "impetuous . . . stream" (179-80). It is not incidental that his "prize" (186) should be "yon Juno of majestic size, / With cow-like udders, and with ox-like eyes" (163-64). The parody of male potency is joined to the caricature of the fecund female, again recalling Timon's Brobdingnagian goddess. Some sort of correlative relation exists between the height and depth of waters (Curll's stream "smoking flourish'd o'er his head" [180]) and the psychic state of duncery, itself a parody of the abundant life of waters in *Genesis* and of the creative principle informing that life.

In this context, Curll's vomit is another nether stream (though, like his urine, flowing upward), and it links with all the other lower waters in the book. It will flow forever and be "for ever green!" (156). And, in a further play on the waters of life, Curll's vomit is the reality of the illusions he perpetrates, and the reward for his vaticide is to be memorialized by the goddess with other dissemblers in eternal pain. This, then, is the anagogic meaning of Dulness's waters flowing as tributaries through her kingdom, reminding us of those other and different streams in *Windsor-Forest* and of the river-god who presides over them. Moreover, the water-deities are the instrumental agents of the mother-goddess, and signify the goals of the aspiring imagination of dunces. For, from the beginning of the book, an intimate relation exists between illusion and obscene love. As Dulness says to Curll:

> Son! Thy grief lay down,
> And turn this whole illusion on the town:
> As the sage dame, experienc'd in her trade,

By names of Toasts retails each batter'd jade;
(Whence hapless Monsieur much complains at Paris
Of wrongs from Duchesses and Lady Maries;).

(131-36)

The selling of diseased sex is equivalent to retailing bad writers for good, and the "hapless Monsieur" poxed in Paris further anticipates the Smedleyan embrace of Lutetia, Nigrina, and Merdamante. Their jetty bowers are the same bowers of bliss offered by Duchesses and Lady Maries as one illusion deepens into another. In the diving contest, as Smedley rises from the amorous clutches of the mud-nymphs, parodying the tale of Hylas and the water-nymphs, he is supreme "in majesty of Mud; / Shaking the horrors of his sable brows" (326-27). Smedley is the river-god of *Windsor-Forest* reborn, but only as a distant and grotesque reminder of Father Thames, whose "Tresses dropt with Dews, and o'er the Stream / His shining horns diffus'd a golden Gleam" (*Windsor-Forest*, 331-32). All the various associations of water aggregate here to focus upon the negation of the god. England is not newly fruitful, her imperial destiny explicit. On the contrary, her river-god is a dunce in the service of Dulness, a pathetic reminder of the union between Anne and Thames celebrated in the earlier poem.

Pope's imagined kingdom of gods and goddesses is again informed with the strife of antithetical powers. The second book is a fantasia of love and death, a hopeless dream of heroic enterprise and brave reward that characterizes the enchanted reality inhabited by the dunces. And it concludes as it should, in the spreading torpor that overtakes them, and in the visit of the "nightly Muse" (421), the last delusory female of the book, who conveys her chosen bards to those special places that they by right divine inhabit: to "stews," and "round-house," and the "neighb'ring Fleet" (422, 424, 427). These are the principal terms of Pope's "complex evaluation" here, and over this fantasia an almost forgotten and surely neglected Cibber presides in majestic ignorance as the real form of his kingdom comes into view.

And the real form arises from the Lethean episode that begins Book III as Cibber's head "repos'd" on "Dulness' lap" (2). Descending into that capacious lap, he sinks to the shore of "th' oblivious Lake" (44), the generative basis of Dulness's creation, the mighty waters from which arise the life of duncery. There is something here of a parallel between Corinna's lake and Curll's fall in Book II and Cibber's descent into the underworld where the souls of bad poets are prepared for their mortal existence. Like sin and death, Brown and Mears "unbar the gates of Light" (28), and the souls of the dull come forth in volumes. Cibber's descent is the sleep of reason, but it is also the awakening into a vision of the past and future kingdom of Dulness. Over these waters presides the "great Father" (42), Settle, who prophesies Cibber's emergent eminence, and as Cibber is the "greater Son" (42) he is the new monarch come to displace the old in what is the endless revival and renewal of Dulness's dominions.

What Settle grants to Cibber is a vision of the kingdom he will inherit. As such it parallels the Adamic vision preceding the expulsion from Eden, but perhaps an equally allusive context is provided by the four faces of the temple of Fame, whose four sides speak the glories of the imagination. In the *Dunciad*, the four geographical areas of the world reveal the triumphs of Dulness and enforce, in relation to the earlier poem, the negations she signifies. If we think for the moment of Dulness and Fame as alternative realities, we see that they correspond to one another in much the same way as selfhood to self-love. The conflict between Dulness and Fame is what history has been about, even as the struggle between selfhood and self-love informs man's passage through the world. When the selfhood creates its foul goddess, history turns into a nightmare, for the nature of Dulness is warfare upon earth. As Settle remarks, "How keen the war, if Dulness draw the sword!" (120). The "armies" gathering "to assert her cause!" (128) are like Satan's legions forming in heaven, but in this case they are gathering to advance the restoration of Dulness in England. Dulness's energies are thus "imperial" (124), and another allusive reference incorporates, by inversion, the imperial energies released at the close of *Wind-sor-Forest*. The inversion of English destiny spins the advances of *Windsor-Forest* backward upon themselves, and the bloody reign of William is come again: "This fav'rite Isle, long sever'd from her reign, / Dove-like, she gathers to her Wings again" (*Dunciad*, III, 125-26).

Aubrey Williams has observed that metaphors of "prog-ress" vein the *Dunciad*. In the third book they are ex-tended: "Rising in China, the shadows cover Egypt, Rome, Spain, Gaul, Arabia, and finally move toward Britain."[33] Behind the Augustan progress-piece he locates Denham's *The Progress of Learning*, deriving it in turn "from the medieval and renais-sance idea of *translatio studii*, the idea of a transplantation from age to age and from country to country of cultural treasure." A related, but different, conception is explicit in Temple's concep-tion of cultures rising and falling back into barbarism following the expiration of their vitality. And this notion is the one Pope follows here. "Instead of a *translatio studii* we have what we may call a *translatio stultitiae*, a transplantation of the rule of Dulness to one country after another."[34] If we think of this idea as one informing the history of cultures, we yet need to understand the agencies that realize the idea historically. And this is where the conception of selfhood comes in again. When Pope wishes to explain how Dulness seizes her advantage, he has Settle tell Cibber that "All nonsense thus, of old or modern date, / Shall in thee centre, from thee circulate" (59-60). The idea is a varia-tion of the concentric circles proceeding outward from self-love; if self-love is social, the selfhood is antisocial, and the history of a culture's fall is, in effect, the history of the selfhoods that reign within it. We may also understand here something of the impor-tance of Pope's figuralism, of the prophetic line that runs down to Cibber, and why by the end of the third book he has become the type of George II and of Augustus Caesar (317-22). Pope is saying that history is the lengthened shadow of a man, a reflection that enforces the importance of Bolingbroke at the center of the *Essay on Man*. In the *Dunciad* the night of barbar-ism and the night of Cibber's mind are correlative realities, and

Cibber is the kingdom of Dulness carried within the mind. This is also why Settle says to him: "Son; what thou seek'st is in thee! Look, and find / Each Monster meets his likeness in thy mind" (251-52).[35]

The Virgilian parallel casts Cibber into the role of Aeneas, and Settle into that of Anchises, whereas the Miltonic parallel implies Cibber as Adam, Settle as Michael. The former association inverts the epic encounter, but the latter establishes the entire envisioning of sorrowful human history that Michael offers Adam. Michael's purpose is to send Adam from paradise, "though sorrowing, yet in peace." Settle's task is ironically comparable: it is to provide Cibber with a vision of his extended influence, the kingdom he is about to inherit. Adam's fall is into death and into time (into history). Cibber's fall is into his own mind, out of which history is generated. Michael shows Adam what his sin has brought into being, what his fall has created. Settle does much the same for Cibber, though there is nothing fortunate about it. In the nature of this fall, "Hell rises, Heav'n descends" (237). Pope is speaking in this passage of theatrical absurdities, of grotesque stage effects that debase the dramatic art. But the metaphor of theater incorporates more than a dramatic performance and points to the imitative basis of the art itself. The validity of drama is confirmed by its proximate relation to the world as known; in the tragic drama that world is heightened, "higher than Nature," as Dryden says,[36] but not deformed. This is standard Augustan dramatic precept, but the theater revealed to Cibber is "a new world to Nature's laws unknown" (241). The *translatio stultitiae* is the history of the Fall manifest in time; the Cibberian drama is the imaging of that Fall, its immediate imagined form. What Pope seeks here is both an idea and its embodiment. At this moment in Book III Pope parodies Adam's delight at Michael's prophecy of the Messiah: "Joy fills his soul, joy innocent of thought" (XII, 249). And he inverts Michael's rebuke of Adam's happy expectation that the Savior shall free him from Satan ("'Not by destroying Satan, but his works / In thee and in thy Seed" [XII, 394-95]) in Settle's reminder: "Son; what thou seek'st is in thee." What is *in* Adam are Satan's works; what is *in* Cibber are those of Dulness. Thus Pope's theater is a theater of mind—Cibber's mind—and Dulness's works are the reality of nature gone mad. In this context, "The Forests dance, the rivers upward rise, / Whales sport in woods, and dolphins in the skies" (245-46).

The theater is equally the theater of the world, and on that stage the realities of Cibber's mind are represented. Such realities are inevitably those of Dulness herself. For the generative basis of all these visions is Dulness's lap, the womb and tomb of nature. That Cibber "mount[s] the wind" on "grinning dragons" (268) reinforces the immanence of the whore and her beast, for the beast is the form the selfhood assumes. Cibber thinks he is riding it, but it in fact is riding him. Whether we call this beast Satan or Leviathan makes little difference; it is the power the *Essay on Man* confronted and defeated but which is now loose again. As the vision consolidates, it takes the shape of "one vast Egg [that] produces human race" (248). What it will hatch is Cibber and his demon, and the entire sorrowful history that is born from the egg.

Given this activity as characteristic of the *Dunciad*, Frye's judgment is curious: the "Augustan conception of 'nature' begins with a physical world outside the mind. . . . Hence the relation of the individual man to nature is uncomplicated by the presence within man of a divine power visualizing eternity."[37] In the *Dunciad*, however, a demonic power has taken possession of Cibber and clouds his vision, for the kingdom of Dulness is within the mind before it is anywhere else. Frye argues that the "wedge driven by Milton between the 'true' Christian and the 'false' heathen mythology expands for the Augustans into a cleavage which almost destroyed mythopoeic poetry."[38] But Pope does not permit this destruction. He circles back upon the epic tradition, and here particularly upon Milton, to draw from it a vision of man coveting the Satanic illusion within temporality. And this activity does not rise abruptly in his poetry; it is figured in Belinda, Eloisa, Atossa, Timon, Balaam, and here in Cibber.

Sitter's comparative treatment of the *Temple of Fame* and the

Dunciad leads him to observe that both poems "have a slender thread of narrative which helps give them unity, but their essential 'design' is the relation of a vision rather than the narration of a story."[39] The remark is so generally true that it insists upon a wider application. The design of the *Dunciad*, its mythopoeic basis, links it with the *Essay on Man*, for each poem is an allegory of origins. In the *Essay* it is an allegory of the human family of passions and the master passion, of self-love and reason. When Pope refers to Dulness as the "Mother of Arrogance, and Source of Pride!" (IV, 470), he is specifying the kind of anti-imaginative act that creates the selfhood, and identifying as well the origin of the selfhood within consistent allegorical terms. Her progenitive energies create the source of the selfhood, pride, and the alliance between pride and erring reason in turn results in the deification of the goddess. From this vantage, one senses again the enlarged design of the poetry, a vision in which the various parts fold intricately into one another.[40] Belinda is an early and lesser manifestation of the great mother, self-deified through the "sacred rites of Pride." Eloisa is enthralled by (and in thrall to) the jealous god of love, and the nature she inhabits is ruled by "Black Melancholy." Pope's characters act within the controlling contexts of the deities they profess, or within the contexts of those deities who possess them. And this reflection takes us back to the sacred six within the hallowed quire of Fame's temple, and to Albion reborn through the union of Anne and Father Thames.

Commenting on that type of fable he called "marvelous," Pope noted that it "includes whatever is supernatural, and especially the machines of the Gods." And, defending Homer against his detractors, he added:

> For we find those Authors who have been offended at the literal Notion of the Gods, constantly laying their Accusation against *Homer* as the chief support of it. But whatever cause there might be to blame his *Machines* in a Philosophical or Religious View, they are so perfect in the Poetick, that Mankind have been ever since contented to follow them: None have been able to enlarge the Sphere of Poetry beyond the Limits he has set: Every Attempt

of this Nature has prov'd unsuccessful; and after all the various Changes of Times and Religions, his Gods continue to this Day the Gods of Poetry.[41]

In another context (not that of the *Dunciad*), Sitter states that Pope's " 'system' as a whole aims at a modern vindication of the ways of God to man, but it is a vindication through poetry. Despite the example of Milton, or more importantly *because* of it, one might well wonder what room is left for a poet in such matters."[42] The remark provides what seems the appropriate response, but Pope's mythmaking, which rationalizes and supports the ethical context of his poetry, also describes the "room" he creates for himself. The poetic space he inhabits is a derived space—as Pope's statement on Homer's gods suggests—and thus an area that focuses our attention upon poetic traditions and Pope's control and assimilation of them. It is not merely a matter of Homer and Virgil (though that is no mere matter), but of Horace and Theocritus, of Chaucer and Spenser, of Dryden and Boileau, of Tasso and Ariosto, and the adaptation of these, and of others beyond these, to the purposes of Pope's "design."

Many modern scholars have made us aware of the allusive content of Pope's works. The less discernible element is the unity of a poet's imagination. In recent years the former subject has attracted general critical attention, and we have heard much of fathers and sons. But Pope is not a rebel, and he has many fathers who shape his imagination. Pope does not destroy myth. That job is done by the Wartons and Collins and Gray, and those who served and supported their idea of poetry. The "marvelous" inhabits Pope's poetry as it does Homer's; the fable is the entire design he chooses to communicate consistent with probability. Once we penetrate the myth, however, we recognize the presence of an imagination—a vision and a design—that challenges our best efforts, not of historical recovery alone, but of comprehension and engagement.

The infected reality with which the fourth book begins

("Sick was the Sun, the Owl forsook his bow'r" [11]) envisions a new nature as prison-house: "*Science* groans in Chains," "*Logic* [is] gagg'd and bound," "fair Rhet'ric languish'd on the ground" (21-24). The usurping forms of sophistry, billingsgate, chicane, and casuistry impersonate their imprisoned opposites, as acts duplicative of Dulness's usurpation of the sleeping Britannia. The monarchical setting reveals Dulness enthroned, but Pope wants something more than just this eminence. To achieve his purpose he creates the image of the perihelion, whereby the motions of the dunces are disposed like planetary bodies about the universal center that is Dulness. This new center is itself superimposed over the old center provided by Phoebus Apollo, so that the universe of Dulness is in effect another usurpation, and dunces "false to Phoebus, bow the knee to Baal" (93). Pope may be recalling here the legend of Apollo's first feat, the seizure of Delphi and the destruction of its guardian, the dragon Python, embodying the dark forces of the underworld. Dulness regains the center from which she had been dispossessed, and establishes in Baal a nature religion whose prominent feature is marked sensuality. At this point several distinct images converge. Pope speaks of those who bow the knee to Baal as "impious," as those who "preach his Word without a call" (94). The relation among sun, Phoebus Apollo, and Christ ("preach his Word") defines the qualities of a center that has been taken over by the goddess. Three distinct and correlative realities converge: the sun as natural center of the universe, Apollo as god of oracles and prophecy, and thus patron of poetry and music, and Christ as Son and the Word incarnate.

The goddess's reign imposes a triple usurpation, an extinction of the natural, pagan, and Christian illuminations by her own darkness. Once this center has been assumed, her next act is to parody the resurrection of the dead through the achievements of bad scholarship: "revive the Wits! / But murder first, and mince them all to bits" (119-20). The resurrection extends to Busby's "Spectre" (139), which rises from the grave, and to Bentley's, which quits his sleeping form. From this conception in turn arises the dominant metaphor of the fourth book, encasements or enclosures within which man is entrapped. Warburton's note to lines 255-71 speaks of Dulness bringing "all human minds to *one dead level*":

> For if Nature should chance to struggle through all the entanglements of the foregoing ingenious expedients to *bind rebel wit*, this [i.e., authority] clasps upon her one sure and entire cover. So that well may Aristarchus [i.e., Bentley] defy all human power to *get the Man out* again from under so impenetrable a crust.[43]

Warburton's comments are in response to Bentley's challenge, after he has finished with his scholars, to "hew the Block off, and get out the Man" (270). But not even a Barrow can "work on ev'ry block" (245). From the initial image of the prison-house, and through the imagery of a false resurrection extended to the wits, the image of death and rebirth expands to include the suffocating enclosure in which Bentley's pupils have been imprisoned and from which none will ever again be released. Another darksome round.

Much of Book IV is built on enclosures of one kind or another, all of which parody the theme of death and rebirth and thereby maintain associative contact with the waters of Book II. The flower "thron'd in glass" (409) by the horticultural virtuoso, the antiquarian who cherishes the mummified body of Cheops, the numismatic who swallows antique coins, are all celebrated within the same imagery, and this imagery links to those who "bind [God] in matter" (476), who create a God "Such as Lucretius drew, a God like thee: / Wrapt up in Self, a God without a Thought" (484-85). The God wrapped up in self is nothing other than the selfhood deified, and thus locked into itself in such a way that no advance or escape is possible. And lest we have any doubts about Pope's meaning here and the terms of relation, Dulness "Wraps in her Veil" (336) her favorites, her act a binding and enclosing, from which no escape (resurrection) is possible. Such enthusiasts as the horticultural virtuoso, the antiquarian, and the numismatic are in their ways equivalent to religious enthusiasts (like Shaftesbury, for example) who wrap "Nature's Cause" (468) in nature, "And reason downward, till we doubt of God'' (472). When this process is complete, nature and art, both shrunken by the educational system Bentley has described, are themselves prepared to be the enclosures within which the imagination is imprisoned, thus attesting to the truth of Silenus's observations on the modern student: "Bounded by Nature, narrow'd still by Art, / A trifling head, and a contracted heart" (503-4).

As the poem moves toward the final metaphoric reality of Dulness, the world is seen as a place of ludicrous or terrifying enclosures, of reductionisms that seek an end in annihilation. Philosophy "Shrinks to her second cause, and is no more" (644), Religion "veils her sacred fires" (649). And the image of contraction follows upon the image of enclosure. The "Cup of Self-love" (517 n) is another container inducing the enchanted vision of self-sufficiency, so that the totality of things that are loved is contracted to an image furnished by "Kind Self-conceit," who "to some her glass applies, / Which no one looks in with another's eyes" (533-34). Her "glass" is Belinda's mirror re-emergent, another variation of the narrowly circumscribed reality of duncery. As the boundaries of self-love progressively contract (though it is the nature of the selfhood to think they are expanding), Dulness moves in to fill the void. And this is what the cup of self-love signifies: it contains the waters of oblivion (as Pope's and Warburton's note suggests) imported from the Lethean chambers of the third book (and the waters of death from the second book), which presumably are still having their effect upon Cibber, who continues to sleep on the goddess's lap.

If we step back from Book IV we witness a world shrinking, much like a huge spherical object passing rapidly from our sight. And if we think of this object as peopled, we can imagine them shrinking proportionately. In Blake, Adam is called the "Limit of Contraction," meaning that man has "fallen as far as man can fall without losing his imagination altogether and the ability to recreate himself along with it."[44] Pope's myth is of man falling beyond the limit of contraction, of a shrinking that, just as it reaches the point of total annihilation, inverts itself and comes forward as a "Sable Throne" (629). When the limit of contraction is passed, when man has fallen so as to lose his imagination and the culture that supports and enriches it, he does not simply vanish. He is returned to a state of undifferentiated matter that is chaos. This is, for Pope, the limit of contraction, the second and final Fall presided over by the black sun, which has usurped the center about which I spoke earlier, and it symbolizes the unconscious or state of unworked matter. It is man after his history and his culture and his society have been destroyed; it is what remains after he has been shrunken to his essential identity or imprisoned within the nature that Dulness represents.

When Frye comments on Blake's symbolism, he says that the "work which throws most light on Blake here is the Wisdom of Solomon, in which the plague of darkness, for instance, is treated as a symbol of the brooding terrors of the opaque self-hood in language very close to Blake":

> For while they thought they were unseen in their secret sins, they were sundered one from another by a dark curtain of forgetfulness, stricken with terrible awe, and sore troubled by spectral forms.[45]

It does not really matter whether Pope (or Blake) is recalling the Bible; what does matter are the correspondent terms of Pope's vision in the *Dunciad*: the forgetfulness that accompanies selfhood, the spectral identities of Busby and Bentley, and the dark curtain of universal night. This is the fulfillment of the archetype, the final embodiment of the reality of selfhood.

Within the polarities defined by the *Essay on Man* and the *Dunciad*, all of Pope's poetry may be disposed. It has no coherent existence except by reference to these poems, and the canon continues to unfold and allusively sustain itself through the complexities of internal reference and expanded restatement and reformulation. No one of the poems discussed in this book could be withdrawn without diminishing the mythopoeic context that has been established, and my methodology should provide the terms by which other works, not considered here, may contribute to the enlarged intellectual pattern. I have not pretended to anything like definitiveness (whatever that may be), but I have presumed to create an idea of Pope's poetic that posits the tenacious coherence of his imagination. The structure, I think, stands intact, and demands that we encounter it as an entity similar in its own ambitious proportions to those created by Milton or by Blake.

5 Conclusion

Even as early as the *Essay on Criticism*, Pope is shaping his greater subject and stating its terms. Each *"ancient Altar"* of poetry "still green with Bays" (181) reaches out to the *Temple of Fame*. Those *"Bards triumphant"* (189) "Whose Honours with Increase of Ages *grow*, / As Streams roll down, *enlarging* as they flow" (191-92) anticipates the aggregative streams of *Windsor-Forest* and the cumulative flow of Father Thames. Within the *Essay on Criticism*, "Pride" (209) and *"Dulness"* (393) enact their roles. The *concordia discors* emerges as a controlling principle (488-89). Wharton of *To Cobham* is anticipated in *"Lust of Praise"* (521). The rebellious night of the *Dunciad* is figured (552-55, 690-91), and as the *Essay on Criticism* draws to a close the *Dunciad*'s dying and shrinking arts and sciences are reversed in a vision of rising and strengthening cultures. Almost from the beginning, Pope's poetry signals its major themes, and the *Essay on Criticism* moves toward the as yet unconstructed myths of his mature verse. To circle back over his work is to heed the impulses within it and to be sensitive to the directions it will take. For the *Essay* seeks its hypotheses within the still unfledged formulations of the later poetry. The mature Pope is implicit in the young poet.

Because we are accustomed to think of Pope as almost exclusively a satirist, we have lost some sense of the range and scope of his work. Milton, we say, is incidentally a satirist, as is Blake. For the work of those two poets, we employ the term *epic*; for Pope's, we qualify the noun with *mock*. And there is sufficient justification for doing so. Rosenblum properly observes: "According to a long tradition satire is the bastard genre, a farrago, a mixed dish, a hastily set down affair without the style and unity of the more elevated genres."[1] Consequently, we are willing to turn satire over to its more immediately persuasive concerns, to insist upon its direct bearing on some topical issue that sponsors and occasions it. Paulson argues that "however much mimesis or representation is involved, the generic end is rhetorical."[2] And even Rosenblum, who wants to take satire in another direction entirely, agrees that the "satirist's efforts are tied to history."[3] There is of course much truth to this statement. Blake's efforts are "tied to history," as the political reading of his poems makes clear. However, the satirist seems sometimes not merely linked to history but bound and limited by it; his topicality is a peculiar kind of burden that minimizes the universality of his poetry and forces us to rummage in footnotes for the references we require.

Pope's poetry is directed at particular persons, and this effort reveals the immediately *historical* meaning of his performance. But beyond such concerns satire must create its fictive condition, develop its envisioning method, or else exist as some clever piece of journalism. *Gulliver's Travels* is a parody of travel literature, of the fabulous reports brought back from voyages of English and European adventurers. But if it were only this, it would be of little continuing importance. Within the envisioning method of the tale, we find it is another story of the fall of man from his middle station, a confusion of human identity. Gulliver's voyage turns into a quest for man, and in the fourth book Gulliver is lost within the vision of pure reason and spirals downward to madness. The work exists to justify our dubiety about human reason, even as Milton's epic exists as another kind of justification. *Gulliver's Travels* is an imitation of an action, the action of man losing his footing and falling again. And if we admire the work, we admire equally the transvaluation that Swift has achieved, the curious investment by which a tale of fantastic adventures is transposed into the tragedy of another fall. Behind it we hear the resonating myth of *Paradise Lost*, of temptation and despair. For Gulliver is tempted to believe that a reason superior to his own destroys the validity of his own, and he despairs over the emergent identity of man as Yahoo. If Swift comes round on the Fall as a collapse of faith in the middle station, it is nothing less than a variation played on the Miltonic vision. Man falls, not necessarily by aspiring, but by despairing, by rejecting absolutely the Yahoo that is part of him, and by longing to be entirely what he is only partially. Man performs his own mutilations. Yet Pope owes even more to his great predecessor than does Swift, and we have been describing his debt for some time now.

From the beginning, Pope is looking for "a place to stand, an angle of vision," as Mack suggests.[4] Earlier I argued that *Windsor-Forest* is Pope's attempt to reconstitute Dryden's myth of England, and I suggested the terms by which the poet complicates his intentions. Pope's doubts there create the satirist; that is, they make the satiric angle necessary to him. But this is exactly the occasion of difficulty, for it raises problems as to our legitimate expectations. We may need therefore a scheme whereby Pope's texts are accommodated to the phases of satire. It seems likely that the *Essay on Man* can be comprehended within Frye's "satire of the low norm," in which the poet himself adopts the role of *eiron* and the selfhood is cast as a variation of the *alazon*. Within this phase, what "is recommended is conventional life at its best: a clairvoyant knowledge of human nature in oneself and others, an avoidance of all illusion and compulsive behavior, a reliance on observation and timing rather than on aggressiveness."[5] In the role of *eiron*, the poet counsels prudence, explains, justifies. As *alazon*, the selfhood is "a Goliath encountered by a tiny David."[6] But the *Dunciad*, differing widely from the *Essay*, corresponds to satire's sixth phase: "Its settings feature prisons, madhouses, lynching mobs, and places of execution. . . . Sinister parental figures naturally abound, for this is the world of the ogre and the witch."[7]

Quite possibly all of Pope's satires could be so catalogued, and when we were finished we would have some idea of his variety and flexibility of mode. We could argue that his works *fill out* the satiric spectrum as do those of no other English satirist. But even so we would need to understand why these phases exist within Pope's poetry. Belinda is at considerable remove from Cibber, though each is possessed of a self-love that is somehow failing to perform its prescribed function. If Belinda is brought to the point where escape from the conventions of her society is possible, Cibber is not. The more we examine this difference, the more we recognize that the *Rape of the Lock* and the *Dunciad* require for their fulfillment subtle variations of the sublime. In the *Rape* the sublime is urged toward the ridiculous; Belinda's outraged cry concluding the fourth canto is the apotheosis of the bathetic moment. But in the *Dunciad*, particularly in the fourth book, the sublime is recreated as terrible. We witness another variation of this strategy in the *Essay on Man*. The tumultuous imagery of contending passions in the second epistle rises toward its resolution in the poet's envisioning of the divine datum acting upon man like the Creator within his creation: "Nor God alone in the still calm we find, / He mounts the storm, and walks upon the wind" (109-10). Perhaps more complexly, Eloisa's anguished cry, "Present the Cross before my lifted eye, / Teach me at once, and learn of me to die" (327-28), is an example of the sublime as sublimation, an occasion for a defensive or substitutive stratagem, an "alienation from particular forms of primary experience."[8]

That Pope can use the egotistical sublime for satiric purposes suggests his attention to the forms of self-deception that run through his poetry. Timon crawling like an insect upon the inflated body of nature is possessed not only of bad taste but of an absurd lustfulness, and the comic sublime fixes him in permanent futility. To ring these changes on the sublime argues the centrality of the conception to Pope's imagination. He is almost constantly assessing the follies and dangers of the sublime, except at such moments, as in the *Essay on Man*, when he enlists it in his own aid. And this observation in turn leads us to recognize that the sublime moment as narcissistic occasion is the focal point of Pope's attack, and directs us not only toward the *Rape, Eloisa,* and the *Dunciad*, but also toward the *Epistle to Arbuthnot*, wherein Pope himself serves as the example of such possession. The inversion of the sublime moment is a fall, an art of sinking. Narcissism turned inside out is the grotesque, the discovery that the fair outside conceals a very nasty inside. This is Swift's game in *A Tale of a Tub*, and although it is used most conspicuously by Pope in the *Dunciad*, it emerges very early in his work. In *Windsor-Forest* it appears as an attempt to gratify the passions by transmuting their object from war to hunt, another effort of sublimation whereby a lesser pleasure is substituted for a greater one.

There are numerous attempts at substitution in Pope's poems: the past for the present in the *Temple of Fame*, the future for the present in the *Rape of the Lock*, to name two. Such shifting temporalities, and the values they imply, are another effort to divest present action of its narcissistic potential, to hedge action within whatever constraints Pope can build around it. Only after his death is there in English criticism a large-scale theoretical commitment to the values of the sublime, and this commitment is consonant with the emergent passions enacting themselves within the theater of the mind. This is one form of demonism highly cultivated by mid-eighteenth-century writers. It seems obvious that Pope was aware of the demonic within the sublime as the efflorescence of the narcissistic element, its logical consequence. In other words, what has caused the initial Fall was likely to bring about another and more disastrous one. This sort of thinking makes the *Essay on Man* an inevitable document in the warfare against the self, an effort to turn narcissism against itself by revealing its inside: "Then drop into thyself, and be a fool."

But the clarification of an inside is precisely the point at which myth enters. In the *Epistle to Bathurst*, the "Daemon makes his full descent," he "Sinks deep within . . . [Balaam], and possesses [him] whole." Balaam's narcissism is linked to a sublime sexuality, as Pope's metaphor makes clear: Satan descends "In one abundant show'r of Cent. per Cent.," and the result for Balaam is that "What late he call'd a Blessing, now was Wit, / And God's good Providence, a lucky Hit." Balaam converted into his own best admirer is the process Pope describes; Satan has dropped into Balaam, and the man he occupies is now a fool. Much the same sort of possession occurs in the *Dunciad*, where Dulness usurps the sleeping form of Britannia. The point of the sublime is that it is a kind of possession, an obsession that almost necessarily evokes from Pope images of the demonic. The aged beauties of the *Epistle to a Lady* were like martial queens ("In Youth they conquer, with so wild a rage"), but they end like "Hags [who] hold Sabbaths, less for joy than spight." The price for this kind of freedom is a Faustian payment. Bad taste, the desire for power, the tyranny of beauty, and other forms of domination are all reducible to a narcissism that is self-consuming.

Recognitions of this sort may have summoned the Horatian *Imitations*; as the story goes, they seem to have been prompted by Bolingbroke's rather casual suggestion. But they bear upon the greater predicament of Pope's own self-consciousness. The attempt to affiliate himself with history is an effort to raise up a plausible alternative to the sublime moment, to offer, in fact, a critique of alienation, of that which calls us from ourselves *(First Epistle of the First Book)*. Pope achieves this brilliantly in the *Imitations*, but those poems have a way also of turning into a critique of action, of man-in-the-world. Bolingbroke, Peterborough, and Pope at Twickenham are superior to men of power because they have not lost themselves to the narcissism that action fosters. The quietist tendencies of Pope's outlook imply a qualification of the maxim that self-love is social. It is not always so. But at least we can see how important the proposition is for Pope and why he works so hard at it. Self-love has to be social if man is to be guarded against the sublime that rises from within.

A mind like Eloisa's searches for confirmation of her desires in nature, and nature can be put to the same uses in any act of egoism. Thus Pope keeps inventing the specters occasioned by the desiring self, keeps transforming man into the metaphorical reality of his creation, as with Timon or Villiers or Balaam. When Warton asks rhetorically, "What is there transcendently sublime or pathetic in Pope?" it is a very bad question because there is a great deal of the sublime in Pope, although it is not often there to be celebrated. And so the Wartons tried to get beyond him and back to the Spenser and Milton they knew and valued, back to romance and fine fabling. They hoped to revive an English and pan-European tradition that had been blighted by the Frenchified literature of the Restoration and lost in Pope's poetry of ethical and didactic intent. Weiskel makes the interesting observation that "in bathos, our laughter is a defense against the anxiety of losing or falling out of what meaning we've got—it is directed against the unfortunate who has fallen out of the great social bond without knowing it."[9] And this is true, but, as Pope knew perfectly well, the art of sinking is corollary to the art of rising. It was just as possible to rise out of the great social bond, and his fear of this necessitates the attack on selfhood.

It seems clear that Pope felt acutely the danger of a pull away from history. Rosenblum states that the *Dunciad* is "a record of Pope's sense of his situation in history,"[10] but it is also clear that the poem assumes the form of a metahistory, a form that enfolds history within itself and gives it meaning. Frye notes that "History as the total form of all genuine efforts of human culture and civilization is the canon or Scripture of human life."[11] In this sense, the *Dunciad* is history, but history spinning backward toward chaos, and it is obvious that Pope came to feel that history was no longer moving in the right directions or being employed so as to control the aberrant impulses arising in the present. For Pope to begin with *Windsor-Forest* is to admit the need to purge history of its indecencies, but to end with the *Dunciad* is to confess the impossibility of doing so. It is likely that the personal need to posit a secure past motivated the

writing of the *Temple of Fame*. What history apparently offered
Pope, among other things, were models for behavior: "Such an
one did good or got an honest reputation by such an action: I
would mark it down in order to imitate it where I had an opportunity."[12] Satire could serve a similar purpose. Pope marked
down Bolingbroke, Bathurst, Burlington, and others as suitable
models. *The First Satire of the Second Book* insists upon the alliance
between satire and history.

Yet it is precisely this kind of partnership that the Wartonian reaction at mid-century dissolves, and history is made the
occasion for the sublime. Thomas Warton's titles alone tell part
of the story: *The Grave of King Arthur, Written in a Blank Leaf of
Dugdale's Monasticon, Written at Stonehenge.* The past becomes
the enchanted haunt of the enthusiast:

> Long have I lov'd to catch the simple chime
> Of minstrel-harps, and spell the fabling rime;
> To view the festive rites, the knightly play,
> That deck'd heroic Albion's elder day;
> To mark the mouldering halls of barons bold,
> And the rough castle, cast in giant mold;
> With Gothic manners Gothic arts explore,
> And Muse on the magnificence of yore.
> *(Verses on Sir Joshua Reynolds' Painted Window, 9-16)*

The past as an incentive to moral action is transformed into the
past as a source of personal emotion, valorized as an occasion
for strong affective response. The readiness to translate history
or nature into the occasion for sublime experience attests to the
challenge to Augustan humanism. In Collins and Macpherson,
in the Wartons and in Gray's later poems, the sublime is the
dominant emotional reality, and inevitably the goddess of the
Dunciad is re-created as the natural sublime:

> Night, sable goddess! from her ebon throne,
> In rayless majesty now stretches forth
> Her leaden sceptre o'er a slumbering world.
> Silence, how dead! and darkness, how profound!
> Nor eye nor listening ear an object finds;

Creation sleeps. 'Tis as the general pulse
On life stood still, and Nature made a pause;
An awful pause! prophetic of her end.
                              (*The Complaint*, "Night I," 18-25)

The centrifugal action of Pope's widening circles, opening from self-love to social, is reversed as the greater realities of history and nature bear back upon the self at the center, the self for whom history and nature exist. The performing self at the center is charged with the power or energy of its sensations, becoming a part of that which it perceives and finding its own justification thereby. Seen in this light, Pope's poetry moves toward figuring the forms of the sublime, which his own critical positioning as satirist requires. This is to come toward the problems of a culture in the only way available *after* Dryden; following, that is, the collapse of Dryden's Restoration myth of Albion reborn.

It is not too much of a digression to call attention to the images of power and negation that haunt Restoration comedy and Rochester's poetry. Obviously, there is some crisis of energy in the later years of the seventeenth century, and, equally obviously, the contractual basis of society is not sufficient to hold personal desire in check. Pope's entire career is explicable in relation to this fact, and the past is culled for the restraints it may impose. In the name of history, however, the Wartons obviate what Pope would have recognized as a culture; in effect, they release the giant selfhood to its own visions of power. In doing so they write the first chapter of modern literary history and define the opening gambit of a modern sensibility. Joseph Warton attacks Pope where he takes him to be weakest, in his refusal to capitulate to the sublime or the pathetic. But in fact Pope's entire existence as a poet depends upon summoning criteria that contextually contain and limit the performing self while simultaneously indicating that such a performance is self-consumptive. It is in this special way that Pope stands between Milton and Blake, and his primary vision is the forms of alienation precipitated by the egotistical sublime. The visionary poet of Thomas Warton's *Pleasures of Melancholy* thrills himself with terrible reflections on isolation:

> O then how fearful is it to reflect,
> That thro' the still globe's awful solitude,
> No being wakes but me!
>
> (56-58)

Warton's experience is of a sentient and intelligent world nullified, contracted to the "I" at its center, exultant in the sublime singularity of his own feelings, an "I" who is nothing other than the "you" of the *Essay on Man*. At such a moment the sensation of transcendence arises from within; the "sacred Genius of the night" is invoked to send "mystic visions" such "as Spenser saw . . . or Milton knew" (62-66). The process is adequately glossed by Kant. He remarks on the *"astonishment* amounting almost to terror, the awe and thrill of devout feeling, that takes hold of one." This, he says, "is not actual fear. Rather is it an attempt to gain access to it through imagination, for the purpose of feeling the might of this faculty combining the movement of the mind thereby aroused with its serenity, and of thus being superior to internal and, therefore, to external, nature."[13] In another context, Edmund Burke speaks of the pleasure it is "to see nature in those great, but terrible scenes. It fills the mind with grand ideas, and turns the soul in upon herself."[14] To turn the soul in upon itself is to experience sensations of power, to court the alienation that sublimity engenders.

In part at least the Wordsworthian sublime aggregates feeling independent of the occasioning circumstance ("emotion recollected in tranquillity") as a way of rising superior to time and place. Albert Wlecke comments on the way in which, for Wordsworth, "the mind is given a sense of its own 'pure grandeur' by an 'influence habitual,' a constantly recurring encounter with the mountain's 'outline' and its 'steady form.' "[15] The assimilation of the "*enduring* sublimity of such a phenomenon" confers upon the mind powers which it recognizes as its own, hence the *egotistical* sublime. The appropriation of power creates a new self-love, the orientation of which is not toward society but toward eternity, toward the freedom from all forms of inclusiveness that limit and restrain the self, that incorporate it. For

Pope, however, the passions and the egotistical sublime may easily become correlative agencies. The dunciadic reality is the sublimity of self: "Son [says Settle]; what thou seek'st is in thee! Look, and find / Each monster meets his likeness in thy mind." For Pope in the *Essay*, various reticulations, spatial and intellectual, contain the desiring self. Sublime space is kept in relation to bathetic space ("Then drop into thyself, and be a fool"). For Wordsworth, sublime space "is phenomenologically generated by the mind's sense of itself spreading outward." The effect of this process is "of being carried quite away from the world of ordinary, always confining localizations."[16] The Popeian spider that "lives along the line" (*Essay on Man*, I, 218) inhabits an architectonically established space. For Wordsworth, to the contrary, sublime space has no such structure; phenomena pass into the "types and symbols of Eternity" (*Prelude*, VI, 639).

It is in this context that I wish to take Brower's remark that Pope, following Dryden, "reaffirmed the public role of the poet."[17] Yet, as this is true, Pope's public role remains also admonitory and highly consistent with a quietist impulse, oriented toward the formulation of a self-identity seeking and establishing its integrity in retirement. I am not now confounding Pope with Cowperian or other modes of retirement poetry. We can see what Cowper makes of this theme in the third book of *The Task*:

> Oh, blest seclusion from a jarring world,
> Which he, thus occupied, enjoys! Retreat
> Cannot indeed to guilty man restore
> Lost innocence, or cancel follies past;
> But it has peace, and much secures the mind
> From all assaults of evil; proving still
> A faithful barrier, not o'erleaped with ease
> By vicious custom, raging uncontroll'd
> Abroad, and desolating public life.
>
> (675-83)

The garden is the protected place into which the self retreats, cherishing its isolation, fearfully constructing its defenses. Twickenham was a crucial metaphor for Pope's imagination,

realized over and again in the special places, the centers, with
which he endows his human actors. All great writers seem to
shelter in some imagined variation of the bower, advancing
from it as does Blake, or driven from it, as is Wordsworth in his
middle years. Yet if for Pope the center holds, the circumference
beyond turns inconsistently. There exists in him some sort of
major tension between the self and the world that the imagination cannot resolve: "Alas! to Grotto's and to Groves we run, /
To Ease and Silence, ev'ry Muse's Son" (*Second Epistle of the
Second Book*, 110-11).

For if the imagination can figure the shapes of its anxieties—as for example in the oedipal relation between Dulness and
her son, or in the Cibberian egotistical sublime—it can do little
other than expose the self-defeating characteristics of each manifestation. It is this predicament that sponsors the Popeian alliance with history, a way of forcing the self into contexts that
mock its special claims. And if society is nothing more than a
structure of contracts, what preserves these contracts when the
self has no further use for them? Most eighteenth-century
humanists tried to answer this question by invoking the concept
of *nature*, which could be employed to serve psychological,
social, or theological purposes. Pope was very much excited by
the idea of the ruling passion, because it linked man to God in a
very special way. The informing datum was the truth of nature
and of human nature, the ruling passion continuing evidence of
God's grace and charity (his immanence) in man. Yet this fact
could engender anxiety simply because it was obvious that
in many people the ruling passion was not doing its job, or,
with Wharton of *To Cobham*, was performing as a caricature of its
divine purpose. Within the world at large, sudden catastrophes
and turbulences were merely referred to the divine plan. At any
moment, suffering man was likely to be stranded within a system determined and yet not determinable. In the *Essay on Man*,
part of Pope's plan is to rationalize human limitation through a
sympathetic formula. Man is saved from himself by his limitations, lest he die of a rose in aromatic pain. Such a strategy
is intended obviously to allay anxiety, but Pope's program

somewhat reductively forces the self to observe merely its own datum. The function of the imagination is thus to fulfill those predeterminations of identity that the ruling passion implies. To rebel against this program is to rebel against oneself and God. As a formula, it is another variation of the Miltonic interdiction, though it is presented as a grace.

After Pope, the Wartons went rummaging through history to find hypothetical identities into which the self could move, habitations for the imagination that were to be exploited as sources of power. The distant consequence of this activity is to be found in Keats where, in the odes, the poet builds a consciousness that owes no obligations to the world, that generates realities beyond the data provided by things and objects. Weiskel observes that the "egotistical sublime which takes the path of desire is going to run directly into the problem of fictionality,"[18] by which he means those fictions of identity that the self generates. Pope knew more about this subject than he is commonly given credit for. In the *Second Epistle of the Second Book*, poets "dispose of all poetic Merit, / Yours *Milton's* Genius, and mine *Homer's* Spirit" (135-36); "Let me be *Horace*, and be *Ovid* you" (144). Such fictions of identity are imposed by the world—in this case London, where poets lose themselves: "can *London* be the Place? / Who there his Muse, or Self, or Soul attends?" (89-90). Given this situation, the imagination is going to have a difficult time building a bridge between the self and the world. Either the self is incorporated into the world or the world is incorporated into the self.

It is obvious that after Pope's death the latter alternative was the prevailing line taken by the poets, but it should be equally clear that despite the gratifications afforded by satire, Pope leaves his reader-in-the-world with some degree of frustration. That is, there are a number of short circuits between the self and the self-in-the-world. The *Essay on Man* wants to show that these seemingly improper connections are only illusions, functions of ignorance and pride, and that the connection requires no adjustment, only our understanding of how it works. Pope refuses to legitimize radical discontinuity, even to the point of insisting that the history of consciousness is unbroken. Homer and nature are the same; man is what he was. Consciousness cannot change its mode of perception without ceasing to be that which makes it what it is, without falling, degenerating, becoming less than itself. The self is thus referred to those categories (history, nature, God) that constitute being, and the irreducible justification for art lies in the authentication of these categories.[19] The Wartonian attack upon Pope is in one sense Warton's election of the "Northern side" of Fame's temple, the "Gothic Structure" (119), and it is based on the desire to reclaim for consciousness what belongs to it, while clearing out from consciousness what has been merely imposed upon it. Pope defines the self by reconstituting the myths within which it exists; the Wartons come to break them, to discover a pure subjectivity that is antecedent to the myths and has a furtive existence in legend and fable. This mode of thought lies at the heart of the romantic repudiation of Pope, a renunciation of law that permits the re-creation of an authentic subject-object relationship. It is Pope's *inauthenticity* that has been central to his rejection. Thus the Wartons leap out of the Popeian context and proceed to turn it against itself. Pope is the one now caught within the darksome round of ethical and didactic prescriptivism, the great apologist for the greater Engineer, an agent of the God who only seemed to be other than the jealous god.

In the *Rape of the Lock* the egotistical sublime is initiated as a dream of desire, and in the *Dunciad* Cibber sleeps his nightmare on Dulness's lap. St. John has to be recalled by Pope at the beginning of the *Essay on Man* and instructed to awake. There is a pervasive quality of nervous vigilance in Pope's poetry, of the need for awakened resistance, that inevitably recalls the Miltonic context, sleeping Eve and whispering Satan. The *Essay* is a poem of inexhaustible restraints built to contain and thwart the selfhood. Nowhere in English poetry is there in evidence a more militant alertness, as though every faculty is at attention to detect the rebellious stirrings of desire, and every effort is required to resist subversion. Such anxiety is reflected in the aggressive wit of the Tory intelligence, and in its cautionary aphorisms that tell the difference between charms and merit, between taking on the new or abandoning the old. The price of stability is eternal vigilance. This atmosphere (so to speak) of Pope's poetry has been widely noticed; it is part of the rear-guard mentality that defines the eighteenth-century humanist. We feel, in reading Pope, the narrow boundaries separating liberty and license, truth from delusion, and we feel them because we have been carefully instructed in the proposition that every vice is the defect of a virtue, that at any moment the betraying inversion may take place, and that what is divine in man will be usurped by what is demonic in him.

Perhaps it is this sense of Pope, more than anything else, that sponsors the Wartonian reaction, the idea that the sublime must not merely risk the demonic but invite it. And it may be that what Warton offers is a veiled indictment of Pope's fearfulness, a deeper intuition obscured by the charge that he is ethical and didactic. What seems at issue here is that the dark energies courted by Burke, Collins, and the Wartons have a fecundating, nighttime existence in the underlife of dream, the primitivism that haunts the mind like primordial imaginings. Thus Pope builds barricades against them, as he does against evil, with which they are virtually identical. For evil is always a usurpation in Pope, an uprising by powers not alien to the mind but, if anything, altogether too indigenous. Pope deals with evil by suppression and constraint, by summoning as a principal weapon in the warfare the wit that identifies and shames its antagonist. This mode of combat—for it is nothing else—arises from the premise that evil is absolutely itself, nothing less or other than what it has been eternally, and may be one of the reasons why Pope's enemies are treated so harshly and with increasing rigor.

In Coleridge, strategies of inclusion seem primed to play a major part. The cruel mother of *The Three Graves* is victimizer and also a victim of the exclusion from which she suffers. We sense that Geraldine's redemption is to be a major part of the unfinished *Christabel*. In Wordsworth, we recognize that the terror inhabiting nature is a purposeful part of its moral order. And

Blake advises us to make friends with devils. But when we turn back to Pope we see that such necessities are alien to his idea of identity and play no role in contributing to the stability of the self. The self admits of no such accommodations, and it may be just this fact of unmediated opposition that threatens the vitality of the human image he creates. Clearly, the mid-century writers of whom I have spoken want to use more of the materials of humanity. Put it another way. To go beyond Pope it was necessary to unlock hell, to risk the rising within being that would enlarge being, and finally to demilitarize the guardian faculties that play so large a role in the *Essay on Man*. I am of course speculating, but not without an evidential basis. Blake tells us to make war on pieties, on those forces that masquerade as guardians but are in fact the jailers of our energies. The flaming sword does not exclude the demonic; it excludes only those who would, through exclusion, narrow and contract Eden to one dull round of repetitive and insipid virtue. To sketch out the matter in these terms is to suggest a certain sympathy for the mid-century enterprise, but it is also to imply that Pope had done his work too well. Pope *had* re-imagined Milton, leaving behind him no room for an immediately comparable act.

The distinction between selfhood and self-love results in an unmediated dualism, a binary opposition that inevitably promotes a sustained militance that lies at the root of being. The selfhood can never be driven out because it is part of what constitutes human nature. It can never be transmuted into what it is not because it is eternally itself. And it can never be accommodated to self-love because it cannot share the same sphere of interest. The selfhood can thus only be figured as usurper, seducer, demon. The forms of its manifestations may be—and are—various, but within the family of self-love and reason it can play no role except that of intruder and destroyer. When we look to Collins, however, we recognize that the process he initiates at mid-century is the resurrection of the demonic into its divine form. The *Ode to Fear* is about the restoration of fear from its ensnarement within the oedipal demonic to the ''divine emotions'' of Shakespeare. ''If,'' says Collins (and the *if* is a condition of his allegiance), I can feel fear as did Shakespeare, then "I, O Fear, will dwell with thee!" Fear is the fallen woman of the poem, but she is also a power that Collins seeks to appropriate without the "paralyzing anxiety" that normally accompanies submission to her.[20] What has gone out of English poetry is the divinization of darkness, the power that self-love rejects. J. B. Beer says about Coleridge that he seeks to re-create Eden not by destroying the serpent, but "by raising it up to its former glory."[21] The procedure defines a dialectic in search of a synthesis; Pope's antitheses define an opposition into which no third term can enter. The alternative family in Pope is provided by Milton's vision of Satan, sin, and death, the family that usurps Eden and closes it forever.

Since Eden was closed, man could settle for the middle kingdom and cultivate his garden. Or he could seek to repossess Eden by wresting it from God, which would involve, as Weiskel observes, "an alliance with the dangerous passions."[22] The former way was taken by Cowper and Goldsmith and Johnson. It consists of shoring up the residue of possibility, and it provides a practical text for living within a diminished world. The other way was taken by Collins and the Wartons, though they indecisively came quickly to fear their enterprise and refer it to the fictions of fine fabling and highland superstition. But in order for a new poetry to come into existence, it was necessary to publicize Pope's limitations, and this was Joseph Warton's strategy in the *Essay on the Genius and Writings of Pope*. It was equally important to establish a traditional basis for the new poetry, and this task was undertaken by Thomas Warton in his *History of English Poetry*. In brief, Pope was to be minimized within a more various and capacious idea of history than he was said to possess. He was diminished within a poetry of fine fabling, and the primitivist aspects of the Wartonian poetic appear to us now as verifications of Popeian anxiety; his anti-sublime was enfolded within what was offered as a judicious critique of didactic and ethical poetry. But the Wartons were anticipated and even expected. The *Sober Advice from Horace* ironically praises the "primitive and the naturalistic, which become the standards for

measuring man's conduct. It effectually denies the value of cus-
tom, tradition, and disciplined development of the individual
mind and soul in accord with inherited wisdom."[23]

The Wartons thought they were liberating the passions; in
fact they were opening Pandora's box. Implicit in their reaction
was the dissolution of *epoch*, of the historical moment as conditioning and determining poetic obligation. As the historical
moment vanishes from view, satire disappears with it, and the
proposition that self-love is social is negated entirely. The characteristic eduction of overflow ("Nature and her overflowing
soul," says Wordsworth) drowns the containing structures of
Pope's *nature*, whereas Pope's *history* is overwhelmed by the
legendary past the Wartons release into poetry. Eloisa ensnared
by her own passion is metamorphosed into Thomas Warton's
Eloise,

> whose mind
> Had languish'd to the pangs of melting love,
> More genuine transport found, as on some tomb
> Reclin'd, she watch'd the tapers of the dead;
> Or thro' the pillar'd iles, amid pale shrines
> Of imag'd saints, and intermingled graves,
> Mus'd a veil'd votaress.
>
> (*The Pleasures of Melancholy*, 96-102)

Warton's covert eroticism ("veil'd votaress") too readily substitutes the passion-gratifying novitiate for the desiring woman.
The ego is not balked or baffled by its situation, but glides easily
from thoughts of a living lover to thoughts of death, and the
erotic element glides right along with it. In this perfect moment
of freedom the self absorbs its surroundings, the passional life
feeds on shrines and graves; the deflection of the self from its
primary object (a living lover) is not loss but gain, enabling the
self to feed more deeply on sensations unknown to it before.
Isolation is the necessary condition for "More genuine trans-
port."

It is hard to measure here the distance between Warton's
Eloise and Wordsworth's hermit, who "by his fire sits alone,"

but clearly the sublime moment demands solitude, insists that what is most valuable in human experience is private and not to be shared. The tradition of heroic self-exile begins here, but it is occasioned by doubts that arise earlier—doubts bearing on the relation of the poet to the world—and by Pope's own uncertainties about the imaginative act that can bridge the distance between the self and the world. As such an act, satire is liable to leave the satirist stranded within the criteria he has summoned. If Dryden's Albion goes *out* in 1688, so too does Pope's *history* in 1743, and within the metaphoric darkness roam the shapes of a dispossessed sensibility seeking new aggregations of power. I take it that this is what Collins's various invocations to feeling are all about, but feeling does not lead back to history but out of it.

What Frye calls "Sensibility" marks the alienation of the ego; an incisive economic analysis of this literary phenomenon would be Marxist at the core. Feeling is the medium through which the self establishes its worth and opposes itself to the world. Primitivism is a return to the hiding places of power, sources that remain yet uncorrupted by social mechanisms of exchange and recognition. At mid-century there was a great surge of poetry focused either upon private experience, as in much of Collins, or upon the reconstruction of affective relations between human beings determined by the shared fact of death, as in Gray's *Elegy*. Macpherson and Chatterton do not merely choose poetic personae, they become Ossian and Rowley. Gray's poetry speaks insistently of the discontinuities that mark the stages of individual growth and development, and Wordsworth's poetry resolutely haunts the places where his earlier selves linger, waiting to be reabsorbed into the mature personality. We experience a leap of interest in the workings of the individual consciousness and in the interiorization of experience. The protected place becomes the self, building its defenses against the world and generating through the treasured instrumentality of the imagination a world within that can be set against the outer world. The imagination refuses to be melted down, absorbed into a system of priorities wherein its value is merely one among many equivalences all serving the god of finance. Under these pressures, the unconscious is cultivated as an underground resistance movement. It has been said that the sublime is "especially at home in the modern theology of the unconscious,"[24] and there is good reason why it should be. But for Pope, coming at the problem from the other end of history, the sublime subverts the sociality implicit in self-love, and this truth he embodies in Dulness.

At mid-century the sublime is increasingly translated from its ontological purposefulness, as in Shaftesbury and Addison, into the egotistical sublime. Allied with the unconscious and increasingly affiliated with the imagination, the sublime emerges as the front line of defense against an encroaching social facelessness, which Blake recognized as uniformity, but which is the withered truth of eighteenth-century uniformitarianism. It is far too much to expect from Blake a usable critique of Pope. Blake is writing in an age when the City of God is clearly the City of Satan. This is not yet entirely true for Pope, though his suspicions that it might be come through visibly enough. We are accustomed to thinking of romantic poetry as profoundly revolutionary. Nothing signifies this fact more than the pervasiveness of elegy, and Wordsworth is the most elegiac of poets. The death of the old self is the precondition for the birth of the new, and the elegiac mode defines the self emergent from a context of loss and dedicated to its own reconstructions. Obviously, the *Dunciad* signals not the real beginnings of romanticism, but the real necessities that will ultimately call it forth.

As Popeian man sinks from view, Wordsworthian man rises on the horizon of a new poetry, isolated within the residue of grace and determined to rebuild the self by aggregating the shifting temporalities of a personal past and present. And the self-love that is social is converted into a self-love seeking to fortify itself against the world. To build with Wordsworth a new nature that is of the imagination's making is a programmatic strategy attesting to the special value and uniqueness of the self and of the imagination that is its informing spirit. I am arguing of course that English romanticism for all its diversity is necessitated by the death of Pope's myth, even as Pope was summoned by the collapse of Dryden's Albion. Elsewhere I have proposed the terms of the mid-century reaction and the inadequacies of it to which the early romantics were particularly sensitive.[25] If I am now knitting Pope into this story, it is because the literary history of the eighteenth century is that extended moment in time when the old world dies and modernism is born. And for much too long students of literature have found in Pope merely the obligatory terms of Blake's rebellion. Frye, for example, suggests that when the "proper study of mankind is the natural man . . . the most fertile themes of the creative imagination will be gossip, slander, and domestic trivia."[26] Edwards, to the contrary, enlists our interest in Pope as a rebel against "Augustanism," the rebellion functioning presumably to manifest Pope's sense of his own plight: "the later poems show an increasing strain being exerted on the Augustan expressive manner by views of experience that are essentially 'grotesque.' "[27]

Neither of these views is at all accurate, and although Frye diminishes Pope, Edwards tricks him out in the honorific garb of poetic rebel. For my part, I am suggesting that Pope demands our interest in the way usual to poets: he sustains and validates the work of his great predecessors by making that work his own. His "Augustanism" accommodates the continuing subject, embodying it in ways far beyond those available to his best contemporaries. He represents not only what the next age could make of Milton, but also what the age could make of the myth of the Fall. In *Dunciad* IV, man has fallen as far as it is possible to fall, into the chaos of his own mind, into that state of undifferentiated or unworked matter that is the unconscious. It is within this residual element that the Wartons located inspiration, an irreducible primitivism in which the passions flourished, what those coming at the problem from the perspective of a psychoanalytic criticism would identify as regressive narcissism. For one legacy of the Fall is the anxiety sponsored by a declining control over one's own human powers. Thus Collins invokes those powers in his various odes and attempts to appropriate them to himself as sources of vision. He keeps summoning the passions, much as Eloisa keeps recalling profane love as the center of her being until, at last, one context folds over another and Abelard is re-imagined as the type of Christ. At mid-century, however, the passions are exploited as the vehicles of inspiration, the stuff of which imagination is made. But nothing saves Collins from being himself exploited by the passions he summons.

Fear and vengeance are themselves the instrumental agencies of the Fall, the constituent elements of the selfhood that has decisively defeated self-love and organized a new center under the authority of Dulness. At this stage the master passion is deformed, and the various separate passions become functionaries in the service of selfhood. The self, one might say, is now prepared to worship itself, a narcissistic redundancy that results in the evocation of such passions as pity or fear or vengeance— the mistakenly conceived energies of the mind that are made to substitute for imagination. This emotional primitivism is equally a religious primitivism, a kind of paganism of the selfhood, the superstitious veneration and deification described in Epistle III of the *Essay on Man*. A curious typology seems to freeze Collins and the Wartons within the prophetic scheme of the *Dunciad*, and the mid-century effort to redeem the imagination appears to have resulted only in a sort of demonization of the passions, or, in Blakeian terms, in a possession of the imagination by the specters that inhabit it. Pope deals with a similar situation very lucidly in the *Rape*; Belinda slides easily from eternal female into *femme fatale*. Her own suppressed eroticism is the occasion for awakening eroticism in others, and the unsatisfied passions she evokes are, in a strikingly Blakeian sense, the "murders" she commits.

That Coleridge was particularly alert to this kind of betrayal from within at least partially explains why his poetry is so often occupied with exorcisms, with driving out the "night-wandering" man who worships the powers by which he is victimized. The "deep romantic chasm" in which a woman wails for her demon lover suggests an addiction to the enslaving passions, the powers that make us feel alive while they corrupt the imagination to their service. It seems also that much of Blake's job was to clear out these specters and identify them within an anatomy of the mind, a task that now appears to have been made mandatory by the requirements of a new poetry, a new alignment with the Miltonic myth, and a new conception of the imagination. Within the limits of my own inquiry, I have attempted to set forth Pope's relation to the modernist moment, as well as to describe how the reality of the Fall informs his vision and determines the bearing of its parts. One intended result of this exploration is to steady our comprehension of eighteenth-century poetry and to invite an understanding of Pope within other, and increasingly well-established, coordinates of the Miltonic and epic legacy.

It is worth noting again that by 1742-43, Pope had closed the book on his own vision. He had destroyed the myth of the special place and created the monster passion that permanently subverts the master passion. That the Wartons should have called for more and greater passion than they found in him is merely one of the ironies of literary history. The greater passion had already been created and named by Pope as the selfhood or Dulness; its human form was Nimrod or Timon or Balaam. The Wartons called it inspiration, but it did not turn out to be so for the poets allied with them. And if we circle once more and finally over our premises, we see that Pope's poetry constitutes the effort to find a special place that can stand intact and invulnerable, to find a circumference that flows from the human center. His imagination was a warning to the future. The artists who came after him would be obliged to build the world anew, not in the spirit of Wartonian sensibility, but from the beginning, from innocence to experience, from the self discovering the premonitions of its own divinity and seeking where it could for confirmation.

Notes

References for Pope's poetry, cited in the following notes as TE and given parenthetically throughout the text, are to the Twickenham Edition: The Poems of Alexander Pope, ed. John Butt et al. (London: Methuen; New Haven, Conn.: Yale University Press, 1939-69), 11 vols.

1. Introduction

1. Northrop Frye, *Fearful Symmetry* (Princeton, N.J.: Princeton University Press, 1947), p. 11.
2. It is important to state that my purposes do not include consideration of the Homeric translations. The subject requires a special category of critical discourse necessarily attentive to issues raised by translation, to the topic of Homeric influence in Pope's original poetry (thereby opening questions of source and allusion lying largely outside my inquiry), and to theoretical problems of the Augustan poetic. It should be clear, however, that interconnections between Pope's other poetry and the Homeric texts are more than merely occasional. Maynard Mack observes, for example, that "Hera's cestus, as Pope interprets it, belongs to the same world of discourse as Belinda, her Cross, and her Lock; and that either Homer's erotic set-piece has affected Pope's image of Belinda, or the image of Belinda has affected his Homer, or both" (TE, 7:ccxlv). Much more in this vein may be cited from Mack's remarkable introduction to the Twickenham edition. The professional student will understand the contrapuntal value that such commentary provides my own inquiry, and the ways in which interpenetrating texts enhance the logic of imaginative design that I wish to establish.
3. Thomas Edwards, Jr., *This Dark Estate: A Reading of Pope* (Berkeley: University of California Press, 1963), pp. vii-viii.
4. John Sitter, *The Poetry of Pope's Dunciad* (Minneapolis: University of Minnesota Press, 1971), p. 117.

5. Richard Blackmore, "Preface to *Prince Arthur*," *Critical Essays of the Seventeenth Century*, ed. J. E. Spingarn (London: Oxford University Press, 1957), 3:237-38.
6. Maynard Mack has described the conception of the ruling passion as being "central to the second Epistle, where it is obvious from the imagery that Pope is thinking of character as a creative achievement, an artistic result, something built out of chaos as God built the world. The ruling passion, which God sends, affords a focal point for this activity. The direction of the character is thus a *datum* . . ." (TE, 3:i, xxxvi).
7. Reuben Brower, *Alexander Pope: The Poetry of Allusion* (New York and London, Oxford University Press, 1959); Earl Wasserman, "Pope: *Windsor Forest*," in *The Subtler Language: Critical Readings of Neoclassic and Romantic Poems* (Baltimore: The Johns Hopkins University Press, 1959), pp. 101-69; *Pope's Epistle to Bathurst: A Critical Reading with an Edition of the Manuscript* (Baltimore: The Johns Hopkins University Press, 1960); "The Limits of Allusion in *The Rape of the Lock*," *JEGP*, 65 (July 1966); 425-44.
8. Ronald Paulson, "Satire, Poetry, and Pope," in *English Satire*, Leland H. Carlson and Ronald Paulson (Los Angeles: William Andrews Clark Memorial Library, 1972), pp. 55-106; Sanford Budick, "Pope and the Hidden God," *Poetry of Civilization* (New Haven, Conn.: Yale University Press, 1974), pp. 111-56.
9. Pat Rogers, *An Introduction to Pope* (London: Methuen & Co., 1975), p. 67; Brower, p. 13.
10. J. P. Stern, *A Study of Nietzsche* (New York: Cambridge University Press, 1979), p. 174.
11. Maynard Mack, " 'The Shadowy Cave': Some Speculations on a Twickenham Grotto," *Restoration and Eighteenth-Century Literature*, ed Carroll Camden (Chicago: University of Chicago Press, 1963), p. 86.
12. Brower, p. 14.
13. Wasserman, "Limits of Allusion in *The Rape of the Lock*," p.443.
14. Roland Barthes, "The Structuralist Activity," *Critical Essays* (Evanston, Ill.: Northwestern University Press, 1972), p. 217.
15. *The Iliad of Homer*, TE, 7:lix.
16. Brower, p. 213.
17. *Ibid.*, pp. 215, 239.
18. Sitter, p. 68.
19. Edwards, p. 78.
20. Samuel Johnson, *Lives of the English Poets*, ed. G. Birkbeck Hill (Oxford: Clarendon Press, 1905), 3:217, 219.
21. *Ibid.*, p. 217.

2. The Word and the Desiring Self

1. Wasserman, *Subtler Language*, p. 163.
2. Brower, *Poetry of Allusion*, p. 62.
3. Budick, *Poetry of Civilization*, p. 121.
4. D. A. Traversi, *An Approach to Shakespeare* (New York: Doubleday & Co., 1956), pp. 267-68.
5. Sigmund Freud, *A General Introduction to Psychoanalysis* (New York: Garden City Publishing Co., 1943), p. 152.
6. William Empson, *Seven Types of Ambiguity* (New York: New Directions, 1949), p. 193.

7. See G. W. Knight, *Laureate of Peace: On the Genius of Alexander Pope* (London: Routledge & Kegan Paul, 1954), pp. 79-110.
8. Roland Barthes, *On Racine* (New York: Hill and Wang, 1964), p. 37.
9. Freud, p. 153.
10. Wasserman, "Limits of Allusion in *The Rape of the Lock*," p. 433.
11. René Girard, *Violence and the Sacred* (Baltimore: The Johns Hopkins University Press, 1977), pp. 81-82.
12. Cf. Hugo M. Reichard, "The Love Affair in Pope's *Rape of the Lock*," *PMLA*, 69 (1954):893: "At first glance the shade of *honour* meant here seems to be 'chastity, purity, as a virtue of the highest consideration,' but on inspection the force of the word fades into 'reputation for this virtue, good name' *(OED)*."
13. Paul de Man, *Blindness & Insight: Essays in the Rhetoric of Contemporary Criticism* (New York: Oxford University Press, 1971), p. 48.
14. Cf. Murray Cohen, "Versions of the Lock: Readers of '*The Rape of the Lock*' " *ELH*, 43 (Spring 1976): 53-73. Cohen remarks on the opening of Canto III: "Close by those Meads for ever crown'd with Flowers, / Where Thames with Pride surveys his rising Tow'rs": "The actual towers are cast as reflections of the towers imaged on the water's surface. The reader cannot tell the original from the reflection, and his confusion reveals the curse of Belinda's irreligious cosmos in which reality is the reflection of itself" (p. 63). Cohen is right about Belinda but wrong about the Thames. The river god is imported from the close of *Windsor-Forest* where he was observing Augusta's "Temples rise, the beauteous Works of Peace" (*Windsor-Forest*, 378).
15. Thomas Weiskel, *The Romantic Sublime: Studies in the Structure and Psychology of Transcendence* (Baltimore: The Johns Hopkins University Press, 1976), pp. 43-44.
16. Frye, *Fearful Symmetry*, p. 140.
17. TE, 2:302-3.
18. Weiskel, p. 36.
19. Cf. Brendan O Hehir, "Virtue and Passion: The Dialectic of *Eloisa to Abelard*," *TSLL*, 2 (Summer 1960): 219-32. There are some similarities between my reading of the poem and O Hehir's, but I am interested in a referential frame that keeps *Eloisa* in relation to the larger context of Pope's texts. O Hehir is interested in a reading of one poem, but only slightly occupied with the deployment of the language of love.
20. In the *Rape of the Lock* Belinda's "Name" is inscribed "mid'st the Stars." In the *Temple of Fame* Pope speaks of his "rising Name." Pope's fascination with *name* and naming suggests a peculiar burden of identity and identification, and doubtless would, if pursued, lead into Arbuthnot's admonitions: "I'd never name," and "No Names." The eighteenth-century trick of anonymously floating a satire suggests the oddity of the unnamed namer.
21. Cf. Ralph Cohen, "On the Interrelations of Eighteenth-Century Literary Forms," *New Approaches to Eighteenth-Century Literature* (New York: Columbia University Press, 1974), pp. 33-79). Cohen is concerned with the decorum of literary forms and the terms of interrelations between and among genres. He makes the case for a less scrupulous decorum than is commonly assumed. See especially p. 38.
22. Edwards, *This Dark Estate*, p. 25.
23. Cf. the entry under "Sacrifice" in J. E. Cirlot, *A Dictionary of Symbols* (New York: Philosophical Library, 1962), p. 264.

3. The Generic Self and Particular Persons

1. J. M. Cameron, "Doctrinal to an Age: Notes Towards a Revaluation of Pope's *Essay on Man*," *Essential Articles for the Study of Alexander Pope*, ed. Maynard Mack (Hamden, Conn.: Archon Books, 1968), pp.353-70.
2. TE, 3:i, xi-lxxx; Douglas White, *Pope and the Context of Controversy: The Manipulation of Ideas in An Essay on Man* (Chicago: University of Chicago Press, 1970).
3. Johnson, *Lives of the English Poets*, 1:183.
4. Martin Price is the only other critic of whom I am aware who uses the term in relation to the *Essay*. But for Price the "voice of the selfhood is one of the two voices of the *Essay*; the other is the complex one assumed by the poet which moves with remarkable tact from satire to comedy, from comedy to consolation" (*To the Palace of Wisdom: Studies in Order and Energy from Dryden to Blake* [New York: Doubleday, 1964], p.133). Price has no interest in the psychological myth of the poem, nor does he submit the work to a study of the interactions between self-love and reason. In his terms the "selfhood" is only another adversary, external to the speaker and constituting the "you" of the poem. Finally, Price suggests that the "central contradictions of Pope's *Essay* lie in the conflict between an aesthetic vision and a moral one," which Pope "cannot resolve" (p. 142).
5. Frye, *Fearful Symmetry*, p. 73.
6. Dustin Griffin, *Alexander Pope: The Poet in the Poems* (Princeton, N.J.: Princeton University Press, 1978), p. 153.
7. Paulson, "Satire, Poetry, and Pope," in *English Satire*, p. 62.
8. Weiskel, *Romantic Sublime*, p. 151.
9. I am reminded here of Kenneth Burke's childhood prayer: "God loving me / Guard me in sleep / Guide me to Thee." Thus Burke: "if we test this by the Hopkins method of *ablaut* punning, we find that the verbs of lines two and three, predicates of the noun in line one, merely restate the noun, thus G —— d; G —— d; G —— d. In sum: 'to guard' and 'to guide' are pun-conjugations of the verb, 'to god.' I should thus here treat 'guard' and 'guide' as 'god-words' in the psychic economy of the person who wrote this prayer" (*The Philosophy of Literary Form*, 3rd ed., [Berkeley: University of California Press, 1973], p. 57). Conversely, reason, which is a "guard" but no "guide" is half a god-term, and reason's desire to be both guard and guide defines an over-reaching.
10. Elizabeth MacAndrew speaks of "the Benevolists' replacement of the traditional faith in Reason as the foundation stone of morality with the concept of feeling (Sentiment) as man's moral arbiter. All men are endowed by their Creator with a Moral Sense, the innate power that enables them to tell right from wrong instantaneously" (*The Gothic Tradition in Fiction* [New York: Columbia University Press, 1979], pp. 23-24). Pope seems not to employ Francis Hutcheson's concept of the "moral sense," but to understand self-love as informed by an intuitive faculty (instinct) superior to discursive reason but quite distinct from sentiment. At first it may seem that self-love is a variation of Burnet's "Natural Conscience," the "principle of distinguishing one thing from another in Moral Cases, without ratiocination" (Ernest Tuveson, *The Imagination as a Means of Grace* [Berkeley: Univesity of California Press, 1960], p. 48). But Burnet's principle leads, as Tuveson argues, to an emphasis upon "sensation," which is what MacAndrew is speaking about above. It is more likely that Pope, unlike Shaftesbury, goes back to the

mens of the Cambridge Platonists, "a transcendent intuition of the mind" (Tuveson, p. 52), to develop his concept of instinct. On the other hand, Thomas Burnet leads, through Shaftesbury, to the Benevolist tradition, which in turn leads through the mid-century poets, finding its greatest literary expression in Gray's *Elegy* and the sentimental novel. Pope has nothing to do with this tradition, for Benevolism conceives of feeling as a moral principle, and neither feeling nor reason is privileged within the *Essay*.

11. "When Love was Liberty, and Nature Law" (III, 208) echoes Eloisa's enthusiastic comment, "When love is liberty, and nature, law" (92). But love cannot be liberty or nature law when, as in the earlier poem, nature has fallen under the suasion of the jealous god, and what Eloisa takes to be equivalence is in fact an illusion sponsored by the demon who possesses her. In the *Essay* the line is invoked to commend a classless society.

12. Frye, p. 398.

13. Cf. Frye's discussion of this topic, p. 349.

14. Maynard Mack, *The Garden and the City* (Toronto: University of Toronto Press, 1969), p. 9.

15. *The Spectator*, ed. Donald Bond (Oxford: Clarendon Press, 1965), 3:570, 571.

16. Paulson, p. 63.

17. Geoffrey Hartman, *Wordsworth's Poetry: 1787-1814* (New Haven, Conn.: Yale University Press, 1971), p. 230.

18. *Ibid.*, p. 229.

19. *Ibid.*

20. Cf. "The Design," TE, 3:i, 8.

21. *Ibid.*, p. 7.

22. See Mack's introduction to the Twickenham edition of *An Essay on Man*. He observes of Pope that "though his theme is analogous to Milton's, Pope cannot and does not probe it to Milton's depth, one reason being that he has no characters involved in dramatic action" (p.lxxiii). On this basis Mack decides that the *Essay* is a "poem of abstractions, but of abstractions put to work in an artistic whole" (p.lxxx). The conclusion defines the conventional wisdom, the *Essay* viewed as a poem of "ideas most relevant to the theme of constructive renunciation—theodicy and ethics" (p.lxxx).

23. Angus Fletcher, *Allegory: The Theory of a Symbolic Mode* (Ithaca, N.Y.: Cornell University Press, 1964), p. 243.

24. Maureen Quilligan, *The Language of Allegory* (Ithaca, N.Y.: Cornell University Press, 1979), p. 188.

25. William Empson, *Structure of Complex Words* (London: Chatto & Windus, 1951), p. 346.

26. Miriam Leranbaum, *Alexander Pope's 'OPUS MAGNUM,' 1729-1744* (Oxford: Clarendon Press, 1977), p. 128.

27. Earl Wasserman, *Pope's Epistle to Bathurst*, p.37.

28. *Epistles to Several Persons*, ed. James Wellington (Coral Gables, Fla.: University of Miami Press, 1963), p. 28.

29. Wasserman, *Pope's Epistle to Bathurst*, pp. 39, 37.

30. *Ibid.*, p. 36. Recent approaches to the *Epistle to a Lady* tend to emphasize either its "symbolic" values, by which is meant the "general truths" inherent in Pope's portraits, or the power of the poem to *overflow*, "reaching beyond literature into reality." For the first position see P. M. Spacks, *An Argument of Images* (Cambridge, Mass.: Harvard University Press, 1971), pp. 157-68. For the second consult Irvin Ehrenpreis, "The Cistern and the Fountain: Art and Reality in Pope and Gray," *Studies in Criticism and Aesthetics, 1660-1800*, ed. Howard Anderson and John S. Shea (Minneapolis: Uni-

versity of Minnesota Press, 1967), pp.156-75.

31. See Francis Hutcheson, *An Essay on the Nature and Conduct of the Passions and Affections* (London, 1728; facsimile ed., Hildesheim: Georg Olms, 1971): "Every passion or Affection in its *moderate Degree* is innocent, many are directly *amiable*, and *morally good*: we have *Senses* and *Affections* leading us to *publick Good*, as well as to *private*; to *Virtue*, as well as to external Pleasure" (pp. 86-87). A great deal of attention is given to the passions in the later seventeenth and early eighteenth centuries, much of the literature probably known to Pope. Benjamin Boyce discusses the subject at some length in his chapter, "The Ruling Passion and the Complex Personality," in *The Character-Sketches in Pope's Poems* (Durham, N.C.: Duke University Press, 1962), pp. 105-30. See also Addison's *Spectator*, no. 183 (September 29, 1711), in which he creates his fable of the family of pleasure and of pain: "There were two families which from the beginning of the World . . ." (*The Spectator*, 2: 222).

32. Fletcher, p. 34.

33. Chester F. Chapin, *Personification in Eighteenth-Century English Poetry* (New York: Columbia University Press, 1955), p. 19.

34. Empson, *Seven Types of Ambiguity*, p. 151.

35. Fletcher, pp. 286-87.

36. *Ibid.*, p. 48.

37. Paul Fussell, *The Rhetorical World of Augustan Humanism* (Oxford: Clarendon Press, 1965), p. 87.

38. Leranbaum, p. 65.

39. *Ibid.*, p. 66.

40. Wasserman, *Pope's Epistle to Bathurst*, p. 21.

41. *Ibid.*, p. 42.

42. Thomas Edwards, " 'Reconcil'd Extremes': Pope's *Epistle to Bathurst*," *Essays in Criticism*, 11 (July 1961): 302.

43. Howard Erskine-Hill, *The Social Milieu of Alexander Pope* (New Haven, Conn.: Yale University Press, 1975), p. 307.

44. Wasserman, *Pope's Epistle to Bathurst*, p. 20.

45. *Ibid.*, p. 21.

46. *Ibid.*, p. 52.

47. *Ibid.*, p. 31.

48. Steven Zwicker, *Dryden's Political Poetry: The Typology of King and Nation* (Providence, R.I.: Brown University Press, 1972), p. 26.

49. *Ibid.*, p. 25.

50. *The Correspondence of Alexander Pope*, ed. George Sherburn (Oxford: Clarendon Press, 1956), 2:228.

51. *Ibid.*

52. Samuel Johnson, *A Dictionary of the English Language*, 2nd. ed. (London, 1756).

53. It seems that Pope's concept of "sense" is another agency of self-love, though in this case it responds to beauty, as instinct or intuitive reason responds to the good. Tuveson notes that the "old model of the mind as a kind of army commanded by the reason is replaced by the idea of a group of specialists sharing responsibility. One controls the moral area; another, that of self-preservation, involving knowledge of the external world; and it is logical to add a third, which would respond to beauty" (*Imagination as a Means of Grace*, p. 50). Pope's family of self-love, reason, and ruling passion expands, particularly in the later works, to include sense, and this accommodation occurs as the aesthetic dimension is given greater significance in

To Burlington.
54. Leranbaum, p. 113.
55. Weiskel, p. 54.
56. Wasserman, "Limits of Allusion in *The Rape of the Lock,*" pp. 442-43. Note especially Wasserman's comments on Pope's use of Martial's Polytimus.
57. "But besides this kind of Fable there is another in which the Actors are Passions, Virtues, Vices, and other imaginary Persons of the like Nature. Some of the Ancient Criticks will have it that the Iliad and Odissey of *Homer* are Fables of this nature; and that the several Names of Gods and Heroes are nothing else but the Affections of the Mind in a visible Shape and Character. Thus they tell us, that *Achilles*, in the first Iliad, represents Anger, or the Irascible part of Human Nature: That upon drawing his Sword against his Superior in full Assembly, *Pallas* is only another name for Reason, which checks and advises him upon that occasion. . . . As for the Odissey, I think it is plain that *Horace* considered it as one of those Allegorical Fables, by the Moral which he has given us of several parts of it" (*The Spectator,* 2:220-21).

4. The Self-Regarding "I" and the Egotistical Sublime

1. Leranbaum, *Pope's 'OPUS MAGNUM,'* pp. 129, 130.
2. Griffin, *Poet in the Poems,* p. 188.
3. *Ibid.,* p. 192.
4. Thomas Maresca, *Pope's Horatian Poems* (Columbus: Ohio State University Press, 1966), p. 50.
5. Brower, *Poetry of Allusion,* p. 290.
6. Frye, *Fearful Summetry,* p. 11.
7. TE, 4:xxx.
8. Fortescue was added to the *First Satire* in 1751 by Warburton. Howard Weinbrot discusses both the *First Satire* and the *Epistle to Arbuthnot* at substantial length in his new book, *Alexander Pope and the Traditions of Formal Verse Satire* (Princeton, N.J.: Princeton University Press, 1982). I regret not being able to consult his work before my manuscript had gone to press.
9. John Aden, *Something like Horace* (Nashville, Tenn.: Vanderbilt University Press, 1969), p. 14.
10. TE, 4:94.
11. U. C. Knoeplfmacher, "The Poet as Physician: Pope's *Epistle to Dr. Arbuthnot,*" *MLQ,* 31 (1970): 440.
12. Irvin Ehrenpreis, "Personae," *Restoration and Eighteenth-Century Literature,* ed. Carroll Camden (Chicago: University of Chicago Press, 1963), p. 32.
13. *Ibid.,* p. 33.
14. Received opinion on the subject of *To Arbuthnot* is well represented by Lilian Feder. She remarks that the "emphasis on his humanity and his high moral standards becomes an essential and consistent feature of Pope's Horatian *persona*; he continues to emphasize these qualities in his portrait of himself in the *Imitations of Horace, An Epistle to Dr. Arbuthnot,* and *The Epilogue to the Satires.*" See "Sermo or Satire: Pope's Definition of His Art," *Studies in Criticism and Aesthetics, 1660-1800,* ed. Howard Anderson and John S. Shea (Minneapolis: University of Minnesota Press, 1967), p. 147.
15. Weiskel, p. 120.
16. "Advertisement" to the *Imitations,* TE, 4:3.

17. Weiskel, *Romantic Sublime*, p. 130.
18. Cf. Maresca, p. 186.
19. See Rosemond Tuve, *Allegorical Imagery: Some Mediaeval Books and Their Posterity* (Princeton, N.J.: Princeton University Press, 1966), especially pp. 40-47.
20. G. K. Hunter, "The 'Romanticism' of Pope's Horace," *Essays in Criticism*, 10 (1960): 404.
21. Tuve, p. 44.
22. Barthes, *On Racine*, p. 38. See also Anthony Wilden, "Lacan and the Discourse of the Other," in Jacques Lacan, *The Language of the Self* (Baltimore: The Johns Hopkins University Press, 1968): "what the subject must seek is what Lacan calls the symbolic identification with the father—that is to say, he must take over the *function* of the father through the normalization of the Oedipus complex. This is an identification with a father who is neither Imaginary nor real: what Lacan calls the Symbolic father, the figure of the Law" (p. 165). This remark bears on my discussion here and elsewhere in the text of the relation between Pope and Bolingbroke in the *Essay on Man*, and on that between the jealous god and God ("the figure of the Law") in *Eloisa to Abelard*. Cf. Wilden's essay as it develops the relation between knowledge and recognition, and issues in a discussion of " 'ontological insecurity' " ("to be an object for the other is to have lost one's being as a person," [p. 166]).
23. Hunter, p. 391.
24. Fletcher, *Allegory: Theory of a Symbolic Mode*, p. 133 n.
25. Ralph Rader, "The Concept of Genre and Eighteenth-Century Studies," *New Approaches to Eighteenth-Century Literature* (New York: Columbia University Press, 1974), pp. 79-117. See especially Rader's comments on the *Rape of the Lock*, p. 104.
26. Johnson, *Lives of the English Poets*, 3:241.
27. Frye, p. 75
28. Erich Auerbach, *Mimesis: The Representation of Reality in Western Literature* (Princeton, N.J.: Princeton University Press, 1953), p. 73.
29. Cf. John Sitter, *The Poetry of Pope's Dunciad*: "This Limbo where no distinction is made between a Corneille and an Ozell, between human genius and an ape, is the spiritual womb and tomb of the worldly Cave of Poverty and Poetry . . . " (p. 20).
30. Auerbach, p. 196.
31. Jung relates a relevant "pathological fantasy of two insane artists," which he derives from Lombroso: "Each of them thought he was God Almighty and the ruler of the universe. They created or produced the world by making it come forth from the rectum, like a bird's egg from the oviduct (or cloaca). One of these artists was gifted with real artistic sense. He painted a picture of himself in the act of creation: the world came forth from his anus, his member was in full erection, he was naked, surrounded by women and by all the insignia of his power" (*Symbols of Transformation*, in *Collected Works*, 2nd ed., [Princeton, N.J.: Princeton University Press, 1956], 5:190).
32. Brower, p. 332. When Dustin Griffin discusses the use of "low materials" in the *Dunciad* he refers their function in Pope's imagination to the Freudian principle of "negation," in which "the subject matter of a repressed image or thought can make its way into consciousness on condition that it is denied" (230 n; cf. Freud, *Collected Papers of Sigmund Freud*, ed. Ernest Jones [New York: Basic Books, 1959], 5:181-85). I am reminded by Griffin's dis-

cussion that "negation" is corollary to "condensation," in the sense that both processes depend upon the principle of ambivalence. The word (fire or rising) opened to alternative meanings in the *Temple of Fame* corresponds to an opening of the self to images of attraction that are effectively denied, or, in the case of the dunces, projected onto others as part of the satiric attack. Such strategies serve the dual purpose of projection and repression; the self discovers the forbidden territory within and employs it as the very substance of folly while simultaneously rejecting its attractions. I consider these tactics as part of the overall engagement with ambivalence, the large-scale contours of which form a major part of my own inquiry. Equally, I find this subject relevant to the concern with the "other" that runs through Pope's works. This entire subject seems to me to open impressively into the theme of predator and prey, and into the covert symbolization of castration, which in turn bears upon the processes of negation and the splitting of the ego. See Wilden's essay in Jacques Lacan, *The Language of the Self*, pp. 278-81; Freud, *An Outline of Psychoanalysis* (1940) [1938], *Standard Edition*, 23:204. It is obvious that the language of disavowal (rejection), and the discovery of that on which disavowal is predicated, forms a very considerable part of Pope's engagement with language and with the structures of desire on which identity is based.

33. Aubrey Williams, *Pope's Dunciad: A Study of its Meaning* (Baton Rouge: Louisiana State University Press, 1955), p. 43.
34. *Ibid.*, pp. 44, 46-47.
35. Cf. Sitter's discussion of this same topic, p. 36.
36. "An Essay of Dramatic Poesy," *Essays of John Dryden*, ed. W. P. Ker (New York; Russell & Russell, 1961), 1:102.
37. Frye, pp. 161-62.
38. *Ibid.*, p. 164.
39. Sitter, p. 80.
40. Donald Siebert's recent reading of the *Dunciad* ("Cibber and Satan: The *Dunciad* and Civilization," *ECS*, 10 [Winter 1976/77]: 205-21) argues against the prevailing tendency to emphasize the poem's darkness and pessimism, a tendency Siebert defines as "the School of Deep Intent" (p. 204). However refreshing his reading, his appraisal of the *Dunciad* depends upon considering it independently of the poet's other works. Thus he is unable to bring to his reading a sense of Pope's mythopoeic imagination, and concludes that the *Dunciad* is, "after all, a work of satire," and "no satire worth its name ever presented its subject fairly or realistically" (p. 221). Siebert's re-evaluation suggests a major justification for my entire enterprise: the need to see poems in relation to other poems.
41. "Preface" to the *Iliad*, TE, 7:7.
42. John Sitter, "The Argument of Pope's *Epistle to Cobham*," *SEL*, 17 (1977): 447.
43. Warburton's note to lines 255-71, TE, 5:369.
44. Frye, p. 130.
45. *Ibid.*, p. 133-34.

5. Conclusion

1. Michael Rosenblum, "Pope's Illusive Temple of Infamy," *The Satirist's Art*, ed. H. James Jensen and Malvin Zirker (Bloomington: Indiana University Press, 1972), p. 29.

2. Ronald Paulson, *The Fictions of Satire* (Baltimore: The Johns Hopkins University Press, 1967), p. 3.
3. Rosenblum, p. 32.
4. Maynard Mack, " 'The Shadowy Cave': Some Speculations on a Twickenham Grotto," *Restoration and Eighteenth-Century Literature*, p. 86.
5. Northrop Frye, *Anatomy of Criticism* (Princeton, N.J.: Princeton University Press, 1957), p. 226.
6. *Ibid.*, p. 228.
7. *Ibid.*, p. 238.
8. Weiskel, *Romantic Sublime*, p. 59.
9. *Ibid.*, p. 21.
10. Rosenblum, p. 53.
11. Frye, *Fearful Symmetry*, p. 340.
12. Joseph Spence, *Observations, Anecdotes, and Characters of Books and Men*, ed. James M. Osborn (Oxford: Clarendon Press, 1966), 1:241.
13. "Analytic of the Sublime," *Kant's Critique of Aesthetic Judgement*, ed. J. C. Meredith (Oxford: Clarendon Press, 1911), pp. 120-21.
14. Cited by J. T. Boulton, ed. *A Philosophical Enquiry into the Origin of our Ideas of the Sublime and Beautiful* (London: Routledge and Kegan Paul, 1958), p. lvi.
15. Albert Wlecke, *Wordsworth and the Sublime* (Berkeley: University of California Press, 1973), p. 61.
16. *Ibid.*, p. 54.
17. Brower, *Poetry of Allusion*, p. 11.
18. Weiskel, p. 157.
19. See Paul de Man's discussion of this topic: "Ludwig Binswanger and the Sublimation of the Self," *Blindness and Insight* (London: Oxford University Press, 1971), pp. 36-51.
20. Weiskel, p. 122.
21. J. B. Beer, *Coleridge the Visionary* (London: Chatto & Windus, 1959), p. 71.
22. Weiskel, p. 133.
23. G. Douglas Atkins, "Strategy and Purpose in Pope's *Sober Advice from Horace*," PLL, 15 (Spring 1978): 172.
24. Weiskel, p. 43.
25. Wallace Jackson, *The Probable and the Marvelous* (Athens: University of Georgia Press, 1978).
26. Frye, *Fearful Symmetry*, p. 162.
27. Edwards, *This Dark Estate*, p. 132.

Index

Wallace Jackson is the author of *The
Probable and the Marvelous: Blake,
Wordsworth, and the Eighteenth-Century
Critical Tradition* (1978) and of articles on
such figures as Dryden, Defoe, Addison,
Wordsworth, Blake, Hogarth,
Gainsborough, and Turner. He received
the Ph.D. degree from the University of
Pennsylvania and teaches in the
Department of English at Duke
University.

The manuscript was edited
by Saundra Blais.
The book was designed by Don Ross.
The typeface for the text is Mergenthaler
VIP Palatino, based on an original design
by Hermann Zapf in 1950. The display
typeface is LeGriffe.
The text is printed on 50-lb S. D.
Warren's "66" text paper. The book is
bound in Joanna Mills' Arrestox B grade
cloth over binder's boards. Manufactured
in the United States of America.